# THE WAY TO
# WHOLENESS

# THE WAY TO
# WHOLENESS

LESSONS FROM LEVITICUS

# RAY C. STEDMAN

Discovery House is affiliated with Our Daily Bread Ministries, Grand Rapids, Michigan.

Requests for permission to quote from this book should be directed to: Permissions Department, Discovery House, P.O. Box 3566, Grand Rapids, MI 49501.

Interior design by Nicholas Richardson

ISBN of this edition: 978-1-62707-502-2

**Library of Congress Cataloging-in-Publication**
Stedman, Ray C.
The way to wholeness : studies in Leviticus / by Ray C. Stedman.
p. cm.
Includes bibliographical references and index.
ISBN 1-57293-119-1 (alk. paper)
1. Bible. O.T. Leviticus—Criticism, interpretation, etc. I. Title.
BS1255.52.S74    2004    222'.1306—dc22    2004023140

Printed in the United States of America
Third printing in 2016

# CONTENTS

PART TWO: Basic Human Behavior

# PART ONE

# BASIC HUMAN NEEDS

※————————————※

# CHAPTER I

# THE WAY TO WHOLENESS
### LEVITICUS 20:26

LET'S FACE IT: Most people are not very excited about studying the book of Leviticus. If you have ever made a commitment to read the Bible through, then you probably remember taking an easy and enjoyable trip through Genesis and Exodus. The first two books of the Bible make fascinating, page-turning reading, because every page is drenched in human drama. In Genesis and Exodus we find the compelling stories of such heroes as Abraham, Isaac, Jacob, and Moses. We read about the creation of the universe, the fall of humanity, the heartbreak and triumph of Joseph, Israel's captivity in Egypt, and the story of Moses leading the people out of Egypt, climaxed by the parting of the Red Sea. It's no wonder that Hollywood has made several spectacular movies from the stories in Genesis and Exodus!

But then comes Leviticus. The drama evaporates. Suddenly, you are plodding through a catalog of offerings, ceremonies, dietary restrictions, specifications for the priesthood, and various other instructions that seem alien to our place and time. That is where many well-intentioned students of the Bible run out of gas. That is where many a well-intentioned commitment to Bible reading falters and fails.

So let's admit at the outset that the book of Leviticus is not an easy book to study. It can seem a bit dry—until you understand the meaning and the rich spiritual reality that underlies these ceremonies and instructions. Exploring the depths of God's truth is never boring, never dry. Once we begin to understand what these ceremonies and instructions mean, and their relevance to our lives today, the book of Leviticus truly becomes one of the most fascinating books of the Bible.

Reading the book of Leviticus without grasping its underlying reality can be like walking through a busy factory without a guide. When I first moved to the San Francisco Bay area, I visited a large steel products factory operated by Ed Stirm, one of the founders of Peninsula Bible Church. When I arrived at the building, Ed was busy, so while I waited for him I went out into the factory area and looked around by myself.

My impression was one of chaotic activity and tremendous noise. There were machines pounding and clanging, machines that hammered metal flat, machines that ground up metal, machines that spit out parts of various shapes. There was no apparent harmony or connection between what one machine did and what another machine did. There was so much noise, I couldn't hear myself think! Against this background of mechanical noise, I saw people scurrying here and there, moving dollies loaded with metal and getting in each other's way.

Finally, Ed joined me and took me on a guided tour of the plant. He took me from place to place, showed me what each machine did, what kinds of parts each machine made, and how these parts were assembled. He introduced me to people, told me what they did, and explained how one person's job connected with the work done by another person in the factory. He explained the assembly line and showed me how all the different parts of the operation flowed together. Finally, he took me to the shipping department, where he showed me the completed product as it was being boxed and wrapped.

By the end of the tour, everything that had confused me before now made sense. What had seemed like a mass of chaos and noise a few minutes earlier had become a symphony of motion. It not only made sense, but it had become fascinating.

The same is true of the book of Leviticus. If you come to Leviticus without any background, without understanding how each part of the book connects to every other part of Leviticus and to the Bible as a whole, then it will seem chaotic and meaningless and, yes, boring.

But if you have a tour guide to Leviticus to help you make sense of it all, then I believe you will find it one of the most important and meaningful books of the entire Bible. You'll see that these ceremonies, sacrifices, and restrictions form intricately articulated relationships that reveal the plan of God for our lives.

## HOLINESS AND WHOLENESS: THE KEY TO LEVITICUS

The key to Leviticus is found in a single verse located near the center of the book. All of the secrets of the book are unlocked by Leviticus 20:26:

> "You are to be holy to me because I, the LORD, am holy, and I have
> set you apart from the nations to be my own."

This is the purpose of the book of Leviticus. Here, God tells the people of Israel—and He tells Christians today—"You shall be holy to me." Why? "Because I, the Lord, am holy, and I have separated you from all the nations around you, so that you will be exclusively my people." What God said to Israel so long ago He also says to Christians today. The promises that appeared in picture form in the Old Testament now belong to us who live on this side of the cross. This profound truth will become even more apparent as we move deeper into Leviticus.

Look again at those words that God speaks to Israel and to us: "You are to be holy to me." What does that word *holy* mean to you?

Some people associate holiness with strangeness or peculiarity. They think of holy people as being weird or different. This misconception is fostered by the stereotype of ancient holy men who lived as hermits in the desert, remote from other people, a little crazed perhaps, possibly even seeing strange visions and talking to themselves. If this is your image of a holy person, then you probably don't find anything attractive in holiness. In fact, the word probably repels you.

For other people, the word *holy* suggests a sort of grim religiousness. They think of a holy person as someone who has been steeped in vinegar. Many of us react to the word *holy* the same way the little girl reacted the first time she saw a mule looking at her over a fence. She had never seen a mule before, so when this long-faced animal peered at her, she said, "I don't know what you are, but you must be a Christian—you look just like Grandpa!"

That's the way I reacted to the word *holy* when I was much younger. I thought of holy people as joyless, solemn people who prayed all the time, sang grim, gloomy hymns all the time, and never had any fun. The word *holy* was not attractive to me. In fact, it repelled me.

But my impression of holiness began to change when I encountered several verses in Scripture that spoke of holiness as a beautiful and glorious thing. For example, 1 Chronicles 16:29 tells us, "Ascribe to the LORD the glory due his name. Bring an offering and come before him; worship the LORD in the splendor of his holiness."(These words are echoed in 2 Chronicles 20:21; Psalm 29:2; and Psalm 96:9.) I began to realize that if holiness is a thing of splendor and beauty, then my mental image of holiness must be all wrong—and I began to explore what the Bible truly means by that word *holiness*.

The word *holiness* comes from the same Old English word from which we get our word *wholeness*. The Old English word is *hali* or *halig*, which had such varied shades of meaning as wholeness, completeness, health, and even salvation. So when we talk about holiness, we are truly talking about wholeness and completeness. And when God says to us, "You are to be holy to me because I, the Lord, am holy," He is telling us that we are to be as whole and complete as He is.

There is no blemish in God; He lives in harmony with Himself. He is whole and perfect. That is the beauty and splendor of His holiness. And this beautiful, splendorous, holy God looks at us in our brokenness and says to us, "You, too, shall be whole, as I am whole." When we experience God's wholeness and His holiness, then we become fully what He intended us to be. All of the parts of ourselves are present and functioning as God intended them to function.

That word *wholeness* has power to awaken a longing within us: We are aware of our brokenness, and we long to be whole and complete. Don't you want to be what God made you to be? Wouldn't you want to have every aspect of your personality function in perfect balance? That is what it means to be a whole and holy person. That is the beauty and splendor of wholeness and holiness. That is what God is after in our lives.

And that is what the book of Leviticus is all about. It is, in fact, a theme that runs throughout the entire Bible.

As a human race and as individuals, we are self-conscious about our brokenness, our lack of wholeness. We are aware of our inability to cope with life. We know how powerless we are to control bad habits, chronic sins, temptations and addictions, the things we say and do to hurt the ones we love. We put up a big façade and pretend that we are in control and there is nothing wrong with us. But underneath the façade, we are hurting, full of shame and guilt, and we are running scared.

But God, in Leviticus, tells us that He knows all about our brokenness and pain. He knows that our lives are riddled with sin, shame, and hurt. Our brokenness stands in stark contrast to His holiness. Yet His love reaches out to us, right where we are, and He makes a wonderful promise to us: "You are to be holy to me because I, the LORD, am holy, and I have set you apart from the nations to be my own." This is the wonderful plan and purpose He has for our lives.

## SEPARATE AND SET APART

We were created in perfection.

If you carefully read the creation account in Genesis 1, you may notice an interesting detail: At the end of every creation day, God looks on what He has created and sees "that it was good." Then in Genesis 1:27, the creation account undergoes a subtle but important change: "So God created man in his own image, in the image of God he created him; male and female he created them." And Genesis 1:31 tells us that at that close of the day on which human beings were created, "God saw all that he had made, and it was very good."

Not just "good" but "*very* good."

When Adam first came from the hand of God, he was perfect and whole. He functioned as God intended humanity to function. He bore the beauty and splendor of the image and the likeness of God.

As human beings, we were lovingly fashioned by God, and He looked upon us and said that we were *very* good. But the human race has become misshapen and deformed by sin. Yes, God's image is still stamped upon us, but that image has become marred and damaged. We are no longer whole.

If you accidentally drop a quarter into a garbage disposal while it is running, that quarter will get hacked and nicked and possibly bent. Turn off the disposal and retrieve the quarter, and you'll be able to tell it is a quarter. You'll be able to recognize the image of George Washington that is stamped upon it, but that quarter will no longer be what it once was. It will be marred and damaged. That is what has happened to the image of God that is stamped on you and me.

We were made in the image and likeness of God—and we still have His image, but we have lost His likeness. There is a semblance of God, but the completeness and wholeness of God have been lost.

In his poem "Choruses from the Rock," T. S. Eliot laments that all of human knowledge only brings a greater sense of our ignorance, and all of our ignorance only draws us closer to death. And though we are approaching death, we are no closer to God. "Where," the poet asks, "is the Life we have lost in living?"

Isn't that the question millions are asking today? Where is the Life I have lost in trying to live? I seek knowledge, but I have no wisdom. I seek pleasure, but I have no joy. I keep chasing after happiness, but I have no satisfaction. I seek to make a living, but I have no life.

But here in Leviticus, God steps into the broken mess we have made of our lives and promises to make us whole again, just as He is whole. And He knows how to do it: "You are to be holy to me because I, the LORD, am holy, and I have set you apart from the nations to be my own." How will God make us whole and holy? Through a process of separation.

The reason we are so broken is that we are involved in a broken race. We have been infected by a broken and sin-ridden world. Our attitudes are wrong. Our view of life is twisted and distorted. We mistake illusions for truth, and we end up chasing phantoms. So God must separate us. He must break us loose from conformity to the thought patterns and attitudes of the people around us. He must deliver us from this world, straighten out our thinking, set our minds and hearts right, and untangle our fouled relationships.

But God will not make us whole against our will. If we choose to remain broken, He will allow it. This process is completely voluntary—God never forces us into it. Some will choose to become whole and holy, and some will not. God will deliver only those who trust Him enough to respond to His love.

## CHRIST BEFORE THE CROSS

Once, when I was in my early teens, I saw a deer in a thicket at the edge of a clearing. I had an apple in my hand, so I tried to entice her out into the clearing by holding out the apple. She was a wild doe and very afraid of me, but she was also hungry, and she wanted that apple. She would venture a few steps toward me; then her fear would overtake her and she'd retreat into the woods. Then she'd come out again, stand still, look around for a minute, seemingly indifferent to my presence. All the while, I stood perfectly still, holding out the apple. Finally, she'd edge closer—then a twig would snap, and she'd disappear back into the bushes.

Now, I wouldn't have hurt her. If she'd only known my intentions, she would have been perfectly safe in walking right up and taking the apple from my hand. But she didn't know that.

I was there a long time, at least half an hour, trying to get her to come out of the woods. Finally she came about halfway toward me and stood there with her neck stretched out, trying to muster the courage to reach for that apple. Just as I thought she was going to take it, a car passed on the road nearby, and she was gone! I had to eat the apple myself.

This is a picture of what God contends with in reaching out to the human race. It takes infinite patience and love on His part to reach out to fearful, hurting men and women like us.

That is why God gave us His Book. He starts in kindergarten with us. He starts with pictures and shadows, with visual aids, in order to show us what He is going to do someday. All the ceremonies and offerings of the Old Testament are shadows and pictures of Jesus Christ. When we understand the meaning of these ceremonies and offerings, it becomes clear that Christ is pictured here in the book of Leviticus. God shows us, through His people Israel, His way of healing human guilt and pain. This is God's way to wholeness.

"Well," you might say, "I thought Jesus Christ was God's way to wholeness." That is exactly true. But Jesus is not the way to wholeness only for those who believed after the cross. For thousands of years before Jesus died and rose again, men and women were hurting and broken, just as we are. They needed Christ, too—and He was available to them centuries before He came to earth in human form. How? Through the pictures and symbols of these ceremonies in Leviticus. When people grasped the reality behind those pictures, when they laid hold of Jesus through faith in the One who would someday come to save them, they came to the same joy and peace that we have as Christians.

We see this principle clearly as we read the Psalms. There we see how much David understood of the presence and the grace of God in his life. Some of the psalms give us a picture of the divine nature of the coming Messiah. For example, Psalm 2:7 tells us, "He [the Lord] said to me, 'You are my Son; today I have become your Father.'" Others speak of the Messiah's humanity; for example,

Psalm 8:4–6 tells us, "What is man that you are mindful of him, the son of man that you care for him? You made him a little lower than the heavenly beings and crowned him with glory and honor. You made him ruler over the works of your hands; you put everything under his feet."

Other messianic passages in the Psalms include Psalm 110:1–2, which Jesus quoted as proof of His authority (see Matthew 22:43–44); Psalm 110:4, which speaks of Christ's atoning and priestly role; Psalm 42:9, which speaks of His betrayal; Psalm 118:22–23, which speaks of Christ being rejected by the people; Psalm 22, which speaks of His suffering and death; and Psalm 16:8–10, which speaks of His resurrection. David was a man whose hurt and guilt had been healed by God. He understood that God was his strength and the source of his life. Only God could meet every need of David's heart and work out all the tangled relationships in his family and his personal life.

Like the Psalms, which were written centuries before the birth of Christ, Leviticus is filled with pictures of Christ. All of the sacrifices, rituals, and ceremonies of Leviticus are pictures of Jesus Christ and His work. From this side of the cross, we can see Jesus clearly in the pages of Leviticus.

So Leviticus is not merely a book of history, nor is it merely a catalog of religious rules and regulations. It was not written merely for the people of Israel. It is a tremendously practical and relevant manual on how we are to live as Christians.

But there is even more to this powerful, practical book: When you read Leviticus and understand what it is saying, it will help you to understand yourself. It will reveal to you the person you truly are and the person God created you to be.

We are a mystery to ourselves. We don't even understand how we think. We are baffled by our own experience. We are driven by motives and urges we don't even understand, much less control. Paul expressed this painful dimension of our existence in his letter to the Romans: "For what I do is not the good I want to do; no, the evil I do not want to do—this I keep on doing" (Romans 7:19). That is a penetrating, probing analysis of what is going on in your life and mine.

In the same way, the book of Leviticus shows why we do the things we do. It leads us to a deeper, richer understanding of ourselves. It is designed to meet us where we are, in our sinfulness, our helplessness, and our hurt. As we learn how to accept the healing grace that God offers us, Leviticus will reveal to us the beauty and splendor of wholeness that can be ours.

In Jesus Christ, God took upon Himself the form of a man. He came to this earth, God in human flesh, and He lived among us—a man who was everything God intended human beings to be. He came to us in the midst of our brokenness. Everything He was and did as a man is what we also can be and do. So as you study Leviticus, you will discover not only Christ but also yourself. You will learn what your deepest needs truly are and how God has met those needs in Jesus Christ.

## AN OVERVIEW OF LEVITICUS

The book of Leviticus falls into two basic divisions. Part One speaks to human need. It reveals our condition as human beings and sets forth God's answer to our need. I call the first part of Leviticus (Leviticus 1–16) Basic Human Needs.

Part Two of Leviticus reveals what God expects from us in response to Him. This section shows God's provision for our wholeness, and then it reveals the performance that results from God's provision for our wholeness. I call this second part of Leviticus (Leviticus 17–27) Basic Human Behavior.

*Part One: Basic Human Needs.* In the first sixteen chapters of Leviticus we find four elements that set forth our need and reveal what we are truly like.

1. *Five offerings.* The first element is a series of five offerings. I believe that God gave us five fingers on each hand so that we can remember the five offerings: (1) the burnt offering, (2) the meal offering, (3) the peace offering, (4) the sin offering, and (5) the trespass offering. These five offerings are pictures of what Jesus Christ did for us when He was sacrificed upon the cross. They are also pictures of the great, fundamental needs of human life. These five offerings speak of the two essential ingredients of human existence: love and responsibility.

We can never be complete persons if we lack this first ingredient, love. We can never be all that God created us to be if we are not loved and if we do not love others. Love is an essential ingredient of life. We were made to love and be loved. Nothing hurts and distorts a human soul like the denial of love.

The second essential ingredient is a sense of responsibility. As human beings, we have duties and responsibilities to other human beings and to God. When we live responsibly, meeting our responsibilities to God and others, we gain a sense of self-worth and self-respect that comes from God.

In order to be whole people with healthy relationships, we need to experience both love and responsibility. The offerings that are presented in Leviticus show us the role that love and responsibility play in our lives.

2. *The priesthood.* The second element in this first half of Leviticus is the priesthood. In Leviticus, God provides the priesthood to help us handle the emotional and intellectual problems we face in trying to work out our relationships with love and responsibility.

In the Old Testament, this priesthood consisted of the sons of Levi. That is where the book of Leviticus gets its name. *Leviticus* is the Latin form of the Greek word *leutikos,* which means "Levitical—having to do with the Levites, the sons of Levi." In Old Testament times, God established the priesthood as ministers of God's Law and God's grace to the people of Israel.

In New Testament times, the Levitical priesthood was exchanged for a new priesthood consisting of Jesus Christ Himself—our Lord and High Priest—and all Christian believers. That's right; in the body of Christ, the church, we are all priests one to another. We are to practice the priesthood of all believers. We cannot get along without each other, because we all have problems with which we need help. And when we need help, we can go to Jesus, our High Priest, and to one another in the priesthood of all believers.

3. *The revelation of God's standard.* The third element in this section of Leviticus is the revelation of God's standard by which we can tell the difference between true and false, holy and unholy, wholeness and brokenness, real and phony, life and death.

It seems amazing but it's true: In our natural condition, we cannot tell the difference. There are thousands and thousands of people who are doing things they think are good and helpful, yet they are causing hurt—and they don't understand why their best intentions create pain in their lives and the lives of others. They cry out and say, "What did I do wrong? Why am I in this mess?" It's because they could not tell the difference between true and false, whole and broken.

God loves us and wants us to know the truth. He wants us to be able to tell the difference between true and false. So He has given us the book of Leviticus in which He sets forth the difference between that which is harmful and that which brings wholeness, health, and happiness. Now that God has made His truth known, we have no excuse if we continue to do the things that cause harm.

4. *An opportunity to respond to God.* The final element of this section of Leviticus is an opportunity to respond voluntarily to God. The Lord never imposes His will upon us. We constantly need His help, and we must come to a place where we recognize our need. Once we recognize our absolute brokenness before God, we need to give Him a response. So, in Leviticus, God gives us the opportunity to voluntarily say yes to Him. This opportunity was provided in the Day of Atonement (or in Hebrew, *Yom Kippur*), the observance of which is set forth in Leviticus 16.

But what if, after we recognize our need of God's help in our lives, we say no to Him? He will, of course, allow us to do so. We can say no to God—but there's a very real danger in doing so: We might never return to that place of opportunity again. God is gracious, and He often allows us a long period of time before our rejection of Him becomes final. But we never know, and we should never presume upon God's grace.

*Part Two: Basic Human Behavior.* The second section of the book, Leviticus 17–27, describes the kind of lives we can lead because of the provision that God has made for us. Notice that when God divides Leviticus into two parts, the order of the two parts is very important. Leviticus 1–16 discusses God's provision, because His provision comes first. Then Leviticus 17–27 deals with our behavior on the basis of His provision. God never speaks about our behavior until He has made clear that the basis of our behavior must be His power alone. We cannot live as we were meant to live in our own power. We can only live as God created us to live when we base our behavior on God's all-sufficient provision.

In the church, we often get this backward. A great deal of damage has been done to people by insisting that they behave in a certain way without helping them to understand the power by which to do so. Some Christians, out of an inadequate understanding of the Scriptures, teach people that they must live up to a certain standard of behavior before God will accept them! This is totally wrong, and it is a lie of Satan. It is deadly legalism, not biblical truth.

That is the great misimpression that God seeks to correct through the book of Leviticus. God never expects us to be holy and whole in our own power.

He always provides His power first, so that we can understand the basis upon which we are to act. In Leviticus He gives the pattern for becoming a whole and holy people. Here are the four elements of that pattern.

1. *The blood.* The basis for wholeness is blood. You see this throughout the Old Testament. A river of blood flows through the Old Testament in the form of sacrifices that seem strange to our thinking. There are thousands and thousands of sacrifices offered every year—bulls, calves, goats, sheep, and birds of all kinds.

Though the sacrifices of Leviticus ceased to be practiced centuries ago, they are not, as many people suppose, mere relics of a bygone era. These sacrifices have a powerful, life-changing meaning for us today. They are symbols designed to teach us the truth about ourselves and our relationships, especially our relationship with God.

Many non-Christians look at how important the blood of animals is in the Old Testament and how important Christ's blood is in the New Testament, and they say, "Well, Christianity is nothing but a slaughterhouse religion! It's all about blood! Why is all this blood being shed?"

It's because God is trying to impress us with a fundamental fact: The brokenness of our lives runs very deep. It is a problem that can be solved only by a death. The basis for our wholeness is that a life must be given up, the lifeblood of another must be poured out. Our brokenness cannot simply be mended by our natural efforts. We must have a new kind of life poured into us. We must give up the old before we can receive the new.

God is telling us that we can't have both the old life and the new. As Christians, that is our continual struggle: We keep trying to hang on to the old way of life and refuse to accept the new. The blood of the Levitical sacrifices speaks to the fact that the old must pass away so that we can receive the new. We will explore this principle in greater detail as we move through our study.

2. *Love in relationships.* The second element that becomes clear in the second half of Leviticus is that God tells us to practice love in all the relationships of our lives. The Bible is an intensely practical book. It is not nearly so concerned about what you do in the temple as it is about what you do in your home as a result of having been to the temple. So this book deals with our relationships within the family, among our friends, and with society in general. It shows us exactly the kind of love relationship that God makes possible for us in all these areas.

3. *Enjoying the presence and power of God.* The third element of the last half of Leviticus is the enjoyment of the presence and power of God—humanity in relationship to God, worshiping God, and empowered by the exciting reality of the living God. The most important thing in life is to have a personal relationship with the living God, who is the source of all life and of everything good.

4. *An awareness of the issues at stake.* The final element in the second half of Leviticus is an awareness of the importance of the issues of life and eternity. God demands that we make a choice. No one else can make this choice for us. God never says, "I'm going to make you leave your misery." Rather, He says, "If you prefer being broken and don't want to be healed, then that is up to you. If you so choose, you can stay right where you are, and you can die in your brokenness. But if you want life, then you can choose life, and I will give it to you."

God never forces His will upon us. But He does set before us the choice—a clear and unambiguous choice between life and death. He expects us to respond. He demands that we choose.

Throughout our study of Leviticus we must remember the key verse that unlocks the meaning of the entire book: "You are to be holy to me because I, the LORD, am holy, and I have set you apart from the nations to be my own" (Leviticus 20:26). That phrase "to be my own" has a unique, emphatic sense in the original Hebrew language. It is as if you can put all three tenses in a single word, so that God is saying, "You *were* mine, you *are* mine, you *shall be* mine."

As a Christian, you may have had an awareness that after you committed your life to Jesus Christ, you not only belonged to God at that moment, but there was a sense in which you had belonged to Him all along. The apostle Paul once wrote, "God . . . set me apart from birth and called me by his grace" (Galatians 1:15). Yet, for much of his life, Paul was an enemy of Christianity and a persecutor of Christians! Even so, Paul could look back upon his life and say that he was God's all along.

"You are mine," God tells us. "Even though you have been an enemy, even though you have been fighting me, you are *mine!* You have been mine, you are mine right now, and you will be mine for eternity." Even in our brokenness, our fragmented and imperfect state, God puts His loving hand upon our lives and says, "I have set you apart to be my own. You belong to me!"

I once heard about a service at a rescue mission in a city in the Midwest. It was a service for children, in which children put on the program. One little boy, about six years old, gave a recitation in the program. The boy had a birth defect which caused his back to be misshapen so that he was humpbacked. As he walked across the stage to give his recitation, he was shy and nervous. Not only was he self-conscious because of his physical condition, but it was the first time he had ever attempted a public performance. Doing the recitation was a great struggle for him.

There were two older boys in the back of the room who were chronic troublemakers. Just as the little boy was walking across the stage to begin his recitation, the two older boys in back called out, "Hey, kid! Where are you going with that pack on your back?"

The little boy stopped in his tracks and started to cry.

A man got up from the audience and walked up onto the stage. He knelt beside the little boy and put his arm around him. Then he said to the audience, "It must take a very cruel person to say such a thing. This boy has a condition that is not his fault. And he loves Jesus and he wanted to come out here and recite something for you all to show you what Jesus means to him. And I want you to know that I'm proud of this boy, because he is my own son. I love him just the way he is, and he belongs to me."

And the man hugged his son and led him off the platform.

That is what God says to us: He loves us just the way we are, and we belong to Him. He sees our hurt, our heartache, and our brokenness. He says to us, "You're mine, and you have always been mine. What's more, you will always be mine, and you will be made whole. All your blemishes and deformities will be corrected, all your sins will be set aside, all your tangled relationships will be straightened out. You will be whole, for I am whole. You will be holy, for I am holy."

That is what Jesus Christ is about. That is what the Bible is about. And that is what the book of Leviticus is about.

The rituals of Leviticus speak to us today as they spoke to the people centuries ago. The sacrifices of Leviticus point us to the sacrifice on the hill called Calvary, where the life of God's own Son was poured out for us, so that we might be whole and holy, so that God might set us apart to be His own.

So turn the page with me, and let's begin our exploration of the rich and rewarding truths of the book of Leviticus.

# THE NEED TO BELONG
### LEVITICUS 1

SOMEONE IS COMING. As you read through the Old Testament, you feel this sense of expectation. On page after page, you see a great emphasis on an approaching figure. You get a clear sense that Someone is coming. We see it in prophecies, shadows, and pictures of the future. All of Old Testament history seems to focus our attention on a coming moment in time.

And it is not just the prophetic books, such as Isaiah or Malachi, that tell us that Someone is coming. We can see it clearly even in the books of Old Testament law, in the book of Leviticus. The ceremonies, rites, and sacrifices of Leviticus are written in love, written in blood, and shout to us: Someone is coming!

Because we live on this side of the cross, we know who that Someone is: Jesus the Messiah. This, in itself, is a remarkable testimony to the divine authorship of Leviticus. Only God Himself could have prescribed offerings that so accurately depict the coming of Jesus.

Unfortunately, many people look at Leviticus and see only meaningless rituals, ceremonies, and sacrifices. But these rituals, ceremonies, and sacrifices are far from meaningless. They are pictures drawn by the hand of God to illustrate His truth. The Old Testament is filled with such pictures, and God employs them in His Word to prefigure something that is yet to come. The New Testament calls such pictures "shadows." In Colossians 2:16–17, Paul writes that the Old Testament dietary laws, religious festivals and celebrations, and Sabbath days "are a shadow of the things that were to come; the reality, however, is found in Christ." And Hebrews 10:1 tells us, "The law is only a shadow of the good things that are coming—not the realities themselves."

These pictures are visual aids God uses to impress His truth upon our minds. After all, we human beings are not very smart. We think we are, because we can invent complicated gadgetry like computers and space shuttles. But, in contrast to the wisdom and greatness of God, we know nothing at all. So God teaches us as you might teach a child. Kindergarten teachers never start out by writing complex mathematical formulas on the blackboard for children to learn. They start with simple arithmetic, using pictures to illustrate the concepts involved ("one apple plus two oranges equals how many pieces of fruit?"). That is how God began teaching the human race—with pictures and shadows.

## God's Pictures: The Law and the Tabernacle

In Exodus, the book immediately before Leviticus, we find the story of Israel's redemption from Egypt. Look at the components of that story and see if they remind you of a deep spiritual truth.

The people of Israel were in slavery under a cruel and vicious king. Then a deliverer came who spoke for God. By means of the Passover, God sheltered His people under the blood, which was splashed onto wooden crosspieces that framed a doorway. God's angel of death passed over the people, and the deliverer led the people out of bondage, through the depths of the sea, and into a place of freedom.

In this story, we also see a picture (a type) of how all humanity was in slavery to a cruel king named Satan. The people were in bondage to sin and death. Then came a deliverer, Jesus Christ. He served the Passover meal; then His blood was splashed on a wooden cross, and that cross became the doorway of escape. The angel of death passes over all who place their trust in the deliverer, Jesus. He leads us out of bondage, through the deep places of this life, and to a place of freedom from sin and death.

Exodus also records two more pictures God gave Israel as visual aids: The Law and the tabernacle. Let's look at each of these pictures and see how they illustrate profound and practical spiritual truth:

1. *The Law.* In Exodus 19 we find a dramatic and terrifying scene. Three

months after leaving Egypt, the people of Israel gathered before Mount Sinai. A trumpet sounded—a blast that must have been very much like an air raid siren today. The mountain was wreathed in flame and smoke, the ground shook with a great earthquake, and the people were terrified. God said to Moses, "Come up here! I want to talk to you!" And Moses went up on the mountain alone.

I have never envied Moses that trip, or that awe-inspiring and terrifying encounter. But it was there, on the mountain, that God gave the Law to Moses.

The Ten Commandments (recorded in Exodus 20:3–17) are nothing more or less than God's revelation of His expectations of us. The Ten Commandments tell us the kind of people God designed and created us to be. When He made us in His own image, He made us to live the kind of life that is described in the Ten Commandments. Some of them pertain to our relationship with God: "You shall have no other gods before me. . . . You shall not misuse the name of the LORD your God." Others deal with our relationships with family and neighbors: "Honor your father and your mother. . . . You shall not murder. . . . You shall not commit adultery."

These commandments speak to us with power and authority, because something within us knows they are right. God has, in a sense, written aspects of the Law into every human heart. This is why everywhere in the world, no matter what culture you observe, you will find a sense of responsibility and accountability to God and an awareness that human beings should live up to a certain standard. This sense of oughtness—we *ought* to do this and we *ought not* do that—is evident throughout the human race.

2. *The Tabernacle.* Along with the Law, God gave Moses the pattern of a building—the tabernacle. God told Moses, in effect, "Don't vary the pattern; build it exactly as I have told you." The book of Hebrews tells us that the tabernacle is a picture of humanity and of what God intends to do—and that is to live in us. So God designed the tabernacle the same way He designed us: in three sections, spirit, soul, and body. In the tabernacle there was the outer court (representing the body), the Holy Place (representing the soul), and the Holy of Holies (representing the unfathomable, mysterious aspect of our being called the spirit). God designed the tabernacle as a picture of humanity so that we could understand ourselves and how God intends to dwell within us.

God illustrated His presence in the tabernacle by means of a bright, shining light which seemed to have no visible source. That light was called the

Shekinah, and it was the visible mark of the presence of God. It was not God Himself but only a picture of God, for no human eye can see God. But that light reminded Israel that this is where God intends to dwell—in the human tabernacle, which the tabernacle represents. God's dwelling place is in you and me, His people.

The Law that was given to Moses at Mount of Sinai was the Old Covenant. God said to humanity, "This is what you ought to be." Thus the Law made an absolutely inflexible demand on the human race. God said, in effect, "Any deviation from this Law must be punished because it means that you are failing to be what you were made to be, and this can't be ignored!" And the human race said, "All right, we'll keep the Law." And they tried—

But they failed. Why? Because someone has thrown a monkey wrench into the human machinery: We are all fallen! As fallen creatures, we are incapable of keeping God's perfect Law.

The Law is like the instruction manual for your car, but with a nasty twist. Imagine this: You have bought a new car, you've carefully read the instruction manual, and you've promised yourself that you would faithfully follow every instruction. But every time you go out to drive your car, you find that someone has put water in your gas tank and sand in your oil—nothing works right. That is what it is like for us as human beings when we try to live in obedience to the Law. That Law, which seems so simple to understand and whose demands are so fair and reasonable, becomes in practice a set of demands that we can never hope to meet.

That is why God, after the tabernacle was built, gave the people of Israel a whole series of sacrifices as a picture of the New Covenant, the new arrangement for living. In these sacrifices there is death and blood—yet there is also a priest who helps us with our spiritual and emotional hurts, who pronounces God's forgiveness of sin, and who helps us experience a restored fellowship with God, even though we have broken His Law.

## THE SACRIFICES

The sacrifices of Leviticus are shadows and pictures. The slaying of an animal and the shedding of animal blood cannot save us. But the blood pictures for us what can save us: Jesus Christ. The animal sacrifices are a picture of the sacrifice of Jesus upon the cross. The sacrifices pictured for the people of Israel a future event, which we now look upon as an historical event. When the people of Israel made these sacrifices, their faith was not in the shed blood of animals but in what that blood pictured, even though their understanding of that picture was limited. Though they didn't know Jesus Christ by name and had never heard the gospel that we have heard, their faith was in Him and in the work He would one day perform upon the cross for all of humankind.

The book of Leviticus opens with these words, which speak of the sacrifices that God has ordained:

> The LORD called to Moses and spoke to him from the Tent of Meeting [that is, the tabernacle]. He said, "Speak to the Israelites and say to them: 'When any of you brings an offering to the LORD, bring as your offering an animal from either the herd or the flock'" (Leviticus 1:1–2).

Notice that this whole system of sacrifices was never given from Sinai. It was given from the tabernacle, the place where God had come to live with humankind. This is significant for us. God never placed the demand of the Law upon us without also intending to meet it from within, from the life of Jesus Christ within us, which is God dwelling in us. So God has made a provision for the problem of breaking the Law. He has dealt with the problem of guilt, shame, condemnation, self-hatred, and all the other afflictions that attack us from within and keep us from experiencing the wholeness God created us to have.

Five offerings or sacrifices are presented in Leviticus, and each of those five offerings represents one aspect of the work of Jesus Christ. Each of these offerings followed a pattern that was fulfilled when Jesus Christ died on the cross and met all the requirements of our holy God. These offerings are (1) the burnt offering, (2) the meal offering, (3) the peace offering, (4) the trespass offering, and (5) the sin offering. When Jesus died, He took our place and made these offerings in our stead. That is why God put Him to death.

The five offerings reveal what we are as fallen human beings, as children of Adam, as heirs of the Adamic sin nature. So if you want to understand yourself, then heed these offerings. They represent what Jesus Christ had to become in order to help us. They tell us who and what we are.

## THE BURNT OFFERING

The first of these five offerings is the most basic one, the burnt offering, which followed a five-step pattern:

First step: A selection of the sacrifice. The burnt offering had to be an animal sacrifice, and, as we shall see, it was always a male, without blemish, without any kind of defect or disfigurement at all. Animals were the most valuable possession of the Hebrew people, so an animal was a costly sacrifice taken from their most valuable treasure—their herds.

Second step: They laid hands on the offering. What does that mean? God was teaching the people the principle of substitution—the fact that we human beings are all tied together, we belong to one another, we share life together, and there is a way by which one of us can substitute for another. To deal with our deepest guilt, however, that substitute had to be a spotless, sinless person. And the only human being who ever fulfilled that qualification was Jesus Christ. That is why He is the only one who can substitute for us and redeem us.

This rite of identification, the laying on of hands, is God's expressive way of teaching us that we belong to each other. That is why, in the church today, when we commission a person to do ministry in the church or on the mission field, we will bring that person before the entire congregation and lay hands on him or her. By this symbolic rite we say, "We are with you, we are one with you, we are praying for you and supporting you financially, spiritually, and emotionally." In the sacrificial sense, the rite of identification said that the people were identified with the sacrifice—not with the animal itself but with the sacrifice of the One the animal represented, the coming Christ.

Third step: They killed the animal immediately. God never allowed any compromise on this step. He did not say, "This cute little lamb is innocent of any wrongdoing, so just drain a half pint of blood and I'll be satisfied." God wanted to impress upon us the fact that our sin problem is so deeply rooted in our lives that nothing but death can solve it. It cannot be mitigated or disguised by some temporary expedient. The awfulness of sin requires the immediate death of the substitutionary sacrifice.

Fourth step: They sprinkled the blood and burned the portions of the sacrifice as an act of consecration and commitment to God. The instant the animal died, it became acceptable to God. Death solved the problem of separation and alienation so that the sacrifice could be offered to God.

Fifth and final step: They experienced a ceremonial indication of a restored relationship. Usually they sat down and ate part of the meat of the sacrifice. This is where the Hebrew people got their meat dishes, because they could eat only the meat of their sacrifices. Every animal they killed had to be slain at the door of the Tent of Meeting—that is, the tabernacle. There were some offerings, like the burnt offering, from which they could not eat. But with these God gave them other means of indicating that the relationship was restored and that there was peace again.

The burnt offering was the most frequently offered sacrifice in Israel. Every morning and every evening the priests would give a burnt offering. It was called the continual burnt offering and it had to fulfill certain requirements: The offering had to be a male without blemish, and it had to be totally consumed by fire.

## FIRST REQUIREMENT: A MALE WITHOUT BLEMISH

The first requirement of the burnt offering was that it was always a male without blemish. The people had three choices as to the kind of animal:

> "If the offering is a burnt offering from the herd, he is to offer a male without defect. He must present it at the entrance to the Tent of Meeting so that it will be acceptable to the LORD. He is to lay his hand on the head of the burnt offering, and it will be accepted on his behalf to make atonement for him. He is to slaughter the young bull before the LORD, and then Aaron's sons the priests shall bring the blood and sprinkle it against the altar on all sides at the entrance to the Tent of Meeting. He is to skin the burnt offering and cut it into pieces. The sons of Aaron the priest are to put fire on the altar and arrange wood on the fire. Then Aaron's sons the priests shall arrange the pieces, including the head and the fat, on the burning wood that is on the altar. He is to wash the inner parts and the legs with water, and the priest is to burn all of it on the altar. It is a burnt offering, an offering made by fire, an aroma pleasing to the LORD" (Leviticus 1:3–9).

If you were rich, you brought a bull. But if you could not afford a bull or if you did not have a herd of cattle but only a flock of sheep or goats, then another provision was made:

> "If the offering is a burnt offering from the flock, from either the sheep or the goats, he is to offer a male without defect. He is to slaughter it at the north side of the altar before the LORD, and Aaron's sons the priests shall sprinkle its blood against the altar on all sides. He is to cut it into pieces, and the priest shall arrange them, including the head and the fat, on the burning wood that is on the altar. He is to wash the inner parts and the legs with water, and the priest is to bring all of it and burn it on the altar. It is a burnt offering, an offering made by fire, an aroma pleasing to the LORD" (Leviticus 1:10–13).

Every action described in these verses is symbolically significant in picturing the coming work and sacrifice of Jesus Christ. We will see this more clearly as we go along.

Finally, if you were very poor and had no animals, you could bring a bird:

> "If the offering to the LORD is a burnt offering of birds, he is to offer a dove or a young pigeon. The priest shall bring it to the altar, wring off the head and burn it on the altar; its blood shall be drained out on the side of the altar. He is to remove the crop with its contents and throw it to the east side of the altar, where the ashes are. He shall tear it open by the wings, not severing it completely, and then the priest shall burn it on the wood that is on the fire on the altar. It is a burnt offering, an offering made by fire, an aroma pleasing to the LORD" (Leviticus 1:14–17).

All of this sounds very bloody and gory to our sensibilities today. But God is saying something important to us through all of this death and bloodletting. He is indicating by these sacrificial animals that a provision has been made for everyone, so that God's people can be made whole and holy. No one is left out. Even the poorest can offer something as a burnt offering.

You may remember that when Joseph and Mary took the baby Jesus to the temple in Jerusalem to be circumcised on the eighth day, they gave a burnt offering of a pair of doves (see Luke 2:21–24). It is amazing to realize that the offering they made on that day symbolized the coming sacrificial death of Mary's own son.

Why did God require that this first offering, the burnt offering, always be male? It is because in the Scriptures a male always stands for leadership, initiative, and dominion. Females in Scripture always signify support, following, and response, and there were certain offerings for which a female animal was specified. The people of God were told specifically what to do because these symbols were intended to teach them truths they needed to know.

So the burnt offering had to be a male without blemish or disfigurement. This is a recognition of the fact that in this most basic of all offerings, God was dealing with man as a king, as a sovereign. Man was made to rule. He was never made to be in bondage to anyone. That is why we are restless when we are enslaved or held in bondage of any sort. We cannot stand it, for something deep within us was made by God to rule.

In Psalm 8, David looks up to the heavens and asks, "What is man that you are mindful of him, the son of man that you care for him?" And then he answers his own question: "You made him ruler over the works of your hands; you put everything under his feet" (Psalm 8:4, 6). All the fish and other inhabitants of the seas, all the animals and birds, everything is put under the authority of man. That is man as God created him. And man still feels this. That is why we are not content unless we are running things in this world.

No scientist is content to be excluded from an area of knowledge. No explorer can rest if any mountains are left unclimbed. When Sir Edmund Hillary conquered Mt. Everest, he was asked why he did it. His reply: "Because it was there." All this is a dim remembrance of the dominion God gave man. This dominion is symbolized by the selection of the male for this offering. The sacrifice of the male was the sacrifice of a ruler, of one who has dominion. It symbolizes the sacrifice of Jesus the King.

## SECOND REQUIREMENT: TOTALLY CONSUMED

The second requirement of the burnt offering was that it must be totally consumed. Nobody ever ate the meat of the burnt offering. Look at Leviticus 1:6–9:

"He is to skin the burnt offering and cut it into pieces. The sons of Aaron the priest are to put fire on the altar and arrange wood on the fire. Then Aaron's sons the priests shall arrange the pieces, including the head and the fat, on the burning wood that is on the altar. He is to wash the inner parts and the legs with water, and the priest is to burn all of it on the altar. It is a burnt offering, an offering made by fire, an aroma pleasing to the LORD."

In Leviticus, there were three sacrifices that were said to be "an aroma pleasing to the LORD." The first of these is this burnt offering. God says that there is something about man which, when he recognizes his right to rule and gives himself wholly to it, is pleasing to God. God is thereby teaching us that man was meant to be His, wholly and totally. The whole human being—body, soul, and spirit—is to be the dwelling place of God. Only a human being who is indwelt and ruled by God is able to rule as he was meant to rule.

This is a recognition of the most basic hunger of man. It is a reflection of our need to belong, to be accepted, to beloved, to have an identity, a relationship, a cause to live for, and even to die for. The human soul is forever restless without a sense of belonging. We will never find fulfillment until we find it in committing ourselves totally to God. You and I are searching for someone to love us. That is the most primitive and basic hunger of our lives.

We like to think we have a godlike ability to control our own destinies. We try to run the universe and have everything revolve around us. Our will to complete autonomy and self-determination was well stated by William Ernest Henley in his poem "Invictus," in which he thanks "whatever gods may be" for his "unconquerable soul." He ends his poem with these defiant lines: "I am the master of my fate / I am the captain of my soul."

It is a satanic lie that a human being is master of his or her own fate. God could flick off a little switch inside your body and you would be instantly dead from a heart attack or an aneurysm. You'd have nothing to say about it. No human being runs his own life or controls her own destiny. Humanity is not God. We were not made to exist on our own. We were made to belong to someone else. When God says, "I have set you apart from the nations to be my own," He is telling us what our purpose is, what we were created to be—God's own people, a people who belong to Him.

Perhaps you have detected a paradox at this point. Here are two great truths, linked together in Scripture, which seem to contradict each other: Man was born to rule, but he was also made to belong to God. Man was born to be king over all, but he was made to be under the authority and ownership of God. In fact, human beings are not happy unless they are possessed by God. These truths appear contradictory, but they complement and complete each other.

A number of years ago, a young man in his late twenties came to our church—we'll call him Michael. He was in trouble with the law because he had been caught bilking people out of their money. For years Michael had lived as a con artist, taking advantage of people. Now he had been caught, and he wanted to mend his ways and start a new life. As I met with him, I learned his story.

Michael had not known anything about his origin or identity until he was fourteen years of age. He had grown up in foster homes. At age fourteen, he got an after-school job in a store, and while working there, he embezzled five thousand dollars. He used the money to hire a private detective agency to trace his family background. Every cent of the stolen money went for that purpose. He couldn't rest until he knew who he was and where he came from—and he was even willing to risk imprisonment to find out. The detective agency was able to uncover the information the boy wanted and reported back to him.

The agency told Michael that he was the illegitimate son of the daughter of an American missionary couple. While in the Philippines with her parents, the girl had fallen in love with a young Filipino man, and she'd had a baby out of wedlock. Because this was a matter of shame and embarrassment to the missionary family, the parents arranged to have the baby taken back to the States and placed in foster care. That baby—who was Michael—grew up in an orphanage and never knew his family background until he paid five thousand dollars in stolen money to find out.

The years of not knowing who he was or where he belonged had taken a toll on Michael. He was in the grip of that ancient paradox: He was born to rule and born to belong to another. Yet he had no sense of belonging, because he didn't know where he came from. His lack of identity and belonging drove him to steal in order to find his origins, and after the first theft, he kept stealing until he finally got caught and didn't want to live as a thief anymore.

In a real sense, we are all born as Michael was. Until we find God and allow

Him to become the Master of our fate and the Captain of our soul, we are doomed to feel lost, cast adrift in the universe, without a sense of where we came from, without a place of belonging.

That is what the burnt offering tells us: Our most basic quest in life is to belong to someone, to be identified with someone, to be loved and accepted and possessed by someone. There is nothing more pitiable and pathetic than that person who feels no one loves him, no one cares for his soul.

## THIRD REQUIREMENT: DEATH

A third requirement of the burnt offering is that it must involve a death. In these offerings, death is always a picture of the sacrificial death of the Lord Jesus Christ on our behalf. Only by means of the death of an acceptable substitute—which is Jesus—can human beings ever satisfy their great longing to be possessed by God. So we must give ourselves to God through Christ, acknowledging that He owns us, that we belong to Him: "You are not your own; you were bought at a price" (1 Corinthians 6:19–20).

Many people rebel at this idea. They say, "I don't want God to run my life; I don't want to be God's little robot." But God does not exploit us or treat us as robots or slaves. He loves us more than we love ourselves, and He wants us to be fulfilled and satisfied. Only when we truly belong to Him can we truly be free and happy. That is one of the great paradoxes and life-changing truths of the Christian faith.

You can find a certain amount of satisfaction in having a family to belong to, and in knowing where you came from in a human sense. But you will never find complete satisfaction by merely knowing your human origins. Your hunger for belonging can find its ultimate satisfaction only in a relationship to God through Jesus Christ. It is the death of Christ that opens the door to that relationship.

I once shared a speaking platform with Dr. Henry Brandt, the noted Christian psychologist. He told a story about when he and his wife were dating and talking about marriage. They told each other that they wanted to give themselves to each other's happiness. He said, "I'll never forget the night my wife said to me, 'Henry, dear, I want to spend the rest of my life just making you happy!' I thought, *Isn't that great!? This beautiful woman wants to dedicate her life to making me happy!* I thought it was tremendous—and then we got married."

The first week of their marriage, Henry Brandt told his wife, "Every Thursday night I go out with the guys. Tonight is Thursday night, so I'll be out late. Don't wait up for me." His wife, he said, reacted very strangely! She said, "But you can't leave me all alone!" He said," There are lots of things you can do, and I'll just be out one night a week." She said, "You can't do that! You're married now! You have to stay here with me!" And Henry Brandt wondered to himself, *What happened to her promise? Here is her first chance to make me happy, and she has blown it completely!*

Eventually, Dr. Brandt realized that there is a great deal of joy in the fact that a husband and wife truly belong to each other. Even so, the deepest yearning for belonging can never be fully satisfied apart from a relationship with God through Jesus Christ.

This is what the burnt offering says to us: Only through the death of Christ, which brings us into a relationship with the living God, can this universal desire for belonging be met. That is what accounts for the great sense of joy and relief so many people feel at the moment they surrender their lives to Jesus Christ. It is a feeling that says, "Now I belong! God is my Father! I'm in a family. I'll never be alone again! I belong to God!"

## FOURTH REQUIREMENT: THE SACRIFICE MUST BE CONTINUAL

The fourth and final requirement of the burnt offering is that it must be continual. This requirement is given in Leviticus 6, where God gives additional instructions to the priests about how to make these offerings:

> "The fire on the altar must be kept burning; it must not go out. Every morning the priest is to add firewood and arrange the burnt offering on the fire and burn the fat of the fellowship offerings on it. The fire must be kept burning on the altar continuously; it must not go out" (Leviticus 6:12–13).

What is God saying by that? Simply that this is the most basic relationship of your life. No other need can ever be met until this need is met. Every morning and every evening the people were to offer the burnt offering. It would consume the wood and the meat all through the day and all through the night, so that the fire never went out. The burnt offering was the central and most basic of the five offerings. Through the symbolism of the burnt offering, God says that you can never satisfy any other hunger of your life until you have satisfied your hunger for God's love. Until you are His—body, soul, and spirit—you can never know peace.

If you want to solve any other problem of life, you must begin by coming into a relationship with God the Father through His Son, Jesus Christ. You must be able to say, "I belong to the Father. I am a child in His family. I know Him as my heavenly Father. I am loved by Him." A relationship with God is the starting point for restoring every other relationship in your life.

This, then, is the meaning of the burnt offering: It satisfies our need to belong, because it represents the continual sacrifice of Christ in our lives, Christ the One without spot or blemish, the One who was completely consumed, who died and rose again, and who opened the door to a relationship with God the Father. Because of the burnt offering sacrifice of Jesus Christ, that relationship can never be broken. We will never be abandoned, never forsaken, never lost. We have our identity and our place of belonging in God.

CHAPTER 3

※————————※

# THE NEED TO RESPOND
## LEVITICUS 2

THERE IS NO more universal food than bread. Almost every culture around the world has its own version of it: white bread, wheat bread, rye bread, pumpernickel, sourdough, French bread, muffins, croissants, matzo, pita, tortillas, and on and on. Bread is symbolic of life and in fact is called the staff of life because we lean on it as a person leans on a wooden staff for support. Bread is also one of our most important social ties, for we break bread together as a sign of friendship and hospitality.

Here in Leviticus, as in our everyday lives, we see that bread, and the grain flour from which bread is made, has a symbolic importance far greater than we usually realize. In Leviticus 2, we come to the second of the five sacrifices, called "the grain offering" in the New International Version. Many other versions call it "the meal offering," while the Revised Standard Version calls it "the cereal offering." In the King James Version it is called the "meat" offering because "meat" was the old English word for "food." There is, however, no meat, no animal flesh whatsoever, in this second sacrifice. Of the five sacrifices in Leviticus, this is the only bloodless sacrifice, involving no animal death.

The grain sacrifice could be offered in any of three forms. The first form was that of simple, fine flour, which is a biblical symbol of idealized or redeemed humanity:

"When someone brings a grain offering to the LORD, his offering is to be of fine flour. He is to pour oil on it, put incense on it and take it to Aaron's sons the priests. The priest shall take a handful of the fine flour and oil, together with all the incense, and burn this as a memorial portion on the altar, an offering made by fire, an aroma pleasing to the LORD. The rest of the grain offering belongs to Aaron and his sons; it is a most holy part of the offerings made to the LORD by fire" (Leviticus 2:1–3).

This sacrifice or offering was clearly intended to be food for the priests. Leviticus 2:4 describes a second form in which the offering could be presented:

"If you bring a grain offering baked in an oven, it is to consist of fine flour: cakes made without yeast and mixed with oil, or wafers made without yeast and spread with oil. If your grain offering is prepared on a griddle, it is to be made of fine flour mixed with oil, and without yeast. Crumble it and pour oil on it; it is a grain offering. If your grain offering is cooked in a pan, it is to be made of fine flour and oil. Bring the grain offering made of these things to the LORD; present it to the priest, who shall take it to the altar. He shall take out the memorial portion from the grain offering and burn it on the altar as an offering made by fire, an aroma pleasing to the LORD. The rest of the grain offering belongs to Aaron and his sons; it is a most holy part of the offerings made to the LORD by fire.

"Every grain offering you bring to the LORD must be made without yeast, for you are not to burn any yeast or honey in an offering made to the LORD by fire. You may bring them to the LORD as an offering of the first fruits, but they are not to be offered on the altar as a pleasing aroma. Season all your grain offerings with salt. Do not leave the salt of the covenant of your God out of your grain offerings; add salt to all your offerings" (Leviticus 2:4–13).

So the people could bring the grain in the form of loaves or cakes of unleavened bread which could be baked, grilled, or pan-fried.

The third form of this offering is found in Leviticus 2:14:

"If you bring a grain offering of first fruits to the LORD, offer crushed heads of new grain roasted in the fire."

The people could take freshly harvested wheat and shake the grain out by hand and crush it. That was then acceptable as a cereal offering. It is obvious that the essence of this offering was that it was bread, the staff of life. This theme is the key to the grain sacrifice. All through the Old Testament you find people offering the grain sacrifice, often in the form of three loaves of bread. And in the tabernacle there was the showbread—the twelve loaves that God had commanded to be displayed on a special table before Him at all times (see Exodus 25:30).

Why was the sacrifice of bread so important in Leviticus? The reason becomes apparent when you turn to the New Testament and see how Jesus spoke of Himself. After the great miracle when He fed five thousand people with a few loaves and fishes, Jesus told the people, "For the bread of God is he who comes down from heaven and gives life to the world. . . . I am the bread of life. He who comes to me will never go hungry, and he who believes in me will never be thirsty" (John 6:33–35). He told the people that He Himself was to be their food. We are to feed upon the character, person, and life of Jesus, because He is the bread of life from heaven.

The words of Jesus give us a clue as to what the grain sacrifice depicts. It is a description of humanity as God intended it to be. Humanity was displayed in its perfect form only in Jesus Christ—the perfect, unsullied, God-pleasing humanity of the Lord Jesus.

Many people today think that the gospel, the good news, is that Jesus Christ died on the cross so that we might go to heaven when we die. But that is only part of the gospel. The truly good news is that Jesus Christ died for you in order that He might live in you today. It is the life of Jesus in us today that is the exciting part of Christianity. If you are not linked with His humanity and all that He is, then you are not enjoying the fullness of the Christian experience, because that is what Christianity is all about.

"I have been crucified with Christ," wrote the apostle Paul, "and I no longer live, but Christ lives in me" (Galatians 2:20). The perfect humanity of Jesus Christ is available to live in us and through us. All the fullness of His life, the fineness of His character, the balanced quality of His humanity—all of this is available to us. As His character becomes more and more our character, we can offer our humanity back to God to use as He pleases. When we do, our very lives become "an aroma pleasing to the LORD." That is the fullness of the gospel, and that is what the grain sacrifice is all about.

Fine flour is a beautiful symbol of redeemed or idealized humanity. In Scripture, fine flour is used to symbolize either the perfect humanity of Jesus Christ or the redeemed and refined humanity of those who are new creations in Christ. If you take a pinch of fine flour and run it through your fingers, you'll find that you can't feel any coarseness, any granularity, any roughness. It is smooth, powdery, and consistent.

This is why fine flour is such an apt picture of the humanity of Jesus, and of humanity, as God intended us to be. Now, if we wanted to symbolize our natural humanity as it is, apart from Jesus Christ, it would be something like rough-cut oatmeal, coarse with chips of husk and straw and other chaff. But humanity as God made us to be, and as He intends us to be, is a balanced life, smooth and refined and consistent.

## WHAT IS INCLUDED

Three things always had to be included in the grain sacrifice and two things always were excluded. Each of these items has great symbolic importance for our lives. The three things always included were oil, incense, and salt. Every mention of the grain sacrifice in any form includes oil and incense. The oil was used in two ways: It was mingled with the fine flour, and it was also poured on top of it. This is very instructive, as we will soon see. The incense was a perfume, a delightful fragrance. The use of salt is specified in Leviticus 2:13:

> "Season all your grain offerings with salt. Do not leave the salt of the covenant of your God out of your grain offerings; add salt to all your offerings."

Again, we have these marvelous visual aids that God uses to teach us what He wants to accomplish in our lives. In our new humanity, which we have received in Christ, God wants to make sure that three elements are present—elements which are symbolized in the grain sacrifice.

The first element is oil, that is a type, or picture, of the Holy Spirit. All through the Scriptures you find that oil symbolizes the Spirit of God. In the grain sacrifice, the oil is to be used in two ways. First, it mingles with our humanity. This speaks of the indwelling Spirit. When you became a Christian by faith in Jesus Christ, the Spirit of God was poured out in your heart (see Romans 5:5). The Spirit came to live in you, and He has become an inseparable part of you, mingled with your humanity. This is called the baptism of the Holy Spirit. By the Spirit, we are all baptized into one body, as Paul says in 1 Corinthians 12:13.

As you live the Christian life, you also need to have the Spirit anointing you and empowering you. To be anointed with the Spirit is to have the Spirit poured out on you. As Paul goes on to say in that same verse, "and we were all given the one Spirit to drink." This was true of Jesus Christ in His life. He was filled with the Spirit from His mother's womb. But then came the day when, in the baptism at the river Jordan, the Spirit of God anointed Him for His ministry.

The second element that must be added is incense, most commonly frankincense, a dried resin extracted from the boswellia tree, which grows from Africa to India. Leviticus 2:2 says, "The priest shall take a handful of the fine flour and oil, together with all the incense, and burn this as a memorial portion on the altar, an offering made by fire, an aroma pleasing to the LORD."

When the Scriptures talk about "an aroma pleasing to the LORD," they speak of something that God desires in our lives—not something outward and showy but something inward and authentic. What this is, I believe, is made clear by various passages in Scripture which speak of the things that delight God. Let's look at just a few.

> I will praise God's name in song
> and glorify him with thanksgiving.
> This will please the LORD more than an ox,
> more than a bull with its horns and hoofs (Psalm 69:30–31).

Don't bother to bring the ox or the bull! Just bring a thankful, cheerful, praise-filled heart! That will please the Lord. And in the New Testament we read:

Through Jesus, therefore, let us continually offer to God a sacrifice of praise—the fruit of lips that confess his name. And do not forget to do good and to share with others, for with such sacrifices God is pleased (Hebrews 13:15–16).

In these and other passages, God tells us that the fragrant, pleasing frankincense of our lives is a thankful, cheerful, obedient heart. That is what delights Him. As we present our redeemed humanity to Him, that is what He wants to see.

The third element that must be added is salt, which is a preservative. In the days before refrigeration, meat was preserved by salting it. Beef jerky is a form of salted, dried meat that you can buy today. It is preserved in much the same way that meat has been preserved for thousands of years.

Jesus once told His disciples, "You are the salt of the earth" (Matthew 5:13). In other words, "You Christians are intended to be the thing that keeps society from becoming rotten and corrupt." He also said, "You are the light of the world" (Matthew 5:14). Light is revealed truth. Salt is truth that is obeyed in the power of the Holy Spirit.

If we want to understand what is wrong with the world today, we need only look to ourselves. The Christian church has been preaching the truth, but it has not been obeying that truth. Until Christians obey what God has said about living moral, merciful, compassionate lives, there is no preservative in society. The world will continue to decay around us. But when the church begins to live as salt and light, living out Christlike love and righteousness toward the world, then the church will be salt and light as God intended it to be.

That is why God says in Leviticus, "Add salt to all your offerings."

## What Is Excluded

There are two things that must be excluded from the grain sacrifice, and both are mentioned in Leviticus 2:11:

"Every grain offering you bring to the Lord must be made without yeast, for you are not to burn any yeast or honey in an offering made to the Lord by fire."

God did not want any yeast added to the grain sacrifice. Why? Because yeast is a leavening agent. It causes bread dough to rise and expand, to puff itself up. Yeast, then, is a picture of that aspect of human nature that puffs us up: pride.

Someone once said, "Human beings are odd creatures. When you pat them on the back, their heads swell up." Pride is a sneaky thing. We in the church have figured out ingenious ways to disguise our pride and make it look like humility! It is said that a church once gave its pastor a medal for humility—but they had to take it away because he wore it! We are all susceptible to the yeast of pride.

Paul said to the Corinthians, "We know that we all possess knowledge. Knowledge [that is, pride in one's knowledge] puffs up, but love builds up" (1 Corinthians 8:1). This is so true. God is saying, "When you come to offer your humanity to me, don't mix in any human ego with it. Don't do this for your own glory. Don't try to take credit for yourself." As Paul says in 1 Corinthians 1:29, no flesh, no human being, shall glory or boast in God's presence. God rejects the yeast of human pride.

The second thing that must be excluded from the grain sacrifice is honey. What's wrong with honey? Normally, nothing. Honey is usually spoken of in positive terms in the Bible, as when the Israelites were promised a land flowing with milk and honey. But here in Leviticus God rejects honey as part of the grain sacrifice.

Honey is not refined like sugar. It is natural sweetness. Honey, in this symbolic sense, refers to the natural sweetness of human nature. There are some people who could be called naturally sweet. They have a sweet disposition. They are charming. They are nice. But God says, "Don't bring your natural sweetness to me because it won't work." The only sweetness God accepts is the sweetness of the perfect humanity of Jesus Christ working in us. He does not want our natural attributes. He refuses the honey we try to mix in with the grain sacrifice of our lives.

## WE ARE MADE TO RESPOND

As you read through Leviticus and the rest of the Old Testament, you find that the people of Israel never offered a grain sacrifice by itself. It was always accompanied by an animal sacrifice. These grain offerings were designed to go with one of the animal sacrifices, and most often with the burnt offering. That is why it is put right next to the burnt offering in the order of the sacrifices. There is the burnt offering, then the grain offering, then the peace offering. The grain sacrifice is always offered in connection with the burnt sacrifice.

This tells us something significant about the meaning of this grain sacrifice. The burnt sacrifice was focused on our human need to be loved and accepted, our need to belong. But if God reaches out to you and says, "You are mine," then that lays a demand upon you, doesn't it? You need to do something; you need to respond to His love. He has reached out toward you; you need to reach back toward Him. That is what the grain sacrifice is all about. It tells us that we can never be fulfilled until we respond to the love of God.

We are made to respond. Usually we respond to others in the same way they approach us. If I approach you with affection and an embrace, you will probably respond to me the same way. If I approach you with criticism and accusation, you will probably criticize and accuse me in response.

God has reached out to us in love, so you'd think we would respond to Him in love as well, but it doesn't always work that way. Why not? Because there are sometimes barriers of fear, suspicion, and selfishness that need to be removed before we are able to respond in love to the love of God.

As long as we are unable to respond, there can be no progress in the love relationship between ourselves and God. The One who loves us and reaches out toward us cannot go any further in developing the relationship as long as we are unwilling or unable to respond. Even God, the Almighty and Omnipotent, can do nothing more with us until we say yes to what He has offered us.

That is why Hebrews 4:2 tells us that when the good news reached the people of Israel, "the message they heard was of no value to them, because those who heard did not combine it with faith." In other words, the people did not respond to the message God gave them. They did not say yes, so God could do nothing more to build a relationship with them. This is why Paul writes this heartfelt plea to the church in Corinth:

> We have spoken freely to you, Corinthians, and opened wide our hearts to you. We are not withholding our affection from you, but you are withholding yours from us. As a fair exchange—I speak as to my children—open wide your hearts also (2 Corinthians 6:11–13).

Paul says, in effect, "There's nothing limiting us. We love you and want to help you. I want to minister to you, but you won't respond. You won't open your heart."

This is why God is often represented in the Scriptures as pleading with humanity. "'Come now, let us reason together,' says the LORD" (Isaiah 1:18). "Come to me," says the Lord Jesus, "all you who are weary and burdened, and I will give you rest" (Matthew 11:28). God is forever pleading with humanity to respond to the love He has demonstrated toward us.

In Hebrews 11:6 the most basic approach to God is described in this way: "Anyone who comes to him must believe that he exists and that he rewards those who earnestly seek him." God has been seeking us, and He says, "Now it is time for you to begin to seek me. I've been reaching out to you. Now it is up to you to respond to me." Draw near to God, and He will draw near to you. This is the law of response in human nature. This is why John says, "We love because he first loved us" (1 John 4:19).

This is why the grain sacrifice is the second of the five sacrifices. In the burnt sacrifice you have God reaching out and saying, "You're mine. I want you." But in the grain sacrifice we must respond and say, "Yes, Lord, I'm yours. I give myself to you." This is what God is after in our lives. Love creates the possibility of response. But if that response is refused, then a relationship is impossible.

This is why many Christians never seem to move beyond a certain level of relationship with God. At a certain point, some Christians stop saying yes to His love. Some of us reach a point where we sense that God wants us to turn over an area of our lives to Him—and we don't want to. We want to hold on to that habit, that character flaw, that addiction, that sin. So we say no to the love of God that reaches out to enfold us. As long as our response to God is no, the relationship is dead in the water. Nothing more can happen.

This is why we sometimes have to go through a time of crisis or trial before we will finally turn to God and say yes. As we noted before, God sometimes has to remove barriers of fear, suspicion, and selfishness from our lives before we are finally ready and willing to respond in love to the love of God. And sometimes the only way to remove those barriers is through a time of crisis. When all the props are knocked out from under us, when we can no longer rely on ourselves but must seek God's help, then we finally turn to God and say, "Yes, Lord! I accept your love for me! Help me!"

Of course, it is far better if we never have to go through such a trial before we will say yes to God. It is much better if, in the quietness of our hearts, we will simply and gratefully respond to the love God has shown us and say, "Lord, here I am. Here is my redeemed humanity, with its oil and frankincense and salt, but with no leaven and no honey. I want to be yours, so that today you can express all that you are through me. I give myself to you. Here I am, Lord. Let's walk together this day."

When you make that response to God, you offer Him the grain sacrifice of your life, just as Jesus, the Son of God, continually offered the beauty of His life, the spotlessness of His humanity, in an ongoing relationship with the Father. Is there some area of your life that you have withheld from God? Is there something in your life that keeps you from responding to His love and saying yes to a relationship with Him?

I pray that you will respond to Him by offering Him your whole heart, your whole life, without any reservation or holding back. Do not shut Him out. He loves you and wants to build a relationship with you. He wants to live through you, so that you can become all you were created to be.

So respond to Him, my friend. Say, "Yes, Lord, here I am. I need your love. I need to belong. I need to be identified with you. And as you have reached out to me, I now reach out to you. Let this be my grain offering to you, so that everything you are, I may be."

Amen!

——————≫————————≪——————

# THE NEED FOR PEACE
## LEVITICUS 3 AND 7

SOME YEARS AGO, a number of artists were commissioned to paint a picture of peace. One artist depicted peace as a calm and tranquil sea under the moonlight. Another depicted peace as a mother and child reading a book together in a sunlit garden. But the picture that won the prize pictured a turbulent mountain waterfall with its noisily plunging waters. Yet, half-hidden behind the waterfall, not far from the thundering waters, was a bird's nest with a mother bird sitting quietly and serenely on her eggs. That was true peace—a safe and quiet little space in the midst of a noisy and raucous world.

In Leviticus 3 we come to the third of the five sacrifices, and we find that this third offering is a picture of peace in the midst of trouble and conflict. This offering has beautiful power to symbolize a truth that affects us deeply in our relationship with Jesus Christ. All five of these offerings are pictures of aspects of the sacrifice of Jesus on the cross, and these five sacrifices follow a logical order. The first sacrifice, the burnt offering, testifies of the universal human need for love. The second sacrifice, the grain offering, speaks of the need for our response to God's love. And when we respond to His love, we experience joy.

In this third sacrifice, God pictures for us our universal need for peace. It is no accident that in Galatians 5:22, where Paul lists the fruit of the Spirit, the order of the first three elements of that fruit are love, joy, and peace. That order was planned by the God who designed human life. That is why these Old

Testament sacrifices are just as eloquent in expressing human need as the New Testament revelation is. This is the evidence which convinces me that the Bible comes from a more-than-human hand. The truth of the Old Testament and the truth of the New Testament corroborate each other, proving both Testaments to be genuine products of God's own hand.

As the Israelites brought these sacrifices, they were learning these truths. It's true, of course, that an Israelite could bring a sacrificial offering in a purely mechanical and perfunctory way, just as some people today attend church mechanically and without sincerity. If an Israelite made a sacrifice to God without his heart being right with God, the sacrifice was worth nothing. It was nothing but a dead ritual, a meaningless act that God would not bless. We can attend church the same way today, singing hymns without meaning the words, hearing a sermon without applying it to our lives, bowing our heads in prayer without bowing our hearts. If that is the way we attend church, we might as well have stayed home and read the Sunday newspaper instead.

God does not want ritual for ritual's sake. The rites and rituals of Leviticus are meaningful only if they reflect the reality of our lives. When an Israelite brought a grain offering to God, he was to do so as a joyful response to God's love. In the grain offering the Israelite was opening up his life to God.

Now here, in the symbolism of the peace offering, God pictures for us how He meets another basic, fundamental need of the human heart—the need for peace. It is impossible to live a fulfilled, satisfying life without peace.

Essentially the Bible talks about two kinds of peace: (1) *the peace of God,* the supernatural sense of peace that comes through God's presence—the peace of knowing that all is well, even in the midst of trouble, because God is in control; and (2) *peace with God,* the experience of God's forgiveness.

This second kind of peace, peace with God, will be pictured for us in the next two sacrifices, the sin sacrifice and the trespass sacrifice. But the peace offering pictures for us the first kind of peace, the peace of God. It is peace not in the sense of an end to hostilities but in the sense of emotional stability, of an untroubled heart. That is what we need: a sense of security, of well being, of confidence that things are under God's control and that all things will ultimately work together for good, even though things are not good right now.

The peace of the peace offering is what was pictured by that painting of the mother bird sitting on her eggs beside the waterfall. That is the kind of peace we can have—peace in the midst of trouble and conflict. That is the peace God pictures for us in the peace sacrifice.

## CHOOSING WHAT IS BETTER—THE PEACE OF GOD

The kind of peace pictured in this sacrifice is best known by its absence. We know when we are not at peace. We have all felt that sense of tension and anxiety, the butterflies in the stomach that won't go away, the inability to get your mind off a troubling subject. No matter what you do, it is there, throbbing inside you. That is the absence of peace.

A lack of peace can create all kinds of disturbances in the body—nervous twitches, indigestion, ulcers, insomnia, and even emotional breakdown and nervous collapse. So the need for peace is a fundamental human need. (If you think the Bible is not practical, you have not even begun to understand this Book. It deals with human life as it really is.)

You probably recall the story of Mary and Martha in the gospel of Luke (Luke 10:38–42). When Jesus visits their home, like any good hostess, Martha goes out into the kitchen and gets busy preparing a sumptuous dinner in the Lord's honor. She is a perfectionist, and she must have everything just so—but Jesus has come unexpectedly, so she is unprepared.

She tries her best, but she becomes nervous and upset when she doesn't have all the kitchen resources she wants to put on a fabulous feast. To put this story in an updated context, imagine Martha opening cupboards, rummaging in her refrigerator, wondering, *What shall I do?* Perhaps she spills flour on the linoleum and the coffee boils over and everything is ruined. Finally, she can't take the pressure anymore. She goes into the living room where her sister, Mary, sits at the feet of Jesus, quietly listening to Him. Martha instantly becomes angry that her sister is not helping in the kitchen. But it's not Mary that she blames. Instead, she blames Jesus!

"Lord," Martha snaps, "don't you care that my sister has left me to do the work by myself? Tell her to help me!" She is probably annoyed with Jesus for showing up without any advance warning. This sort of blaming behavior is characteristic of a troubled heart.

Now, I have always appreciated the fact that Martha at least did not hold anything in. I suspect Jesus appreciated her candor as well. She wasn't the kind of person who goes into an icy silence for weeks. Martha got it off her chest. This little rhyme could well have been written to describe Martha:

> There's a gladness in her gladness when she's glad,
> And a sadness in her sadness when she's sad.
>   But the gladness in her gladness,
>   And the sadness in her sadness,
> Are nothing to her madness when she's mad!

How does Jesus answer when Martha blames Him for her stress and anxiety? He replies, "Martha, Martha, you are worried and upset about many things, but only one thing is needed. Mary has chosen what is better, and it will not be taken away from her." Only one thing is needed, Jesus says. What is that one thing? Peace. Mary chose peace by listening to the One who could set her mind at ease. Martha had missed it by worrying and obsessing over the details of a meal.

But didn't Martha have a right to be upset over the fact that Mary didn't help with the meal? In the original Greek version of this account there is a strong suggestion that Mary had already been in the kitchen and had done her part. She had prepared a simple little repast that was perfectly adequate. But Martha wanted to put on a banquet, and she became frustrated when she didn't have everything needed to put on an elaborate show of a meal.

Martha had missed the point of the Lord's visit, but Mary had chosen the one thing that was needed: peace. That kind of peace—the peace of God that passes human understanding—is what the peace offering is all about.

## FOUR DISTINCTIVES OF THE PEACE SACRIFICE

The New International Version of the Bible, from which we take our text, is a very good and readable translation. For some reason, the editors of the NIV have called the peace sacrifice by a different name, "the fellowship offering," with a note at the bottom of the page that reads, "Traditionally *peace offering.*" Most of the other translations of this text, including the King James Version, the Revised Standard Version, and the New American Standard Bible, use the term *peace offering.* In reproducing the NIV text of Leviticus 3 (and throughout the rest of this book), therefore, I have replaced the word *fellowship* with the bracketed word *[peace]*:

"If someone's offering is a [peace] offering, and he offers an animal from the herd, whether male or female, he is to present before the LORD an animal without defect. He is to lay his hand on the head of his offering and slaughter it at the entrance to the Tent of Meeting. Then Aaron's sons the priests shall sprinkle the blood against the altar on all sides. From the [peace] offering he is to bring a sacrifice made to the LORD by fire: all the fat that covers the inner parts or is connected to them, both kidneys with the fat on them near the loins, and the covering of the liver, which he will remove with the kidneys. Then Aaron's sons are to burn it on the altar on top of the burnt offering that is on the burning wood, as an offering made by fire, an aroma pleasing to the LORD.

"If he offers an animal from the flock as a [peace] offering to the LORD, he is to offer a male or female without defect. If he offers a lamb, he is to present it before the LORD. He is to lay his hand on the head of his offering and slaughter it in front of the Tent of Meeting. Then Aaron's sons shall sprinkle its blood against the altar on all sides. From the [peace] offering he is to bring a sacrifice made to the LORD by fire: its fat, the entire fat tail cut off close to the backbone, all the fat that covers the inner parts or is connected to them, both kidneys with the fat on them near the loins, and the covering of the liver, which he will remove with the kidneys. The priest shall burn them on the altar as food, an offering made to the LORD by fire.

"If his offering is a goat, he is to present it before the LORD. He is to lay his hand on its head and slaughter it in front of the Tent of Meeting. Then Aaron's sons shall sprinkle its blood against the altar on all sides. From what he offers he is to make this offering to the LORD by fire: all the fat that covers the inner parts or is connected to them, both kidneys with the fat on them near the loins, and the covering of the liver, which he will remove with the kidneys. The priest shall burn them on the altar as food, an offering made by fire, a pleasing aroma. All the fat is the LORD's.

"This is a lasting ordinance for the generations to come, wherever you live: You must not eat any fat or any blood" (Leviticus 3:1–17).

Here in Leviticus 3 we notice four distinctives about the peace sacrifice that mark it as different from the other sacrifices we have examined. The first distinctive is that the peace offering could be either a male or a female animal.

> "If someone's offering is a [peace] offering, and he offers an animal from the herd, whether male or female, he is to present before the LORD an animal without defect. . . . If he offers an animal from the flock as a [peace] offering to the LORD, he is to offer a male or female without defect" (Leviticus 3:1, 6).

Leviticus 3:12 says that it was also possible to offer a goat; in any case, the animal could be male or female. That is significant. God makes these distinctions in order to impart truth: The burnt offering could be only a male because it deals with man in his capacity to rule, his dominion over all things. And the one thing that is necessary to a man in order that he be able to rule is that he himself be possessed and loved. That is why a male was absolutely required for a burnt offering.

But here in the peace offering we are not dealing with man in terms of his overall purpose in life, his archetypal relationship. We are dealing now with humanity and the human condition. It does not make any difference whether you are a leader or a follower, whether you are in a position of authority or not. You need peace in any case. Therefore, either a male or a female is an adequate expression of the peace offering. (Now, perhaps, it is becoming clear why the distinctions between the five sacrifices are so important to recognize.)

The second distinctive mark of the peace offering was that all the fatwas to be consumed upon the altar.

> "From the [peace] offering he is to bring a sacrifice made to the LORD by fire: its fat, the entire fat tail cut off close to the backbone, all the fat that covers the inner parts or is connected to them, both kidneys with the fat on them near the loins, and the covering of the liver, which he will remove with the kidneys. The priest shall burn them on the altar as food, an offering made to the LORD by fire" (Leviticus 3:3–5).

Similar provisions for the offering of lambs and goats are contained in Leviticus 3:9–11, 14–15. Look also at Leviticus 3:16–17:

"The priest shall burn them on the altar as food, an offering made by fire, a pleasing aroma. All the fat is the LORD's. This is a lasting ordinance for the generations to come, wherever you live: You must not eat any fat or any blood."

This restriction is explained further in Leviticus 7. Why were the Israelites not permitted to eat any of the fat or blood? Blood is a symbol of the life. This is God's way of impressing upon the Hebrew people, and upon all of us, that life is sacred to God. Life belongs to God. It is His to control. Humanity should treat life with respect and care. The Hebrews were reminded of this fact every time they were told they were not to eat blood.

The fat, too, is the Lord's. In the Scriptures, fat is a symbol of the richness of life. We think of fat-marbled meat as rich meat, the prime cut, and that is exactly what this symbol portrays. The richness of life comes from God and belongs to God.

All that is rich and enjoyable in life comes from God. As Paul writes, "Or do you show contempt for the riches of his kindness, tolerance and patience, not realizing that God's kindness leads you toward repentance?" (Romans 2:4). God showers His love and His richness upon the just and the unjust alike in order that He might show us all that everything that makes life worth living comes only from God. As James puts it, "Every good and perfect gift is from above, coming down from the Father of the heavenly lights, who does not change like shifting shadows" (James 1:17).

The Hebrew people were told to take the fat and carefully remove it, especially the interior fat that was on the inner organs of the body. They were being taught that all the inner richness of life, everything that delights a person from within, is from God, belongs to God, and comes only from God.

## A Picture of the Love and Strength of Jesus

The third distinctive mark of the peace offering is extremely important. We find it described in the law of the peace offering in Leviticus 7:28–34:

The LORD said to Moses, "Say to the Israelites: 'Anyone who brings
a [peace] offering to the LORD is to bring part of it as his sacrifice
to the LORD. With his own hands he is to bring the offering made
to the LORD by fire; he is to bring the fat, together with the breast,
and wave the breast before the LORD as a wave offering. The priest
shall burn the fat on the altar, but the breast belongs to Aaron and
his sons. You are to give the right thigh of your [peace] offerings to
the priest as a contribution. The son of Aaron who offers the blood
and the fat of the [peace] offering shall have the right thigh as his
share. From the [peace] offerings of the Israelites, I have taken the
breast that is waved and the thigh that is presented and have given
them to Aaron the priest and his sons as their regular share from
the Israelites.'"

Only two portions of the peace offering animal were to be eaten: the breast
and the right thigh. But before they were eaten, they were offered, in a sense, to
the Lord. They were not burned upon the altar. That would have ruined them
as food for the priests. They were merely waved before the Lord. The thigh, perhaps heavier than the breast, was heaved up and down before the Lord, rather
than waved. This was a symbolic gesture that these portions were related to
God. Then the priests were to feed on them.

In this seemingly simple requirement is embedded a profound secret of how
to have peace in the midst of trouble, how to get rid of the knots in your stomach and the tension in your mind. As we have already noticed, every one of
these sacrifices involved the death of an animal. Even the grain sacrifice was
always offered in conjunction with the burnt offering. In the Old Testament,
the sacrificial death of an animal always symbolized the sacrificial death of
Christ. He was the fulfillment of the peace offering, and He died in order that
His life might be ours.

The two aspects of the life of Christ that we are to feed on are represented
by the breast and the thigh. In Scripture, the breast is always a symbol of affection and love. It symbolizes the seat of our emotions. And the thigh is always a
symbol of power and strength. It is where the strength of our physical bodies is
centered. So in the breast and thigh of the sacrificial animal we have pictured
for us the love and the strength of Jesus Christ to solve our problems.

We all need the love and strength of Jesus—two mighty forces that exploded from the cross at Calvary. His love tells us that He is alongside us in whatever we are going through. No matter what challenge we face or what pain we suffer, He understands because He has been through it Himself. His strength is reliable and powerful to carry us through any trial. "All authority in heaven and on earth has been given to me," He said (Matthew 28:18). As we learn to rest in His love and trust His strength, we will find peace in our hearts, even in the most troubled circumstances.

Our problem is that we continually try to second-guess God. We ask Him in prayer to supply our needs, to calm our fears, to heal our relationships, just as God's Word says we should. But after we pray, what do we do? We start trying to figure out how God is going to do it. Sometimes we even start giving Him advice and telling Him how He should solve our problem. But when God doesn't solve our problem in the way we expect, in the time frame we demand, we become disappointed, even angry, with God. We say, "Lord, you've failed me! I guess you don't care about me at all! You don't keep your promises!"

What is the real problem? It's that we have forgotten that God has promised that He loves us and that He has power to work it out His own way. He tells us plainly, "For my thoughts are not your thoughts, neither are your ways my ways" (Isaiah 55:8). In other words, "The way you think it is going to work out is not the way I am going to work it out. But if you will trust me, I will work all things together for good." If we will accept God's will for our lives, if we figuratively feed upon the breast and the thigh of His sacrifice, if we will base our lives upon the love and strength of Jesus Christ, then He will work out His good purpose in our lives. That is the source of God's peace in our lives.

This is the teaching of both the Old Testament and the New. In John's gospel, Jesus, the true Sacrifice, put it this way:

> "All this I have spoken while still with you. But the Counselor, the Holy Spirit, whom the Father will send in my name, will teach you all things and will remind you of everything I have said to you. Peace I leave with you; my peace I give you. I do not give to you as the world gives. Do not let your hearts be troubled and do not be afraid" (John 14:25–27).

Notice that Jesus does not give peace as the world gives. When a worldling—a natural and unregenerated inhabitant of this world—is upset and troubled, he seeks peace through three means.

First, he tries to change the circumstances, because he believes that peace comes only from peaceful circumstances. He can be at peace only when his circumstances are peaceful. The problem is that circumstances cannot always be changed. Accidents, illnesses, losses, and financial problems have a way of crashing into our lives and robbing us of our worldly peace.

Second, if the circumstances cannot be changed, the worldling will try to forget his problems by numbing his mind. He tries to anesthetize his pain by going on vacation, or escaping into entertainment, or taking drugs or alcohol. Escaping into forgetfulness is the world's way of finding peace when there is no peace. The problem is that anesthetics eventually wear off—and when they do, the worldling awakens to find that his problems have only grown bigger and more unmanageable than before.

Third, when he sees that he cannot change his circumstances or anesthetize himself against the pain, the worldling blames his problems on other people or on God. His lack of peace is everybody's fault but his. Blame shifting may not produce peace, but at least the individual gains that tiny particle of satisfaction that comes with whining, "It's not my fault!"

Jesus says, in effect, "I'm not going to give you peace the way the world gives peace. I have come not to take you out of your circumstances but to take you through them. And in the midst of the worst that the world can do to you, I give you my peace. Don't let your hearts be troubled, and don't be afraid."

How does Jesus give us His peace? He gives it from within. He gives it to us as we feed upon His love and His strength. When we trust His promises to be true, when we turn over the task of running our lives to Him and leave all of our circumstances in His hands, then we will have peace.

The deepest and most practical meaning of the peace sacrifice was expressed by the apostle Paul in his letter to the church in Philippi:

> Do not be anxious about anything, but in everything, by prayer and petition, with thanksgiving, present your requests to God. And the peace of God, which transcends all understanding, will guard your hearts and your minds in Christ Jesus. . . . Whatever you have learned

or received or heard from me, or seen in me—put it into practice. And the God of peace will be with you (Philippians 4:6–7, 9).

That is what it means to feed on the love and strength of Jesus Christ. That is how we can have the peace of God in the midst of the turmoil and troubles of life.

## A Strange Requirement

I once spoke at a series of meetings at a church in Phoenix, Arizona. While I was there, a man came up to me at the end of the Wednesday night meeting. He gripped my hand and said, "Pastor Stedman, you'll never know what your coming to Phoenix has meant to me. I don't attend this church, but I heard about these meetings, and I had to come last night and tonight. When I walked into this church last night, I was so full of fear and anxiety that I was on the verge of an emotional collapse. I was so upset that I couldn't eat or sleep.

"But as I listened to your messages, I heard Jesus speaking to me, inviting me to put my trust in Him. So I have placed my problems in His hands, and now I'm at peace. I never imagined that such peace was even possible. I just want to thank you for coming and telling me how I could experience the peace of Jesus Christ in my life."

I was tremendously moved by what this man told me. I have to confess to you that there have been many times, even in my Christian experience, when I have experienced deep troubles that have drained all my natural strength. At such times, I have been able to find peace only through the reassuring fact that our God, a God of infinite love and infinite power, was at work in the circumstances of my life.

The fourth and final distinctive of the peace sacrifice is found in Leviticus 7:15–18—and it is a rather startling requirement.

> "The meat of his [peace] offering of thanksgiving must be eaten on the day it is offered; he must leave none of it till morning. If, however, his offering is the result of a vow or is a freewill offering, the sacrifice shall be eaten on the day he offers it, but anything left over may be eaten on the next day. Any meat of the sacrifice left over till the third day must be burned up. If any meat of the [peace] offering

is eaten on the third day, it will not be accepted. It will not be cred-
ited to the one who offered it, for it is impure; the person who eats
any of it will be held responsible."

Isn't that a strange requirement? As an Israelite, you could eat the meat of
the peace sacrifice on the day you offered it if it was an offering of thanksgiving for some particular thing. If it was a general expression of your gratitude
to God, you could save some of the meat for the second day. But under no circumstances were you ever to eat of the meat of the peace offering on the third
day. It had to be burned with fire. If you tried to eat any of it, it was an abomination unto God.

What is God saying through the symbolism of these requirements? He is
giving Israel—and us—some intensely practical life truths. He is saying that
there must be no separation between the peace that you feel and the source of
that peace, the sacrifice which provided it. You must not separate the two. In
other words, you must not depend upon the feelings of peace that are given to
you. Don't try to live on the basis of feelings, but live on the basis of your trust
in the ultimate Sacrifice, who is Jesus alone.

Once we experience the peace of trusting the work of Jesus Christ, we often
say to ourselves, "Ah! I feel much better! That is the feeling of peace I was
seeking! Now I can continue on with my life covered by this feeling of God's
peace!" In other words, we are tempted to shift our trust from Jesus Himself,
the One who brings peace, to the peaceful feelings themselves. We stop trusting Jesus; we begin trusting emotions and feelings. And what happens then?
Within a day or two, we find we are back in the same mess as before. Our heart
is troubled; our mind is disturbed.

Feelings come and go. Only Jesus Himself is the unchanging Rock we can
depend on. He will never let us down. Even though our emotions may change,
His love and strength never change. We can trust the love and power of our
risen Lord, because He can handle our problems and crises in ways we can't
begin to imagine—if we will trustingly place them in His hands.

#### ⫸━━━━⫷

# THE NEED TO CONFESS
## LEVITICUS 4:1–5:13

EVERYWHERE, HUMAN BEINGS avoid, if they can, having to deal with the reality of God. People do not want to even think of God. Most people become distinctly uncomfortable if any reference to God is interjected into a conversation—unless, of course, that reference is in the form of blasphemy. Taking God's name in vain has become acceptable, but talking about the love of God or the demands of God upon our lives is a social taboo! People simply do not want to talk about God.

Why is that? Why is God such a painful subject to so many?

In Leviticus 4 and 5, we come to the fourth of the five Levitical sacrifices, the sin offering. Here we come face to face with a question that hangs over our world but which few people ever attempt to answer: Why do people fear and avoid God?

This is a question that goes all the way back to the dawn of humanity. In the Garden of Eden, Adam and Eve first walked in fellowship with God. In the cool of the evening, God would come and walk with them, and they were in perfect communion. Then Adam and Eve made a choice to obey the tempter's voice instead of God's. The first effect of their disobedience of God was that they hid from God when He came to walk in the garden—

And humanity has been hiding from God ever since.

Why? Because sin produces guilt, and guilt alienates us from God. What was true in the Garden is still true today. People fear God and hide from Him because of alienating guilt. Here in Leviticus 4 and 5, through the means of the sin offering, we see God dealing with the problem of human guilt.

## THE MESSAGE IN THE ORDER OF THE SACRIFICES

Once again, we see that the order of the offerings is significant. This fourth offering comes only after the first three, which have dealt with the basic needs of men and women for love (the burnt offering), joy (the grain offering), and peace (the peace offering). Love, joy, and peace are the basic needs of human life. Without them, we cannot function effectively as human beings. This is the same order that these fruits of the Spirit are listed in Galatians 5:22–23—love, joy, and peace.

Only after symbolically dealing with these basic human needs does God begin to talk about sin and trespass, the next two offerings. In the final two offerings, God deals with another basic requirement of humanity. We need not only the positive virtues of love, joy, and peace, but also to behave as responsible individuals. The sin and trespass offerings call us to act responsibly toward God and toward the people around us.

It is important to notice the order of the five sacrifices because the sacrifices tell us something important about the mind of God. Notice where He begins. While all five of the sacrifices of Leviticus were fulfilled in the sacrifice of Jesus on the cross, each sacrifice expresses a different aspect of His death, a different blessing that flows from His sacrifice. The first three blessings that come to us from the sacrifice of Jesus are love, joy, and peace. That is what the first three sacrifices speak of.

Then, in the final two sacrifices, the sin and trespass offerings, we see yet another blessing that flows to us from the cross of Christ: *the forgiveness of sin.* Now consider this: What is the first blessing we always think of when we reflect on the cross of Christ? Forgiveness! We always start our understanding of the cross with the issue of forgiveness—but that is not where God starts!

When we preach the Christian gospel, the first thing we usually say is, "You're a sinner! You need to be forgiven!" And sometimes we thunder away with hellfire and damnation at people in order to get them under conviction, to make them aware of the guilt that results from their sins. It's true, of course, that God wants to talk to human beings about sin. Men and women can never solve their problems until they solve the sin problem.

But we must remember that this is not where God starts. He begins by talking about love, joy, and peace. He provides these three blessings first. Then He says, "Now let's get at the heart of the problem that separates us." Isn't that marvelous?

That is why, in the story Jesus told of the prodigal son in Luke 15, when the wandering son returned from the far country and his father spotted him on the horizon, the father ran to meet him with his arms wide open. The father flung his arms around his returning son and cried out with joy. And the boy stammered and tried to make the speech of repentance he had memorized all the way home: "I am no longer worthy to be called your son; make me like one of your hired men" (Luke 15:19).

But the father didn't even wait for the boy to finish his contrite little speech. He shouted, "Quick! Bring the best robe and put it on him. Put a ring on his finger and sandals on his feet. Bring the fattened calf and kill it. Let's have a feast and celebrate" (Luke 15:22–23). The father recognized the boy as his son, and he blessed the son with love, joy, and peace before he dealt with his sin problem. To be sure, the son had to make his confession and deal with his sin and guilt—but that isn't where the father started.

We see this same order in Paul's letter to the Galatians, where he writes, "Because you are sons, God sent the Spirit of his Son into our hearts, the Spirit who calls out, 'Abba, Father'" (Galatians 4:6). Now, we tend to turn that order around. We'd tend to say, "Because God has sent the Spirit of His Son into our hearts, we are sons of God." But that is not the way Scripture puts it. It says that because we are sons in Christ, God has sent His Spirit, and all the blessings that the Spirit brings: love, joy, and peace. On the basis of our sonship, God now wants to talk to us about the problem of guilt and alienation in our lives. That is our introduction to the sin offering.

Let's look at the regulations concerning the sin offering, as found in Leviticus 4:1–35:

> The LORD said to Moses, "Say to the Israelites: 'When anyone sins unintentionally and does what is forbidden in any of the LORD's commands—

"'If the anointed priest sins, bringing guilt on the people, he must bring to the LORD a young bull without defect as a sin offering for the sin he has committed. He is to present the bull at the entrance to the Tent of Meeting before the LORD. He is to lay his hand on its head and slaughter it before the LORD. Then the anointed priest shall take some of the bull's blood and carry it into the Tent of Meeting. He is to dip his finger into the blood and sprinkle some of it seven times before the LORD, in front of the curtain of the sanctuary. The priest shall then put some of the blood on the horns of the altar of fragrant incense that is before the LORD in the Tent of Meeting. The rest of the bull's blood he shall pour out at the base of the altar of burnt offering at the entrance to the Tent of Meeting. He shall remove all the fat from the bull of the sin offering—the fat that covers the inner parts or is connected to them, both kidneys with the fat on them near the loins, and the covering of the liver, which he will remove with the kidneys—just as the fat is removed from the ox sacrificed as a [peace] offering. Then the priest shall burn them on the altar of burnt offering. But the hide of the bull and all its flesh, as well as the head and legs, the inner parts and offal—that is, all the rest of the bull—he must take outside the camp to a place ceremonially clean, where the ashes are thrown, and burn it in a wood fire on the ash heap.

"'If the whole Israelite community sins unintentionally and does what is forbidden in any of the LORD's commands, even though the community is unaware of the matter, they are guilty. When they become aware of the sin they committed, the assembly must bring a young bull as a sin offering and present it before the Tent of Meeting. The elders of the community are to lay their hands on the bull's head before the LORD, and the bull shall be slaughtered before the LORD. Then the anointed priest is to take some of the bull's blood into the Tent of Meeting. He shall dip his finger into the blood and sprinkle it before the LORD seven times in front of the curtain. He is to put some of the blood on the horns of the altar that is before the LORD in the Tent of Meeting. The rest of the blood he shall pour out at the base of the altar of burnt offering at the entrance to the Tent of Meeting. He shall remove all the fat from it and burn it on the altar, and do with this bull just as he did with the bull for the sin offering. In this way the priest will make atonement for them, and they will be forgiven. Then he shall take the bull outside the camp and burn it as he burned the first bull. This is the sin offering for the community.

"'When a leader sins unintentionally and does what is forbidden in any of the commands of the LORD his God, he is guilty. When he is made aware of the sin he committed, he must bring as his offering a male goat without defect. He is to lay his hand on the goat's head and slaughter it at the place where the burnt offering is slaughtered before the LORD. It is a sin offering. Then the priest shall take some of the blood of the sin offering with his finger and put it on the horns of the altar of burnt offering and pour out the rest of the blood at the base of the altar. He shall burn all the fat on the altar as he burned the fat of the [peace] offering. In this way the priest will make atonement for the man's sin, and he will be forgiven.

"'If a member of the community sins unintentionally and does what is forbidden in any of the LORD's commands, he is guilty. When he is made aware of the sin he committed, he must bring as his offering for the sin he committed a female goat without defect. He is to lay his hand on the head of the sin offering and slaughter it at the place of the burnt offering. Then the priest is to take some of the blood with his finger and put it on the horns of the altar of burnt offering and pour out the rest of the blood at the base of the altar. He shall remove all the fat, just as the fat is removed from the [peace] offering, and the priest shall burn it on the altar as an aroma pleasing to the LORD. In this way the priest will make atonement for him, and he will be forgiven.

"'If he brings a lamb as his sin offering, he is to bring a female without defect. He is to lay his hand on its head and slaughter it for a sin offering at the place where the burnt offering is slaughtered. Then the priest shall take some of the blood of the sin offering with his finger and put it on the horns of the altar of burnt offering and pour out the rest of the blood at the base of the altar. He shall remove all the fat, just as the fat is removed from the lamb of the [peace] offering, and the priest shall burn it on the altar on top of the offerings made to the LORD by fire. In this way the priest will make atonement for him for the sin he has committed, and he will be forgiven.'"

As we have already seen, in each of the sacrifices in Leviticus there is a certain set of distinctive ceremonies and requirements which marks each sacrifice as distinct from the rest. Each of these sacrifices points out with beautiful accuracy some important aspect of the sacrificial death of Jesus Christ on our behalf. Since Jesus is the fulfillment of these offerings, they all point to Him.

The first distinctive of the sin offering is that it provided for public and private sin. There were offerings available for those who had sinned as a group and those who had sinned as individuals. You find this clearly delineated in Leviticus 4. When a sacrifice was offered for the sin of a group, or a public individual representing a group, the offering always had to be a male. When it was an offering for an individual sin, the animal was a female:

> The LORD said to Moses, "Say to the Israelites: 'When anyone sins unintentionally and does what is forbidden in any of the LORD's commands—
>
> "'If the anointed priest sins, bringing guilt on the people, he must bring to the LORD a young bull without defect as a sin offering for the sin he has committed'" (Leviticus 4:1–3).

Later, we see this same principle again:

> "'If the whole Israelite community sins unintentionally and does what is forbidden in any of the LORD's commands, even though the community is unaware of the matter, they are guilty. When they become aware of the sin they committed, the assembly must bring a young bull as a sin offering and present it before the Tent of Meeting'" (Leviticus 4:13–14).

In the case of a ruler or king, we find this requirement given:

> "'When a leader sins unintentionally and does what is forbidden in any of the commands of the LORD his God, he is guilty. When he is made aware of the sin he committed, he must bring as his offering a male goat without defect'" (Leviticus 4:22–23).

But we find that a female is to be offered when the common people sinned as individuals:

> "'If a member of the community sins unintentionally and does what is forbidden in any of the LORD's commands, he is guilty. When he is made aware of the sin he committed, he must bring as his offering for the sin he committed a female goat without defect'" (Leviticus 4:27–28).

And again:

> "'If he brings a lamb as his sin offering, he is to bring a female without defect'" (Leviticus 4:32).

So once again the distinction is made between the male, as the symbol of the ruler (man in his dominion over all things, as symbolized by any functionary, official, priest, ruler, or king) and the female, as the symbol of the common individual in the supportive relationship.

## PROVISION FOR RICH AND POOR ALIKE

There were also provisions made in the sin offering for people who could not afford large animals like a bull, goat, or lamb. We find these provisions in Leviticus 5:1–13:

> "'If a person sins because he does not speak up when he hears a public charge to testify regarding something he has seen or learned about, he will be held responsible.
>
> "'Or if a person touches anything ceremonially unclean—whether the carcasses of unclean wild animals or of unclean livestock or of

unclean creatures that move along the ground—even though he is unaware of it, he has become unclean and is guilty.

"'Or if he touches human uncleanness—anything that would make him unclean—even though he is unaware of it, when he learns of it he will be guilty.

"'Or if a person thoughtlessly takes an oath to do anything, whether good or evil—in any matter one might carelessly swear about—even though he is unaware of it, in any case when he learns of it he will be guilty.

"'When anyone is guilty in any of these ways, he must confess in what way he has sinned and, as a penalty for the sin he has committed, he must bring to the LORD a female lamb or goat from the flock as a sin offering; and the priest shall make atonement for him for his sin.

"'If he cannot afford a lamb, he is to bring two doves or two young pigeons to the LORD as a penalty for his sin—one for a sin offering and the other for a burnt offering. He is to bring them to the priest, who shall first offer the one for the sin offering. He is to wring its head from its neck, not severing it completely, and is to sprinkle some of the blood of the sin offering against the side of the altar; the rest of the blood must be drained out at the base of the altar. It is a sin offering. The priest shall then offer the other as a burnt offering in the prescribed way and make atonement for him for the sin he has committed, and he will be forgiven.

"'If, however, he cannot afford two doves or two young pigeons, he is to bring as an offering for his sin a tenth of an ephah of fine flour for a sin offering. He must not put oil or incense on it, because it is a sin offering. He is to bring it to the priest, who shall take a handful of it as a memorial portion and burn it on the altar on top of the offerings made to the LORD by fire. It is a sin offering. In this way the priest will make atonement for him for any of these sins he has committed, and he will be forgiven. The rest of the offering will belong to the priest, as in the case of the grain offering.'"

Here is the principle in Leviticus 5:7: The Israelite who cannot afford a lamb is permitted to bring two doves or young pigeons, one for a sin offering and the

The book of Hebrews makes this principle clear, telling us that this is exactly what happened to Jesus:

> We have an altar from which those who minister at the tabernacle have no right to eat. The high priest carries the blood of animals into the Most Holy Place as a sin offering, but the bodies are burned outside the camp. And so Jesus also suffered outside the city gate to make the people holy through his own blood. Let us, then, go to him outside the camp, bearing the disgrace he bore. For here we do not have an enduring city, but we are looking for the city that is to come (Hebrews 13:10–14).

Though our inner life, our inner nature, is now changed and acceptable to God, we are still in the world. We still have to live under its reproach and its rejection, just as Jesus did. We are to bear that reproach with him, recognizing that there is still an aspect of our lives which has not yet been changed. That is why we look forward to the resurrection as the completion of God's work in our lives. All of this is beautifully described in the sin offering.

And there, outside the camp, we are to take the place that Jesus took—the place of humility and rejection before the world. This is a blow to our pride. We don't like it there. But our Lord is there, so God calls us to identify with Him as He has identified with us, and to take our place with Him outside the camp.

The great truth of the sin offering is that God has dealt with our sin nature, and we are no longer linked to it. We are no longer what we once were. With our lives hidden in Christ, we stand accepted before God, loved and favored in His sight.

St. Augustine was a wild and hedonistic young man before he became a Christian. He lived for selfish pleasure. When he gave his life to Jesus Christ, he became a new man. One day, as he walked down the street of the city, an old girlfriend saw him and called out to him, "Gustine!" He turned and saw the girl—then he gathered his robes around him and ran away. The girl chased after him, calling, "Gustine! Gustine! Why do you run? It is only I!" And Augustine stopped long enough to turn and say, "I run because it is no longer I!" Then he dashed off again, fleeing temptation.

That is what the sin offering tells us: In Christ we are no longer what we once were. The body may be the same, but inside we are all new. We are no longer guilty; we are forgiven. God has shown us a way out of our guilt, a way out of our alienation, so that we no longer need to be far off from God. We no longer need to fear God. He is our heavenly Father, and He loves and receives us because we are His children.

To remove our burden of guilt, we need only be honest with ourselves and with God, acknowledge our sin—and allow Him to take the burden off our shoulders. We all have the need to confess our sin, and once we have confessed it, we are truly free.

꩜ ——————— ꩜

# THE NEED TO RESTORE
## LEVITICUS 5:1–6:30

WHEN TOMMY'S PARENTS gave him a BB gun for his birthday, they told him not to aim it at any animals. The gun was only for shooting at paper targets or tin cans on the back fence. Tommy agreed to the conditions his parents imposed. After a few days, however, he got tired of shooting only targets and cans. Spotting a bird in a tree, he took aim, fired—

And the bird fluttered out of the tree, mortally wounded.

Tommy ran over to the bird and watched it slowly die. Overcome with guilt, he buried the little bird in a shallow grave at the base of the tree. Then he looked up and saw his sister, Jane, walking toward him from the house.

"I saw what you did!" Jane said. "You shot that bird and killed it! I'm telling!"

"No, don't" Tommy said. "I'll give you the money in my piggy bank if you don't tell!"

Jane agreed to the bribe.

That night at dinner, when Mom told Jane to wash the dishes, Jane said, "Tommy said he'll wash the dishes for me."

Tommy was about to protest when he saw the smug look on his sister's face. He knew what that meant: *Wash the dishes or I'm telling.* So Tommy washed the dishes.

On Sunday, after Jane left the comics strewn all over the living room floor, Mom told Jane to clean up the mess. Jane said, "Tommy promised he'd clean up the papers."

Again, Tommy was about to protest—then he saw the look on his sister's face. He cleaned up the papers.

After several more days of doing his own chores and Jane's, while feeling horrible inside about the bird, Tommy finally told his mother what he had done.

"Oh, I know all about the bird," Mom said.

"You mean Jane told you? She promised she wouldn't!"

"No," Mom replied. "Jane didn't say a word. I was standing at the window, and I saw you shoot the bird. I saw how sad you were, and I knew you'd come and tell me sooner or later."

"But why didn't you say anything?" Tommy said.

"I just wanted to see how long you were going to let your sister make a slave out of you," said Mom.

That is what guilt is like. We sin, and we try to hide our sin from other people, from God, and from ourselves. Soon, we become a slave to guilt. It makes us do things we don't want to do. It damages our relationships. It destroys our happiness.

In Leviticus 5:14, we come to an issue that affects and afflicts all of us: sin and the guilt that sin brings into our lives. Here we deal with the last of the five fundamental human needs represented by the five sacrifices instituted by God in the book of Leviticus. The fifth sacrifice is the trespass offering—or, as it is called in several translations, including the New International Version and the Revised Standard Version, the guilt offering.

The best word for this sacrifice is *trespass offering*. The word *trespass* means "to commit an offense or a sin; to intrude across a boundary; to infringe upon a law." It is trespass, not guilt, that the original Hebrew word in this passage suggests. So, in quoting the Leviticus passage from the NIV translation, I will substitute the word *[trespass]* in brackets in place of the word *guilt*.

The trespass offering is the fifth and final sacrifice in a series of five sacrifices. It deals with our relationships to other people—to our neighbors, our family members, and to every other human being with whom we come into contact. This offering teaches us how to restore harmony to broken human relationships, so it's as relevant to us today as it was to the Hebrew people in the time of Moses.

It is instructive to notice that this sacrifice comes last in God's order of business. All the other offerings come before this one. The first four sacrifices represent the need for love, expressed by the burnt offering; the need for joy, expressed by the grain offering; the need for peace, expressed by the peace offering; and the need for forgiveness, expressed in the sin offering. Finally, God gets around to talking about how we can get along with each other, with our neighbors, family members, and friends.

This is the reverse order from the way we human beings usually go about it. We are concerned primarily with how to get along with each other. We organize committees and work hard at trying to stop crime, eliminate war, and correct injustice. We set up governments and struggle to solve these issues involving broken relationships between human beings. We think that if we can create the right set of laws and rules and institutional structures, then we will all get along and our social problems will disappear.

God acknowledges that our relationships are important, but He also wants us to know that this is not the place to begin. He reverses the order and says that the place to start is with your relationship to God Himself. That is why, when Jesus summarized the Law, He first said, "Love the Lord your God with all your heart and with all your soul and with all your mind." In fact, He added His own commentary: "This is the first and greatest commandment." Then, next in order of priority, He said, "Love your neighbor as yourself" (Matthew 22:37–39).

It is obedience to the first command—"Love the Lord your God"—that gives us the power to obey the second command—"Love your neighbor as yourself." If you reverse the order, you lose the power to obey. God has to continually remind us how this principle works.

In the trespass offering, we deal with the resolution of problems caused by our sinful actions toward one another. In the previous sacrifice, the sin offering, we dealt with our estrangement and alienation from God as a result of our sinful nature, which is our inheritance from Adam. But here, in the trespass offering, we deal with the sinful deeds we commit against one another and the injustice and injury caused by those deeds.

It is important to understand that not all sins could be forgiven on the basis of the trespass offering, because the people of Israel were under the Law. Under God's grace, all guilt can be forgiven because all sin is against God, and it arises because we are lost children of Adam. God in His mercy has provided a way of redemption for us through the sacrifice of Jesus Christ. So all guilt can be forgiven.

Under the Law, however, there were trespasses that could not be forgiven. For example, if people committed adultery, they were to be stoned to death. An act of sexual perversion or murder was also punished by death under the Law. The reason for these harsh penalties was that these acts strike against the very core of our humanity. Human beings can stand only so much stress in social relationships; when the stress exceeds a certain level, it can be relieved only by the elimination of the offender from society.

That is why God's punishments in the Old Testament, whether against individuals or even against entire nations, seem so harsh and severe to us today. God used these severe measures to keep human sinfulness from breaking down Hebrew society and Hebrew families. It was His way of limiting evil. That is why certain sins were unforgivable under the Law.

Under grace, this is no longer true. There is only one unforgivable sin under grace, and that is the rejection of the Savior Himself. Every other sin is covered by the grace of God, extended to us through the sacrifice of His Son, Jesus.

## UNCLEAN PEOPLE AND UNCLEAN THINGS

As we have seen, each sacrificial offering has a distinctive character. The unique characteristic of the trespass offering is that it required restitution. When an Israelite sinned against another person, he or she needed to go back and right the wrong, as far as it was possible. A broken relationship needs repair, whether that repair involves an apology, a confession, or restoring possessions that were lost or stolen. Human relationships can move forward into the future only when they have been freed of the problems of the past. That is what God teaches us through the symbolism of the trespass offering.

The regulations regarding the trespass offering are found in Leviticus 5 and Leviticus 6:1–7. In that passage, we read:

> "'If a person sins because he does not speak up when he hears a public charge to testify regarding something he has seen or learned about, he will be held responsible.
>
> "'Or if a person touches anything ceremonially unclean—whether the carcasses of unclean wild animals or of unclean livestock or of

unclean creatures that move along the ground—even though he is unaware of it, he has become unclean and is guilty.

"'Or if he touches human uncleanness—anything that would make him unclean—even though he is unaware of it, when he learns of it he will be guilty.

"'Or if a person thoughtlessly takes an oath to do anything, whether good or evil—in any matter one might carelessly swear about—even though he is unaware of it, in any case when he learns of it he will be guilty.

"'When anyone is guilty in any of these ways, he must confess in what way he has sinned and, as a penalty for the sin he has committed, he must bring to the LORD a female lamb or goat from the flock as a sin offering; and the priest shall make atonement for him for his sin.

"'If he cannot afford a lamb, he is to bring two doves or two young pigeons to the LORD as a penalty for his sin—one for a sin offering and the other for a burnt offering. He is to bring them to the priest, who shall first offer the one for the sin offering. He is to wring its head from its neck, not severing it completely, and is to sprinkle some of the blood of the sin offering against the side of the altar; the rest of the blood must be drained out at the base of the altar. It is a sin offering. The priest shall then offer the other as a burnt offering in the prescribed way and make atonement for him for the sin he has committed, and he will be forgiven.

"'If, however, he cannot afford two doves or two young pigeons, he is to bring as an offering for his sin a tenth of an ephah of fine flour for a sin offering. He must not put oil or incense on it, because it is a sin offering. He is to bring it to the priest, who shall take a handful of it as a memorial portion and burn it on the altar on top of the offerings made to the LORD by fire. It is a sin offering. In this way the priest will make atonement for him for any of these sins he has committed, and he will be forgiven. The rest of the offering will belong to the priest, as in the case of the grain offering.'"

The LORD said to Moses: "When a person commits a violation and sins unintentionally in regard to any of the LORD's holy things, he is to bring to the LORD as a penalty a ram from the flock, one without defect and of the proper value in silver, according to the sanctuary shekel. It is a [trespass] offering. He must make restitution for what he has failed to do in regard to the holy things, add a fifth of the value to that and give it all to the priest, who will make atonement for him with the ram as a [trespass] offering, and he will be forgiven.

"If a person sins and does what is forbidden in any of the LORD's commands, even though he does not know it, he is guilty and will be held responsible. He is to bring to the priest as a [trespass] offering a ram from the flock, one without defect and of the proper value. In this way the priest will make atonement for him for the wrong he has committed unintentionally, and he will be forgiven. It is a [trespass] offering; he has been guilty of wrongdoing against the LORD."

The LORD said to Moses: "If anyone sins and is unfaithful to the LORD by deceiving his neighbor about something entrusted to him or left in his care or stolen, or if he cheats him, or if he finds lost property and lies about it, or if he swears falsely, or if he commits any such sin that people may do—when he thus sins and becomes guilty, he must return what he has stolen or taken by extortion, or what was entrusted to him, or the lost property he found, or whatever it was he swore falsely about. He must make restitution in full, add a fifth of the value to it and give it all to the owner on the day he presents his [trespass] offering. And as a penalty he must bring to the priest, that is, to the LORD, his [trespass] offering, a ram from the flock, one without defect and of the proper value. In this way the priest will make atonement for him before the LORD, and he will be forgiven for any of these things he did that made him guilty."

Five different categories of sin were covered by this offering. The first is what we might call sins of guilty silence. You see it in Leviticus 5:1—"If a person sins because he does not speak up when he hears a public charge to testify regarding something he has seen or learned about, he will be held responsible." This is a sin of omission. If a person has knowledge of an injustice being committed but keeps silent and does not help the injured person receive justice, he or she is guilty of a trespass. He has injured society by withholding testimony.

A just society cannot exist where evil is concealed. We all have a moral duty before God to do our part in helping the people around us to receive just and fair treatment. The person who remains silent and says, "I don't want to get involved," is guilty of a sin before God.

The second category of sin is found in Leviticus 5:2–3—"Or if a person touches anything ceremonially unclean—whether the carcasses of unclean wild animals or of unclean livestock or of unclean creatures that move along the ground—even though he is unaware of it, he has become unclean and is guilty. Or if he touches human uncleanness—anything that would make him unclean—even though he is unaware of it, when he learns of it he will be guilty."

This passage introduces the issue of unclean people and unclean things. When the Old Testament set aside an object, animal, activity, or person as unclean, it recognized a fundamental law of what we would today call ecology—the scientific study of maintaining clean, healthy, balanced relationships between people and their environment.

If laws of ecology are broken, the individual who breaks them usually does not suffer the consequences immediately. For example, a person who tosses trash out of his car window as he speeds down the freeway will not be damaged by his thoughtless actions—but if enough people break the laws of ecology, the cumulative effect can eventually disturb the delicate balance of nature and wreak havoc upon society and individual people. We are seeing the effects of unclean activity in our society today in the form of pollution and ecological disturbances. We are reaping the consequences of generations of ecological neglect and thoughtlessness.

Many of the technological advances that were once considered blessings for humanity are now known to have a severe ecological price tag. A good example was the invention of the automobile, which was considered a tremendous advance over the horse and buggy. Today, however, the automobile clogs our cities, chokes our lungs, and threatens our health and our environment. We can't live without our cars—but it also seems that we can't live with them. The fumes from our internal combustion engines have become a bigger problem than we can cope with.

Pesticides, such as DDT, were considered a great boon to the human race when they were first introduced. These chemicals controlled the swarming populations of flies and mosquitoes and helped reduce the incidence of insect-borne disease in humans and animals. But in time we found out that DDT was killing birds and other beneficial creatures and that the poison was accumulating in our bodies and making us sick. We even found that some of the pests it was supposed to kill were developing a resistance to DDT.

This is the kind of problem which God, in His wisdom, deals with in this matter of unclean things. He teaches us that uncleanness will ultimately destroy us. Uncleanness is an offense against society. As we face increasing dangers from ecological problems and from pollution, we need to take careful notice of what the Bible calls unclean.

The third category of sin is found in Leviticus 5:4—"Or if a person thoughtlessly takes an oath to do anything, whether good or evil—in any matter one might carelessly swear about—even though he is unaware of it, in any case when he learns of it he will be guilty."

An oath is a promise or vow to accomplish something. If a person thoughtlessly, carelessly took an oath to do something, even something good, he was guilty before God. Why? Because fallible human beings do not have the power to guarantee that they will perform in an infallible and 100 percent dependable way. That's what an oath is: an absolute guarantee or promise. An oath is a statement of arrogance on the part of a mortal human being who has momentarily lost sight of his own mortality. He is pretending to be the almighty Creator instead of the frail and fallible creature he is.

For all three of these categories of sin, God prescribes the same sacrifice in Leviticus 5:5-6—"When anyone is guilty in any of these ways, he must confess in what way he has sinned and, as a penalty for the sin he has committed, he must bring to the LORD a female lamb or goat from the flock as a sin offering; and the priest shall make atonement for him for his sin." The sacrifice was to be a female animal because this sacrifice deals with humanity's weakness and submission to the laws of nature. The female of the species is, therefore, the appropriate symbol.

I understand, of course, that it is not considered acceptable in these days of political correctness to suggest that women are the weaker sex. I want to make it clear that neither God nor His Word ever suggest that women hold an inferior or second-class status to men. Throughout the Scriptures we see in women a value and strength that is different from the physical strength of men. The way the Bible here pictures the female as the weaker sex reminds me of a British motion picture that was released soon after World War II. The movie was ironically titled *The Weaker Sex*, yet it dealt with the incredible moral, spiritual, and emotional strength of English women during the dark days of the war. The fact that a female animal is used in Leviticus to symbolize human weakness is merely an acknowledgement of an obvious fact of nature: women, in general, are not as physically strong and powerful as men.

The first three categories of sin were sins of guilty silence, sins of uncleanness, and sins of giving a thoughtless oath. These are sins of human weakness, and the sacrifice symbolized the weakness of humanity and our all-too-human tendency to sin without even realizing the sinfulness of our actions or inaction.

## THE NEED FOR CONFESSION

As we have already seen, God made provision for all economic classes to be included in the sacrifices and forgiveness of sins. If a person couldn't afford a lamb, he could bring turtledoves. And if he couldn't afford turtledoves, he could bring a measure of finely ground flour and offer that. So even the poorest could be forgiven and reconciled to God.

There was only one inflexible requirement: that the sinner admit his or her sin. The individual had to confess to the act of wrongdoing against God. It wasn't that God demanded repayment for the sin. Human beings cannot repay God for sinning against Him. But God required that people make restitution, if only to the extent of confessing that the act of wrongdoing was truly wrong. Confession of sin was essential to obtaining forgiveness through the sacrificial offering of the animal.

The truth that is depicted here in these sacrifices is the same truth we read about in the New Testament letters of John: "If we claim to be without sin, we deceive ourselves and the truth is not in us. If we confess our sins, he is faithful and just and will forgive us our sins and purify us from all unrighteousness" (1 John 1:8–9).

God insists that we admit and confess our sin—not because He wants to humiliate us but because confession is necessary in order for us to receive the forgiveness which He has already provided. It isn't that God forgives us at the moment we confess. He has already forgiven us. But we can't accept that forgiveness until we see and understand the truth about what we have done. That is why it is necessary for us to admit our wrongs before we can experience His cleansing forgiveness.

This is a fundamental principle for curing broken relationships within human society. We must come to a place where we face and admit our sins. We must admit our sin specifically, clearly, and unequivocally. It does no good to simply say, "*If* I have offended you, please forgive me." That word "if" cancels out everything else you say. It is a denial of your own recognition of sin. When someone says, "*If* I have done something wrong," he is really saying, "You may see what I did as wrong, but I don't, and I won't admit it. If you think I did something wrong, then I'm sorry you feel that way, but I don't agree." That is not an admission of guilt, and it does not result in healing, forgiveness, or a reconciled relationship.

There are times in human relationships when we must do things that are right but painful, such as confront people who are living in a sinful lifestyle. At such times, we can be sorry that we have to hurt someone by speaking the truth to them in love—yet we are not sinning by doing so, we are doing what is right. A doctor may say, "I'm sorry" when doing something that causes a patient to feel pain—but the doctor is not doing something wrong. Sometimes a doctor must cause a little pain in order to bring about healing. So we need to understand that not every incident of causing pain or hurt to someone else is necessarily a sin.

But when we do sin against other people, God wants us to admit it to ourselves and confess it to God and to the person we have sinned against. God wants us to come to a place where we say, "Yes, I was wrong. I sinned, and I have no excuses to offer. Please forgive me."

Only at this point can a relationship be restored. In most broken relationships, it is necessary for both parties to seek forgiveness. Each person must begin with himself or herself. As Jesus said, "First take the plank out of your own eye, and then you will see clearly to remove the speck from your brother's eye" (Matthew 7:5).

## RESTORED RELATIONSHIPS

Next, we see two other classes of trespass sins. The first of these two is a religious offense, which is described in Leviticus 5:14–17:

The LORD said to Moses: "When a person commits a violation and sins unintentionally in regard to any of the LORD's holy things, he is to bring to the LORD as a penalty a ram from the flock, one without defect and of the proper value in silver, according to the sanctuary shekel. It is a [trespass] offering. He must make restitution for what he has failed to do in regard to the holy things, add a fifth of the value to that and give it all to the priest, who will make atonement for him with the ram as a guilt offering, and he will be forgiven" (Leviticus 5:14–16).

This offense involved something done "in the LORD's holy things," and for it the person was to bring a male because the offense here is greater. This offense was not just a result of human weakness but a breach of the individual's relationship to God, within which man is made to rule in dominion over the earth. Thus the male animal was the appropriate symbol.

Still, this offense was committed ignorantly and unwittingly. The person didn't understand that it was a wrong act at the time. But upon learning it was wrong, the individual could not merely pass it off and say, "Well, I didn't understand that at the time." He was to make restitution—and not just restitution of an equivalent sum. The offender was required to add an additional one-fifth (20 percent). He was to evaluate the offering according to a scale in the temple and add 20 percent of that amount to the sacrifice to make restitution.

This sacrifice addressed sins committed by an individual who acted with deep sincerity, with the utter conviction that he or she was doing the right thing in the name of the Lord, but who later discovered that it was the wrong thing. I think that such sins are very common among Christians today. We think we are doing good things in the name of the Lord when we attack other Christians who do not worship or believe exactly as we do. We think God wants our legalistic efforts, our formalistic rituals, our political action, or our strident condemnation of those who believe differently than we do—yet our hearts are very far from His heart.

Instead of loving God and loving others, we love rules, traditions, ideologies, dogmas, and doctrines. Instead of loving God and loving others, we love to be right and for others to be wrong. Like the preconversion apostle Paul, we become zealous for the things of God, but we have lost sight of God's love and mercy, His message of good news for lost and hurting people. We are sincere and convinced that we are right, yet the things we are doing in the Lord's name are not the things God would have us do. So we are sincere—but we are sincerely sinning against God. That is the kind of sin that is covered by the trespass offering.

And there is one more category of sin that is covered by the trespass offering. We find it discussed in Leviticus 6:1–7:

> The LORD said to Moses: "If anyone sins and is unfaithful to the LORD by deceiving his neighbor about something entrusted to him or left in his care or stolen, or if he cheats him, or if he finds lost property and lies about it, or if he swears falsely, or if he commits any such sin that people may do—when he thus sins and becomes guilty, he must return what he has stolen or taken by extortion, or what was entrusted to him, or the lost property he found, or whatever it was he swore falsely about. He must make restitution in full, add a fifth of the value to it and give it all to the owner on the day he presents his [trespass] offering. And as a penalty he must bring to the priest, that is, to the LORD, his [trespass] offering, a ram from the flock, one without defect and of the proper value. In this way the priest will make atonement for him before the LORD, and he will be forgiven for any of these things he did that made him guilty."

Here, God talks about the need to make restitution in cases of cheating, robbing, stealing, defrauding, or extorting goods from a neighbor; or cases of filing a false income tax return, or cases of harming a person's reputation. What was taken must be restored. Sin has broken the relationship, and the relationship cannot be healed until the offense is admitted. Time will not cure this kind of hurt. Decades may go by, but the hurt will not be healed unless the offender takes steps to seek forgiveness and make restitution.

As a young Christian in my early twenties, I worked for a contractor as a timekeeper. I made out the paychecks (including my own) at the end of each month. One month, I needed some money and asked my boss if I could have an advance of twenty-five dollars, and he graciously consented. I wrote out a check, signed it, and cashed it. At the end of the month, when I was making out the regular checks, I did forget that I had already drawn twenty-five dollars. So I made out my check for the usual amount.

Later, after the boss signed my check and gave it to me, I remembered the advance I had taken. I struggled with myself. I realized that he hadn't remembered it either. I rationalized it, telling myself, "Well, he really owes it to me anyway. I've been working very hard. So I'll just say nothing about it."

My job soon ended, and I went back to school. A couple of years passed, and I couldn't forget the fact that I had taken twenty-five dollars I hadn't earned. One day, under the conviction of the Spirit, I wrote the man a letter and at great cost to myself (this was during the Great Depression), I returned the twenty-five dollars. I didn't know that God's Word said I should add an extra fifth to it, or I would have had to send him thirty dollars! In my letter, I asked for the man's forgiveness, and he sent me a very gracious letter, inviting me to come back and work for him any time—and that was a great load off my soul.

Jesus talked about this very principle when He said, "Therefore, if you are offering your gift at the altar and there remember that your brother has something against you, leave your gift there in front of the altar. First go and be reconciled to your brother; then come and offer your gift" (Matthew 5:23–24). God is more pleased with our integrity and our healed relationships than He is with our religious offerings.

God provided the trespass offering and fulfilled it in Jesus Christ, so that we might heal the broken relationships of the past and live our lives with a clear conscience. If you want to have a vital relationship with God, you may need to heal the broken relationships of the past—relationships with friends, neighbors, and family members. You may need to make restitution and confess your sins and errors. But once you do, those relationships will be healed before God, and you will experience emotional and spiritual freedom for the rest of your life.

In Leviticus 6:8–30, God tells the priests of Israel how they are to administer the burnt offering, the grain offering, and the sin offering to the people:

> The LORD said to Moses: "Give Aaron and his sons this command:
> 'These are the regulations for the burnt offering: The burnt offering
> is to remain on the altar hearth throughout the night, till morning,

and the fire must be kept burning on the altar. The priest shall then put on his linen clothes, with linen undergarments next to his body, and shall remove the ashes of the burnt offering that the fire has consumed on the altar and place them beside the altar. Then he is to take off these clothes and put on others, and carry the ashes outside the camp to a place that is ceremonially clean. The fire on the altar must be kept burning; it must not go out. Every morning the priest is to add firewood and arrange the burnt offering on the fire and burn the fat of the fellowship offerings on it. The fire must be kept burning on the altar continuously; it must not go out.

"'These are the regulations for the grain offering: Aaron's sons are to bring it before the Lord, in front of the altar. The priest is to take a handful of fine flour and oil, together with all the incense on the grain offering, and burn the memorial portion on the altar as an aroma pleasing to the Lord. Aaron and his sons shall eat the rest of it, but it is to be eaten without yeast in a holy place; they are to eat it in the courtyard of the Tent of Meeting. It must not be baked with yeast; I have given it as their share of the offerings made to me by fire. Like the sin offering and the guilt offering, it is most holy. Any male descendant of Aaron may eat it. It is his regular share of the offerings made to the Lord by fire for the generations to come. Whatever touches them will become holy.'"

The Lord also said to Moses, "This is the offering Aaron and his sons are to bring to the Lord on the day he is anointed: a tenth of an ephah of fine flour as a regular grain offering, half of it in the morning and half in the evening. Prepare it with oil on a griddle; bring it well-mixed and present the grain offering broken in pieces as an aroma pleasing to the Lord. The son who is to succeed him as anointed priest shall prepare it. It is the Lord's regular share and is to be burned completely. Every grain offering of a priest shall be burned completely; it must not be eaten."

The Lord said to Moses, "Say to Aaron and his sons: 'These are the regulations for the sin offering: The sin offering is to be slaughtered before the Lord in the place the burnt offering is slaughtered; it is most holy. The priest who offers it shall eat it; it is to be eaten in a holy place, in the courtyard of the Tent of Meeting. Whatever touches any of the flesh will become holy, and if any of the blood is spattered on a garment, you must wash it in a holy place. The clay pot the meat is cooked in must be broken; but if it is cooked in a bronze pot, the pot is to be scoured and rinsed with water. Any male in a priest's family may eat it; it is most holy. But any sin offering whose blood is brought into the Tent of Meeting to make atonement in the Holy Place must not be eaten; it must be burned.'"

In these regulations for three of the sacrificial offerings in Leviticus, we see the importance God placed on the role of the priest in the spiritual life of the Hebrew people. We will explore the need for a priest in more detail in the next chapter.

As we close our study of the need for restored relationships, it is important to remember why God instituted not only a program of sacrifices to God but also a program of restitution and forgiveness between human beings. God understands human nature and human need, because He created us. He knows that we can't live joyfully and effectively when our relationships are in shambles.

When we bring our broken relationships to Jesus, He will heal them, transform them, and restore them. That is the provision God made for us through the trespass offering, and that is the provision Jesus made for us on the cross of Calvary.

※————————※

# THE NEED FOR A PRIEST
## LEVITICUS 8:1–9

IF YOU BUY a new car or computer, you also get the manufacturer's instruction book, which tells you how your new machine works and what to do with it when things go wrong. That is exactly what the Bible does. God created a marvelous machine—you!—and He also wrote an instruction book to tell you how you work and what to do when things go wrong with you. That instruction book is the Bible. The Bible is the greatest book ever written on the subject of human psychology. Our problem is that we tend to ignore its advice.

Many of us like to spend all of our time in the New Testament while essentially ignoring the Old Testament. The problem with this approach to Scripture is that the New Testament contains a great deal of truth that is too advanced for us. That is why we have the Old Testament. The Old Testament starts at the kindergarten level. It uses pictures in much the way a kindergartner's book is filled with pictures. We can't understand the advanced concepts of the New Testament until we have first learned our spiritual ABCs by studying God's picture book, Leviticus.

So far in Leviticus, God has been using animal sacrifices as pictures to show us that we human beings need a sacrifice, a substitute. No one can handle the problems of life alone. No one can solve the sin problem alone. That is the lesson of history and of our individual lives. In picture after picture, sacrifice after sacrifice, God tells us that the solution to our problems is this: We need a substitute, a sacrifice, to die in our place. Only if we accept God's perfect sacrifice as the solution for our problems can we have the basic needs of life met: love, joy, peace, forgiveness, and restored relationships with the people around us. That is what the five sacrifices of Leviticus 1–7 have been teaching us.

Now, as we come to Leviticus 8, the nature of these pictures changes, revealing a new facet of God's truth for our lives: Not only do we need a sacrifice, but also we need a priest. Even though a sacrifice has been provided for us, we still cannot solve our problems unless we have a priest.

## THE PURPOSE OF THE PRIESTHOOD

Why do we need a priest? Because no one can offer a sacrifice by himself or herself. Every individual, whether in ancient Israel or in twenty-first century America, needs a priest. We need a priest because we need instruction. We need someone to explain the meaning of the sacrifice to us. After the meaning of the sacrifice is explained and its value made clear, we need to have the sacrifice applied to our lives. We need help in dealing with the emotional and spiritual problems awakened by our awareness of sin and struggle in our lives. God understands this deep need we have, so He has given us the gift of the priesthood.

The most basic reason we need a priest is that we cannot see ourselves and our lives with clarity. We don't know what our faces look like without a mirror. Without the ability to see ourselves reflected, we would have no idea of the color of our eyes or the shape of our noses. A priest is like a mirror of the soul, a human being who looks into our hearts and reflects back to us what we are really like, so that we can understand ourselves more accurately. God designed the priesthood to be a class of people who are trained and skilled at meeting our needs for a clearer understanding of who we are, what we are like, and why we do the things we do.

The Old Testament priests were, in a sense, the psychiatrists of the Old Testament. They were the ones to whom people came when they had emotional problems and psychological issues such as guilt, fear, anxiety, hostility, and relationship problems. Though I have great respect for modern psychology and psychiatry, I am convinced that these Old Testament priests knew more about human nature than most modern therapists because the early priests were taught by God. So as we study the Levitical priests, it is important to realize that they did much more than merely conduct religious ceremonies. They fulfilled that tremendous need that people have for help with their problems. Our need for a priesthood is just as great today.

## THE ELEMENTS OF THE PRIESTHOOD

In the opening verses of Leviticus 8, God gives us an introduction to His plan for the priesthood, describing for us the essential ingredients that make a priest:

> The LORD said to Moses, "Bring Aaron and his sons, their garments, the anointing oil, the bull for the sin offering, the two rams and the basket containing bread made without yeast, and gather the entire assembly at the entrance to the Tent of Meeting." Moses did as the LORD commanded him, and the assembly gathered at the entrance to the Tent of Meeting (Leviticus 8:1–4).

In those verses, God lists the basic elements of the priesthood. You may have missed the first element on the list, but you find it in the first few words of the passage: "The LORD said to Moses. . . ." The first ingredient of the priesthood is the Word of God. A true priesthood never originates from any human plans or intentions but from God's Word, God's thoughts. The Word of God does not originate from a pope, a council, a convention, a synod, or a committee. It originates with God Himself.

As we will soon see, the priesthood today, in the New Testament era, involves every believer. We are all priests to one another in the church of Jesus Christ; we minister to one another as believers in much the same way that the Levitical priesthood ministered to the people of Israel centuries ago. We need to make it clear, at the beginning, that the priesthood of all believers is God's idea, not a human idea. It is an idea that began with the Word of God.

The second element of the priesthood is Aaron and his sons. Aaron was the brother of Moses. Aaron and his descendants were the only family in the entire Old Testament authorized to serve as priests. In this family, Aaron was to be the chief priest, the high priest. This plan was beautifully designed by God to teach us an important truth about our lives. As the book of Hebrews makes clear, we too have a high priest. Aaron is a symbolic picture of our Great High Priest, Jesus Christ. The priesthood of Jesus is as necessary to our lives as Aaron's was to the life of Israel. When we read about Aaron serving as high priest, we see a picture of Jesus and of what He is to us.

If you don't understand the priesthood of Jesus, you are missing out on a great part of your Christian heritage. This is one reason so many people are bored and uninspired in the Christian life. They don't grasp the provision God has made for them. They don't access the rich spiritual and emotional resources that are available to them to meet their needs and lift their spiritual and emotional depression.

Just as Aaron is a picture of our Great High Priest, Jesus Christ, the sons of Aaron represent every believer in Jesus Christ, serving also as priests. Everyone who knows Jesus Christ as Lord and Savior is a believer-priest to the other members of the human family, to the world at large and to the rest of the body of Christ.

Some Christian denominations have a priesthood of men who have been set apart to serve as priests. I have no objection to a priestly clergy in the church, except that the officially ordained priests should not be viewed as the only exclusive priests in the church. The true priesthood is not limited to a certain class of professional Christians. Every believer, whether male or female, is a priest. This is clearly taught in the New Testament, as these two examples show.

> To him who loves us and has freed us from our sins by his blood, and has made us to be a kingdom and priests to serve his God and Father—to him be glory and power for ever and ever! Amen (Revelation 1:5–6).

> You also, like living stones, are being built into a spiritual house to be a holy priesthood, offering spiritual sacrifices acceptable to God through Jesus Christ (1 Peter 2:5).

So we are all priests in the church, the body of Christ. It's exciting to be priests to one another, because we have the privilege of helping our Christian brothers and sisters deal with the emotional and spiritual issues of their lives. We help one another solve problems in the realms of Christian behavior and Christian relationships. One of the great lessons of Leviticus is that it shows us how we can all serve as priests to one another and to God.

The third element of the priesthood is the element of the priestly garments. Moses was God's representative, acting on God's behalf, and God told him to take with him the priests' garments in preparation for the consecration of the priesthood. In the symbolism of Scripture, garments are always a revelation of the character of the individual who wears them. Later, we will examine the list of priestly garments, and we will see how they picture for us what a priest is and how he functions in our lives on God's behalf.

The fourth element of the priesthood is the anointing oil. In Scripture, the oil of anointing always speaks of the Holy Spirit. This means that a priest, to be effective, must walk in the Spirit. You can never be an effective priest unless you learn the ministry of the Holy Spirit and how He works in you and through you, imparting the life of Christ to others through you.

The fifth element of the priesthood is the sacrifices. God tells Moses to take the bull and the two rams. These always speak of redemption, of the need for dealing with the problem of sin and guilt. Since Aaron and his sons were human beings, prone to sin, they too needed sacrifices. But the sacrifices were also food. The sacrifices were the food that the priests were to feed on and live by.

The sixth element of the priesthood is the fact that God told Moses to bring the congregation together. God insisted on that. He wanted all the adults there, and all the children as well. He wanted the humblest and the greatest in Israel to be present. So God told Moses to assemble the whole congregation—more than a million people. They all gathered so that God might teach them what the priesthood meant in their lives and in the life of the nation of Israel.

The seventh and final element of the priesthood was that they were to assemble in front of the tent of meeting, the tabernacle. As we have already seen, the tabernacle is a picture of man. It was built on the same pattern as humanity itself. The tabernacle was a threefold entity; just as we are composed of body, soul, and spirit. This is God's way of telling us that He Himself will teach us what all of this means and that He will do so from within ourselves, from the place where God meets humanity. Remember that Paul says, "We have not received the spirit of the world but the Spirit who is from God, that we may understand what God has freely given us" (1 Corinthians 2:12).

## WASHED BY THE WORD OF GOD

Next, Moses, under the direction of God, gives us a step-by-step account of the process by which God calls the priesthood into existence. If we read Leviticus purely as a book of instructions to ancient Israel, then this section is going to be dull and boring. But if we see Leviticus as God intends us to see it, if we truly see ourselves and our own priestly role as Christians inscribed upon these pages, then the book of Leviticus will come alive! God's picture of the priesthood is truly a picture of your life and mine. We have a Great High Priest, Jesus, who is pictured for us by Aaron, and you and I are pictured as the sons of Aaron. We find the first step in God's process of creating the priesthood in the next two verses:

> Moses said to the assembly, "This is what the LORD has commanded to be done." Then Moses brought Aaron and his sons forward and washed them with water (Leviticus 8:5–6).

What does the washing of Aaron and his sons signify? We find a clue in the linking of the word and the water in this passage. The Lord commands—that's the word. Then the priests are washed—that's the water.

You will recall that in the gospel of John, Jesus said to Nicodemus, the religious intellectual who came to Him by night, "I tell you the truth, no one can enter the kingdom of God unless he is born of water and the Spirit" (John 3:5). What did Jesus mean? Water stands for the Word. Unless a person is born by believing the Word of God, thus releasing the operation of the Spirit of God into his or her life, that person can never enter the kingdom of God. So the Word, in its capacity to cleanse and purify, is pictured for us by water. Jesus later used the same symbol when He told His disciples, "You are already clean because of the word I have spoken to you" (John 15:3).

In His Great High-Priestly prayer, Jesus said, "I have given them your word and the world has hated them, for they are not of the world any more than I am of the world. . . . Sanctify them by the truth; your word is truth. As you sent me into the world, I have sent them into the world. For them I sanctify myself, that they too may be truly sanctified" (John 17:14, 17–19). That is the fulfillment of the word picture God draws for us here in Leviticus 8. Jesus consecrated Himself as our Great High Priest by the washing of the water of the

Word—and as the only sinless man who ever lived, He is the only one who is fit to do so.

In Leviticus, we see Aaron, a symbolic type of Jesus, consecrated with water by Moses. Then the sons of Aaron are also washed. The priesthood operates by the proclamation of the Word of God; by the Word, the priesthood is prepared for ministry.

## THE MEANING OF THE GARMENTS

After the washing of the priests comes the dressing of the high priest in his garments. We read:

> He [Moses] put the tunic on Aaron, tied the sash around him, clothed him with the robe and put the ephod on him. He also tied the ephod to him by its skillfully woven waistband; so it was fastened on him. He placed the breastpiece on him and put the Urim and Thummim in the breastpiece. Then he placed the turban on Aaron's head and set the gold plate, the sacred diadem, on the front of it, as the LORD commanded Moses (Leviticus 8:7–9).

Notice that this whole ensemble is God's idea. Each piece of priestly clothing has a significant meaning. What are the meanings of these garments? If you follow the pattern of the Old Testament, you are given clues as to what Jesus Christ is prepared to be and to do in your life, for the garments reflect the character and the quality of the Great High Priest. Let's look at them.

First, Moses began dressing Aaron, who was naked, because he had just been washed with water. At the command of God, Moses put an inner garment upon Aaron, a white linen tunic which fit closely around Aaron's body and served as his undergarment. Moses bound it around him with an inner sash (or, in some translations, girdle). After Aaron was fully dressed, these two items were hidden by the outer garments, yet each was symbolically significant.

In Scripture, the tunic or coat is always a picture of the righteousness of an individual. This inner tunic coat is a picture of that inner, hidden righteousness of the Lord Jesus, which only God could see. Jesus had a purity within, a purity that God could see even when people could not. That is why God the Father spoke as he did at the baptism of Jesus, which took place after Jesus had lived almost thirty years in the town of Nazareth.

Many people have wondered what kind of a person Jesus was as a growing boy. Did he ever misbehave and get into trouble? The Father spoke from heaven and said, "This is my Son, whom I love; with him I am well pleased" (Matthew 3:17). Jesus had no spot or blemish within Him, not the slightest taint of sin. He had the inner righteousness that was symbolized by the white linen undergarment worn by Aaron.

A sash or girdle, in Scripture, always symbolizes a servant. This inner sash represents that inner spirit of servitude, a willingness to be a servant. This is the attitude we see again and again in the life of our Lord. The people around Jesus could not always see it, but God the Father saw. The apostle Paul wrote that Jesus "made himself nothing, taking the very nature of a servant, being made in human likeness. And being found in appearance as a man, he humbled himself and became obedient to death—even death on a cross!" (Philippians 2:7–8). It is His inner willingness to stoop and meet us at the point of our deepest need that characterized the life of our Great High Priest.

Over these garments, Moses placed the outer robe. In Exodus 28:31–34 and Exodus 39:22–26, it is described as an exquisite robe of finely woven cloth, all of one piece and colored a brilliant and beautiful blue. This robe speaks of righteousness—but in this case, it symbolizes the visible righteousness of Jesus that human beings could see. Before condemning Jesus to death, the Roman governor Pontius Pilate examined the life of Jesus and concluded, "I find no fault in Him." Jesus had an outward, visible righteousness that was plainly apparent to many.

Over the robe, Moses placed the ephod. The ephod was a long vestment that covered the front and back of the priest, hanging down to the knees. It was fastened at the shoulders by clasps and bound at the waist by a sash. The ephod was the mark of the high priest's authority because it hung from his shoulders, the biblical symbol of power. When Isaiah prophesied regarding the coming Messiah, he wrote, "For to us a child is born, to us a son is given, and the government will be on his shoulders" (Isaiah 9:6). The ephod serves to remind us of the words of Jesus just before He ascended into the heavens: "All authority in heaven and on earth has been given to me" (Matthew 28:18).

We tend to think that while Jesus has power in heaven, human beings can thwart His purposes on earth. That is not true. *All* power is given to Jesus in heaven and on earth. He is able to act as He chooses. Much of the trouble of the church today comes from the fact that we have forgotten the Source of our power. We have lost sight of the fact that we have a High Priest who has all power and all authority. He is the one of whom it is said, "What he opens no one can shut, and what he shuts no one can open" (Revelation 3:7).

Around the ephod was bound a skillfully woven waistband, a band of beautifully decorated cloth intertwined with gold. Here again, the waistband is a picture of the servitude of Jesus, but in this case His outward servant character—His willingness to stoop to meet our need, whatever it is. This means that our Great High Priest, even with all His power and authority, is willing to meet us right where we are.

This waistband reminds us of that moment in the upper room when Jesus, just hours before the cross, bound a towel around Himself and began to wash His disciples' feet. In this way, Jesus manifested His willingness to meet the need of His disciples even when they were too proud to be served. Peter pridefully tried to reject the Lord's servant ministry to him, but the Lord said, "Unless I wash you, you have no part with me" (John 13:8). In other words, "If you do not allow me to serve you, there is no way you can be helped." The high priest, bound with a beautiful waistband, reminds us of the beautiful servanthood of Jesus, who stooped to serve us and meet us at the place of our need.

Over the middle of Aaron's breast, Moses hung the breastpiece. This was a square of gold on which were written the names of all twelve tribes of Israel. Thus Israel was reminded that the high priest held closest to his heart every individual member of the nation of Israel. In the same way, Jesus holds all of God's people close to His heart. He cares about your needs and hurts. He is deeply involved with your life. He knows what you are going through.

In the midst of the breastpiece, Moses placed the two objects called the Urim and Thummim. What were these objects? No one knows. They are never described in the Bible. Even the ancient rabbis lost any conception or description of what these objects were and what they looked like. Their names mean "Lights" and "Perfections."

Though we don't know what the Urim and Thummim looked like, we know what they were for. They were used by the priests to determine the mind and will of God concerning specific events. Whenever a king or even an ordinary person desired to know what God wanted him to do, he went to the priest, and, through the Urim and the Thummim, the priest was able to help him find direction in life.

We are getting very close to the true meaning of these words when we translate "Lights" as "Insights" and "Perfections" as "Outworkings." "Lights" truly are insights into life. And "perfections" truly are the outworkings of circumstances to accomplish the goal God has in mind. When a problem arose, people could go to the priest, and he would use these instruments to gain insight from God into the nature of the problem. Then he received assurance from God that He was working out the problem to a perfect solution. This corresponds exactly to what the Spirit of God does in our hearts through the Word of God and through the counsel of other members of the priesthood of God. The Spirit helps us to gain an understanding of the problem and to have the assurance that He is working out His perfect purposes in our lives.

My mentor and patron saint, Dr. H. A. Ironside, used to tell of a young man who was a recent graduate of a theological seminary. Educated beyond his intelligence, he had arrived at a place where he thought he knew all the answers to every theological question. He traveled to a certain town where there lived an old Christian layman who had never been to a Bible school or a seminary but had taught himself the Word of God under the guidance of the Holy Spirit. In the process, he had gained a reputation as a man of wise counsel.

When the young theologian heard about the wise old Christian layman, he decided to meet the man, question him, and try to stump him with a theological riddle. So a meeting was arranged between the two men. The young man said, "Sir, I hear that you have quite a reputation as a Bible student. I'd like to ask you a question."

"Well," the old man replied, "I don't know if I can answer it, but I'd be glad to try. What is your question?"

The young man said, "Tell me, what were the Urim and the Thummim?"

"Well, sir," the old man said, "I don't really know—and I don't think anyone else does either. The names mean 'Lights' and 'Perfections,' and we know that these were instruments the high priest used to determine the mind of God in certain situations. But I've found that if you change just one letter in these words, you have the instrument by which I can know the mind and will of God for my own life."

The young man was puzzled. "What do you mean?" he asked.

"Well," the old man said, "if you change the R in Urim to an S, you'll make it 'Usim and Thummim.' And when I want to know the mind of God, I just take the pages of my Bible and I use 'em and thumb 'em. By using and thumbing the pages of my Bible, I can learn what I need to know!"

I don't know how theologically accurate that is. But I do think the old man had arrived at a practical approach to seeking the mind of God.

Next, we see that Moses placed a turban on the head of the priest. The turban consisted of a beautiful cloth bound around Aaron's head—a symbolic picture of the mind under control, the intelligence of the priest in submission to the will of God. It represents what Paul describes when he writes, "we take captive every thought to make it obedient to Christ" (2 Corinthians 10:5). Jesus, our Great High Priest, embodies all the treasures of wisdom and knowledge, and He works intelligently on our behalf to carry out the will and purpose of God the Father in our lives. And that is what we are to do as a priesthood of believers, helping one another to understand the mind and thoughts of God.

Finally, in the middle of the turban, Moses set the golden plate which is called the diadem (or crown) of the high priest. Only the high priest wore it. Inscribed on it were the words "Holiness to the LORD." As we have already learned from the book of Leviticus, the word *holiness* means "wholeness." God's purpose is to make us a whole and holy people. This golden diadem is a beautiful picture of how our Great High Priest keeps this great purpose always before Him—the purpose of making us whole before the Lord. That is the purpose the Lord Jesus is working out in your life and mine, and that is the purpose we, as priestly believers, should seek in the lives of our fellow believers.

The book of Hebrews tells us, "For we do not have a high priest who is unable to sympathize with our weaknesses, but we have one who has been tempted in every way, just as we are—yet was without sin" (Hebrews 4:15). Jesus, our High Priest, has known discouragement, hostility, and opposition. He has wept with those who wept. He was angry over injustice and oppression. He understands how we feel and He has experienced the worst pain and suffering of which human beings are capable.

Whatever your problem may be at this moment, Jesus has been where you are. He has a servant's heart, and He knows how to solve every problem you will ever face. Your Great High Priest is ready to meet you at your place of need. The reason we are so weak and faltering as God's people is that we lose sight of this Great High Priest who is powerful and available to us twenty-four hours a day.

Friend in Christ, lift your eyes to your Great High Priest. He is ready to meet you at the door of your tabernacle, at the heart of your own life. He will release in you all of the mighty resources that are available to Him through God the Father.

# CHAPTER 8

# THE WORK OF A PRIEST
## LEVITICUS 8:10–36

CENTURIES AGO IN Germany, a monk named Martin Luther rediscovered certain long-neglected truths in the Scriptures. One of the most radical and transforming of these truths was the priesthood of all believers, which is rooted in 1 Peter 2:9—"But you are a chosen people, a royal priesthood, a holy nation, a people belonging to God, that you may declare the praises of him who called you out of darkness into his wonderful light."

Prior to the time of Martin Luther, the church taught that the priesthood was limited to a select group of men who acted as intermediaries between God and ordinary people. Standing firmly on the clear teaching of the Bible, Luther exploded that idea. He taught that every person who comes to know Jesus Christ is a priest under God and that every believer joins with that Great High Priest, Jesus Christ Himself, in a ministry of mercy, blessing, and ministry to a world. This is the priesthood to which God has called you and me.

The priesthood of all believers is one of a number of truths that Luther rediscovered in Scripture. These truths had such a radical impact on the church in Europe that a whole new movement quickly swept across the continent: the Protestant Reformation.

In the centuries since Luther's day, the idea of the priesthood of all believers has again become a much-neglected truth. Today, few Christians realize that they themselves are a priesthood. They come to church on Sunday morning, absorb the music and the sermon, and go back home unchanged. They take, but they do not give. They listen, but they do not love and serve. They do not experience the excitement of the Christian life, because they do not see themselves as priests.

All Christians were meant to serve God and serve others. All Christians were meant to be in the game, not in the grandstands. My prayer is that God would call us to a vibrant rediscovery of what it means to be a royal priesthood, a people belonging to God, declaring the praises and the good news of Him who has called us out of darkness and into His wonderful light. I pray that God would call us to an exciting rediscovery of what it means for every believer to be a priest of God.

## ANOINTED WITH OIL, ANOINTED WITH THE SPIRIT

As we previously saw in Leviticus 8:1–9, God set aside the high priest—Aaron, the brother of Moses—as a type or picture of our Great High Priest, the Lord Jesus Christ. It is symbolic that Aaron was set aside first, before his sons, because the sons of Aaron are a picture of the priesthood of every believer. As we look at this passage, we discover some powerful, practical truths about the way God wants to work in our lives and use us to encourage, bless, and heal one another in His church.

When Aaron, the high priest, was set aside for service, he was cleansed with water and clad in beautiful priestly garments—a linen tunic or undergarment, an inner sash, the brilliant blue outer robe, the ephod, the beautifully woven waistband, the breastpiece with its golden decoration and the two mysterious objects, the Urim and Thummim. Each item of these priestly garments reveals an aspect of the work that our Great High Priest, the Lord Jesus Christ, does in our lives. The priestly vestments symbolize the fact that Jesus, our High Priest, meets all of our spiritual, emotional, and intellectual needs. With that as our background, we move deeper into Leviticus 8:

> Then Moses took the anointing oil and anointed the tabernacle and
> everything in it, and so consecrated them. He sprinkled some of the
> oil on the altar seven times, anointing the altar and all its utensils
> and the basin with its stand, to consecrate them. He poured some
> of the anointing oil on Aaron's head and anointed him to consecrate
> him. Then he brought Aaron's sons forward, put tunics on them,

tied sashes around them and put headbands on them, as the LORD commanded Moses (Leviticus 8:10–13).

Here we see the anointing of the high priest. It took place before the sons were anointed, and even before they were dressed in their priestly attire. This is symbolically significant. Though this Old Testament passage was written centuries before the earthly ministry of Jesus, it symbolically captures what Jesus did when He came and fulfilled these words.

After Jesus was baptized in the Jordan River by John the Baptist, Jesus saw the heavens open, and the Spirit of God descended like a dove and rested on Him. A voice from heaven said, "This is my Son, whom I love; with him I am well pleased" (see Matthew 3:13–17). This was the very moment that God anointed our Great High Priest, Jesus. The oil that Moses used when he anointed Aaron symbolizes the Holy Spirit, who anointed Jesus after His baptism. These ceremonies in Leviticus are shadowy pictures of the reality that would come when Jesus began His ministry.

Next, after anointing the high priest, Aaron, Moses anointed the sons of Aaron. This act symbolizes the anointing of the disciples by the Holy Spirit on the day of Pentecost (see Acts 2:1–4). Just as Jesus was first anointed by the Holy Spirit, then His disciples, so Aaron was anointed with oil first, then the sons of Aaron.

Moses clothed Aaron's sons with tunics (coats), then tied sashes around them and bound their heads with headbands. Here we see a picture of our ministry as the priesthood of believers. We are to the Lord Jesus Christ in our priestly ministry as Aaron's sons were to Aaron. Just as the garments of the high priest were a picture of his character and of what he could do, so the three items worn by the high priest's sons are a picture of our ministry and of what we can do.

God is speaking directly to you and to me through these symbolic pictures in Leviticus. If you are a follower of Jesus Christ, then this is the ministry God has called you to—and this is the provision God has made for you, so that you can fulfill this ministry.

## THE MEANING OF THE TUNIC

The vestments worn by the sons of Aaron were not just impressive-looking uniforms. They were visual statements of God's redemptive plan for the human race. Each piece of priestly clothing had a specific symbolic meaning.

First, there is the tunic or coat. The tunic is a covering; it symbolizes the righteousness of Christ, which is imparted to us. We are clad in His righteousness. We cannot please God and earn His approval by our works. Many people do good deeds and observe endless religious rituals, all in the hope that if they just do enough, then God will be pleased with them. The problem is that you can never know if you've done quite enough, so you are doomed to feeling discouraged and defeated all the time.

No matter how many good works you do, you will never feel you have done enough. You will always suspect that you fall short—because, in fact, you do fall short! As Paul wrote to the Romans, "For all have sinned and fall short of the glory of God" (Romans 3:23). That's the bad news. Paul then goes on to give us the good news, that we "are justified freely by his grace through the redemption that came by Christ Jesus" (Romans 3:24). We may try to justify ourselves by our good works, but we will always fall short of the glory of God. However, the true High Priest of God has wrapped a tunic of righteousness around us. By grace through faith, we are wrapped in the righteousness of Jesus Christ.

What does that mean for our daily lives? It means that you and I are allowed to make mistakes! It means that we are allowed to fail at times, because it isn't our ministry, our work, our perfection that makes us acceptable to God. It's His ministry, His work, His perfection. The life of Christ, the sacrifice of Christ, and the resurrection of Christ make us accepted in the Beloved. Jesus clothed us in His righteousness. That is the meaning of the tunic or coat worn by the priests, the sons of Aaron.

## THE MEANING OF THE SASH

Next, there is a sash (or girdle) that is tied around the tunic. In Scripture, this sash is always a picture of a servant character. It signifies the willingness that should reside in the heart of every believer to meet and serve other people at the point of their need. It signifies a humble, Christlike desire to stoop to any need, without ever asking what it will cost or what we will get in return.

This sash reminds us of the towel that Jesus wrapped around Himself before He began to wash the feet of His disciples (see John 13:1–17). Jesus didn't hesitate to wash dirty feet, and neither should we. God calls us to pattern our lives after the life of the Master, meeting people in the midst of their human need and their human stink and their human filth. If we would follow Christ, then we must take up the towel and basin, and we must serve.

In 1971, my wife, Elaine, and I went to Charlotte, North Carolina, for a celebration honoring Dr. Billy Graham. It was an exciting event—even President Richard M. Nixon was there. Afterwards, Elaine and I boarded the plane for the flight home to California. Once aboard, we noticed a woman with a tiny boy in tow. As she made her way onto the plane, dragging the unhappy-looking child, she loudly announced, "I have a naughty little boy to give away if anyone wants him! Would someone please take my grandson? You're welcome to him, because he's been nothing but trouble all day!"

The woman was obviously trying to shame her little grandson, and it was working. The boy looked absolutely miserable. The woman kept up this behavior all the way down the aisle, oblivious to the disapproving looks she received from the other passengers. The plane was not full, and I noticed that a number of passengers who were seated near her got up and moved to unclaimed seats.

As it happened, the woman was seated directly across the aisle from us. As the plane was beginning its takeoff run, Elaine looked at the woman and saw that she was all huddled up in her seat with her eyes tightly shut, perspiring and obviously scared to death. Elaine said, "Do you know what that woman's trouble is? She's scared!"

I said, "Would you like to help her?" Elaine had the aisle seat, so she was closer to the woman than I was.

So Elaine unbuckled her seat belt, moved across the aisle, and sat down beside the trembling woman—much to the distress of the flight attendant (changing seats during takeoff, of course, is strictly forbidden!).

Buckling herself into the seat next to the woman, Elaine said, "Are you scared?"

"Scared to death!" the woman said. "I just don't know what to do! I wish I could fly without being so frightened."

"I know just how you feel,' Elaine said. "For years, I couldn't fly without being terribly afraid. But I no longer have any fear of flying."

"How did you get over it?" the woman asked.

"Well, my husband and I came to Charlotte for the celebration honoring Dr. Billy Graham. I'm sure you know about his ministry."

"Oh, yes!" the woman said. "I've seen his evangelistic crusades on TV, and I just love the singing of that man with the wonderful voice—George Beverly Shea."

"Have you ever heard Mr. Shea sing 'He's Got the Whole World in His Hands'?" Elaine asked. The woman said she had. "Well, that song means so much to me," Elaine continued, "because I know that I am in God's hands, and He is watching over me. That assurance has taken away my fear of flying. By the way, it may comfort you to know that Mr. Shea himself is sitting two seats behind you on this plane."

The woman gasped, peered over the back of her seat, then said, "Well, then we don't have a thing to worry about, do we?"

In fact, the woman was so relieved that she was soon back to her old loud, obnoxious, troublesome self! But perhaps a seed of God's truth was planted.

The point is that in crossing the aisle to comfort that woman, Elaine was being a priest to her. She was ministering to that woman, serving her, and symbolically washing her feet. We are all, as Christians, called to be priests and servants to our fellow human beings, meeting them at their point of need. It may mean having to sit next to people that no one else wants to be close to. It may mean putting up with the offensiveness of humanity—but that is what servants do.

What excitement comes into our lives when we allow God to use us this way! What an adventure life becomes when we let God serve others through us. God doesn't want His priesthood confined within houses of stone and stained glass. He wants His priesthood to move out into the neighborhoods, streets, alleys, prisons, schools, shopping malls, and office buildings. He wants His priests to go wherever the people are, serving them wherever they hurt.

Living as priests isn't easy. It will cost us. It will inconvenience us. It will be unpleasant and even downright disgusting at times. Washing dirty feet is never pleasant work. But how can we call ourselves followers of Jesus if we refuse to live as He lived and serve as He served?

## THE MEANING OF THE HEADBAND

The third article of clothing was the headband that was bound around the head of the priest. Just as the turban on the high priest is a picture of the mind bound by the authority of the Word of God, so the headband of the priest is a picture of the mind under the control of the Lord Jesus Christ. As Paul writes in 1 Corinthians 2:16, "We have the mind of Christ." This means that we look at life as Jesus sees it. We set aside all the illusions and delusions of worldly thinking.

These, then, are the three dimensions of our priesthood, as pictured for us by the three primary articles of priestly clothing: The tunic pictures for us the righteousness of Christ, which clothes us and covers all of our sin and guilt. The sash depicts our servant attitude, our willingness to reach out to people in their hurt, need, and filthiness. The headband represents our minds under the control and authority of Christ. When we have this kind of attitude and relationship with God, then we are ready to go out as priests into this poor, broken, suffering world—and God will see to it that we have many opportunities to serve others in His name.

## THE SACRIFICES FOR THE PRIESTS

Next we see that sacrifices had to be offered for Aaron and his sons. As the New Testament letter of Hebrews makes clear, the Lord Jesus, as the Great High Priest, had no need to offer sacrifices for Himself, for He was without sin. But Aaron was a fallen man, and his sons were fallen men. Their sins needed to be dealt with, so they, like the people they served, had need of the sacrifices. First was the sin offering.

> He then presented the bull for the sin offering, and Aaron and his sons laid their hands on its head. Moses slaughtered the bull and took some of the blood, and with his finger he put it on all the horns of the altar to purify the altar. He poured out the rest of the blood at the base of the altar. So he consecrated it to make atonement for it. Moses also took all the fat around the inner parts, the covering of the liver, and both kidneys and their fat, and burned it on the altar. But the bull with its hide and its flesh and its offal he burned up outside the camp, as the LORD commanded Moses (Leviticus 8:14–17).

This sacrifice is God's reminder to us that the basic, fundamental problem of human nature is our sin-distorted, fallen nature. We never can solve a single problem until we deal with the problem of sin in our lives. That is why the sin offering is mentioned in Leviticus again and again. It is God's constant reminder.

There are many books and speakers today who tell us that if we will learn to think differently and discover our hidden potential, then we will find all sorts of personal power to achieve happiness and satisfaction in life. There are good ideas in many of these books and speakers, but rarely do they talk about the fundamental human problem, which is the problem of sin. There is rarely any recognition that the cross of Christ is the only basis upon which our God-given human potential can be fulfilled.

After the sin offering comes the burnt offering, which pictures for us the life that is completely given over and sacrificed to God:

> He then presented the ram for the burnt offering, and Aaron and his sons laid their hands on its head. Then Moses slaughtered the ram and sprinkled the blood against the altar on all sides. He cut the ram into pieces and burned the head, the pieces and the fat. He washed the inner parts and the legs with water and burned the whole ram on the altar as a burnt offering, a pleasing aroma, an offering made to the LORD by fire, as the LORD commanded Moses (Leviticus 8:18–21).

This sacrifice pictures for us the life that was described for us by Paul when he wrote, "You are not your own; you were bought at a price" (1 Corinthians 6:19–20). To the world, these words sound harsh, as if God has taken our lives away from us. But the Christian knows that this is the way to fulfillment. God loves us, owns us, and cherishes us, and that is how we find a deep sense of joy and satisfaction that the world cannot comprehend. We have been bought with a price, the sacrifice of our Great High Priest, and that gives us the right to say, "Yes, Lord! Use me as you will. I am here to be your servant and priest. Consume my life, use me up, because it is only through serving you that my life has meaning and purpose."

In the next few verses, we read of the third offering for the priests, the offering of ordination:

He then presented the other ram, the ram for the ordination, and Aaron and his sons laid their hands on its head. Moses slaughtered the ram and took some of its blood and put it on the lobe of Aaron's right ear, on the thumb of his right hand and on the big toe of his right foot. Moses also brought Aaron's sons forward and put some of the blood on the lobes of their right ears, on the thumbs of their right hands and on the big toes of their right feet. Then he sprinkled blood against the altar on all sides (Leviticus 8:22–24).

What a strange ceremony that is! What does it signify? If you have followed the meanings of these symbols, the meaning is obvious: Blood reminds us that our lives have no meaning or hope apart from the death of Jesus Christ on our behalf. His spilled blood is the source of our life. The priest of God is to have a blood-stained ear, a blood-stained thumb, and a blood-stained toe—and each of these blood-stained places on the body is symbolically significant.

God's priest is to hear God's Word with ears that have been redeemed by the blood of Jesus Christ. He should recognize that the Bible isn't just a collection of interesting stories and nice ideas. It is truth that transforms our lives, because it is essentially the truth of how God redeems us by the blood of His sacrificed Son.

God's priest is to use his hands in service to others, for they are hands that have been redeemed by the blood of Jesus Christ. The thumb is used to stand for the entire hand because, as the body member that enables us to grasp and use tools, it is probably the most useful member of the human body. With our hands, we can feed those who are hungry, bathe those who are unclean, and touch the wounds of those who are hurting. Our hands are the members we use to serve others.

As servant-priests, we serve as blood-stained people—stained by the blood of our Great High Priest. We have no righteousness in ourselves, we are no better than the people we serve, we do not judge others or look down our noses at others. We serve others because Christ first served us and touched our lives with His bleeding, nail-pierced hands. And as we serve, we must be continually reminded of our need of constant cleansing by the blood of Christ.

Finally, God's priest is to use his feet to walk through life as a man or woman whose pathway has been redirected and redeemed by the blood of Jesus

Christ. In these verses, the entire foot is represented by the big toe, which is to be stained with blood. The Bible often represents our lives as a walk, so as we walk through life, we need to be continually reminded of God's cleansing grace, which we need to experience every day of our lives. Our walk must be a blood-stained walk, and our lives must daily speak to the world around us of the blood that flowed down the cross of Jesus Christ.

## THE OIL AND THE BLOOD

The offerings continue with the offering of the fat, inner parts, thigh, and breast, and the offering of the unleavened bread.

> He took the fat, the fat tail, all the fat around the inner parts, the covering of the liver, both kidneys and their fat and the right thigh. Then from the basket of bread made without yeast, which was before the LORD, he took a cake of bread, and one made with oil, and a wafer; he put these on the fat portions and on the right thigh. He put all these in the hands of Aaron and his sons and waved them before the LORD as a wave offering. Then Moses took them from their hands and burned them on the altar on top of the burnt offering as an ordination offering, a pleasing aroma, an offering made to the LORD by fire. He also took the breast—Moses' share of the ordination ram—and waved it before the LORD as a wave offering, as the Lord commanded Moses (Leviticus 8:25–29).

We have previously seen that the fat, the thigh, and the breast symbolize richness, strength, and peace in the inner life, sacrificed and made acceptable to God. The meal offering is a type of the human response which says, "Here I am, Lord! My humanity is at your disposal. I'm ready to be used of you." Next, notice what Moses does with the anointing oil and the blood.

> Then Moses took some of the anointing oil and some of the blood from the altar and sprinkled them on Aaron and his garments and on his sons and their garments. So he consecrated Aaron and his garments and his sons and their garments (Leviticus 8:30).

Here is another demonstration of the accuracy of Scripture. When Moses anointed Aaron as a type of Christ, our Great High Priest, he used only oil, the symbol of the Holy Spirit. But when he anointed the sons, who are a picture of our priesthood, he used oil and blood—oil symbolizing the Holy Spirit and blood representing the redeeming death of Jesus. Our priesthood is based upon a recognition that we are to minister in the power of the Spirit and on the basis of a personal experience of the forgiveness of sin. That is the only right we have as priests to minister to other people.

There is nothing in our fallen humanity that gives us the right to act as priests to other people. If you attempt to serve other people on any basis other than the blood of Jesus and the anointing of the Spirit, you are offering "unauthorized fire before the Lord, contrary to his command" (Leviticus 10:1), an offense which carries dire penalties. The only basis for our priesthood is a humble recognition of our own sinfulness, plus a realization that we are forgiven through the grace of God and the blood of Christ, plus a recognition that the Holy Spirit is pleased to work through us. Next we read:

> Moses then said to Aaron and his sons, "Cook the meat at the entrance to the Tent of Meeting and eat it there with the bread from the basket of ordination offerings, as I commanded, saying, 'Aaron and his sons are to eat it.' Then burn up the rest of the meat and the bread. Do not leave the entrance to the Tent of Meeting for seven days, until the days of your ordination are completed, for your ordination will last seven days. What has been done today was commanded by the Lord to make atonement for you. You must stay at the entrance to the Tent of Meeting day and night for seven days and do what the Lord requires, so you will not die; for that is what I have been commanded." So Aaron and his sons did everything the Lord commanded through Moses (Leviticus 8:31–36).

And no wonder! When Moses told Aaron and his sons to remain at the entrance to the Tent of Meeting (the tabernacle) for seven days "so you will not die," they took him seriously and did as they were commanded. Why? Because God is very serious about issues of sin and obedience.

Why did God command Aaron and his sons to stay in the doorway of the tabernacle? Again, there is symbolic significance at work in this command. The tabernacle is a symbolic picture of the human body. This command symbolizes the fact that God wants us to wait and feast upon the work of Jesus Christ on our behalf. His work is symbolized by the right thigh of the animal, a picture of His strength; the breast, a picture of His love for us; and the bread offering, a picture of the life of Christ, available to us.

Why did God command Aaron and his sons to remain for seven days? Seven is always the number of perfection in the Bible. So the number seven in this command is a clue as to how God works.

We are impatient people. We pray, and then we expect God to respond like the genie in the story of Aladdin and his magic lamp, announcing, "I am here, human master, ready to do your bidding! What do you wish me to do?"

But praying to God is not like rubbing a magic lamp. We are not the master; God is. He is not our servant; we are His. So when we pray to Him, we must be patient, even when He seems to delay. His answer and His timing are always perfect, as symbolized by the number seven. We may have to wait as God works out His perfect plan according to His perfect timing. While we are waiting, He calls us to feed upon the truth of the sacrifice of Christ.

One of the hardest things to do in life is to wait upon the Lord. But a priesthood is made up of people who wait and serve. The only agenda a priest has is God's agenda, so it is our privilege, as His servants, to wait and watch the unfolding of His plan.

Are you living as a priest of God? Are you reaching out to this troubled and fragmented world? Have you discovered the adventure of living as a servant, a channel of God's love and healing power to the hurting people around you?

I urge you to keep your eyes open as you walk through your life. Look for people who are hurting, people who are in need—then serve them in the love of Jesus Christ. Allow the Holy Spirit to anoint you and work through you. As you do this, you will be living not only after the pattern of Jesus, our Great High Priest, but after the pattern of God's eternal commandments in the book of Leviticus.

# CHAPTER 9

# THE PRESENT GLORY
## LEVITICUS 9

SOME YEARS AGO, I went through a time of personal crisis unlike anything I had experienced before. I prayed more intensely than I had ever prayed before, yet I felt no relief. I didn't know it, but at the very time I was feeling totally alone with my pain and oppression, God was actively answering my prayer in a way I didn't realize or expect.

A few days later, I received a phone call from a dear and trusted friend who had been living in another state. He was in town and wanted to stop by and see me. I was stunned. I had reached a point where I felt that I was ready to break down, emotionally and physically, from the strain I was under. Just that morning, I had thought of this man and wished that I could see him and talk with him—and suddenly, miraculously, he had come to town!

We met for lunch, and in the course of our time together, he said a few words that restored my hope and delivered my spirit! I'm not saying that my circumstances changed, but my faith in God's ability to resolve those circumstances soared.

That man had no idea what I had been going through until we talked over lunch. In fact, he couldn't even tell me why he had come to see me. He just felt an urge to do so. I know that God sent him to me to be a priest to me, to speak God's message of healing to me. We all need a priest, and that is why God has ordained every individual in His church to be a priest.

## Living by Resurrection Power

The ninth chapter of Leviticus continues the process of describing how a priest functions in service to God and in ministry to humanity, meeting our basic human needs. Leviticus 9 opens with these words:

> On the eighth day Moses summoned Aaron and his sons and the elders of Israel (Leviticus 9:1).

Notice the symbolic significance of the numbers in this passage. Throughout the Old Testament, God used symbolic numbers to help us understand practical truth, and here He does so again: "On the eighth day. . . ." Eight is the number of a new beginning, a resurrection. The eighth day symbolizes resurrection life. We see the significance of this number not only throughout the Old and New Testaments but also in nature.

For instance, the eighth day is the beginning of a new week. One of the strange mysteries of human life is the week. It is easy to explain why we have months, because they correspond to the phases of the moon. The year corresponds to the time it takes for the earth to orbit the sun. But no one can explain why we have a week of seven days. Nothing in the physical world corresponds to it. Yet from the earliest times, the human family has observed the seven-day week.

Or consider the tones of the musical scale. An octave consists of seven notes; the eighth note on the scale is the first note of a new octave. Eight corresponds to a new note, a new day, a new beginning.

By means of this number, God teaches us something important about the functioning of the priesthood. The ministry of a priest, He tells us, must take place on the basis of resurrection power. A priest must rely on the resurrected life of the living Lord within him (or her—for women also are priests in the priesthood of all believers). A priest functions not in his or her strength but in the power of the new life that is ours in Christ, the new beginning that Jesus made possible when He burst forth from the tomb on the first Easter.

Our natural tendency is to rely upon the natural, human resources of our old life, with its attempt to garner wisdom from human sources. We have all been subjected to the good advice of well-meaning people which, when followed, has only made life more difficult.

A priest who is truly living and ministering in the wisdom and power of the resurrected Lord will dispense the wisdom of God that comes from the Word of God. A priest deals sensitively to the needs of individuals according to the leading of the Holy Spirit. All of this marvelous truth is symbolized for us in these words: "On the eighth day Moses summoned Aaron and his sons and the elders of Israel."

That is why Moses insisted that the priests should not leave the tabernacle for seven days. That is why God told them through Moses, "You must stay at the entrance to the Tent of Meeting day and night for seven days" (Leviticus 8:35). God is saying, in effect, "Do not try to act as a priest upon any other basis except resurrection power, for if you act on any other basis, you will only produce death."

This is a crucial principle for us to understand. Wherever we see deadness and sterility in the church today, we always find evidence that the church has abandoned reliance upon the resurrection power of Jesus Christ. Again and again, we see churches and individual Christians who substitute human power, human insight, human techniques and tactics in place of God's resurrection power, and the result is always death—Christians who become lifeless in their faith, as well as churches that become dead and powerless to authentically influence the world for Jesus Christ. In place of Spirit-led evangelism and ministry, we substitute electronic media and promotional techniques. These efforts may look successful on the outside, but they are empty and hollow on the inside. They are not animated by resurrection power but by human ingenuity.

God wants us to know that He doesn't need money, might, or majorities to win His battles. He always selects a handful of faithful people, and through those few individuals, He works His mighty deeds.

## THE SINNER AND THE SACRIFICE

We know that our God is the great Creator of the universe and that His power is sufficient to meet all of our needs. Why, then, do we so often reject His power and resort to our own? The answer is given in the next section of Leviticus 9, which details for us the sacrifices that were offered in connection with the ordaining of the priests. First, there were the offerings for Aaron.

> He said to Aaron, "Take a bull calf for your sin offering and a ram
> for your burnt offering, both without defect, and present them

before the LORD. Then say to the Israelites: 'Take a male goat for a sin offering, a calf and a lamb—both a year old and without defect—for a burnt offering, and an ox and a ram for a fellowship offering to sacrifice before the LORD, together with a grain offering mixed with oil. For today the LORD will appear to you.'"

They took the things Moses commanded to the front of the Tent of Meeting, and the entire assembly came near and stood before the LORD. Then Moses said, "This is what the LORD has commanded you to do, so that the glory of the LORD may appear to you." Moses said to Aaron, "Come to the altar and sacrifice your sin offering and your burnt offering and make atonement for yourself and the people; sacrifice the offering that is for the people and make atonement for them, as the LORD has commanded."

So Aaron came to the altar and slaughtered the calf as a sin offering for himself. His sons brought the blood to him, and he dipped his finger into the blood and put it on the horns of the altar; the rest of the blood he poured out at the base of the altar. On the altar he burned the fat, the kidneys and the covering of the liver from the sin offering, as the LORD commanded Moses; the flesh and the hide he burned up outside the camp.

Then he slaughtered the burnt offering. His sons handed him the blood, and he sprinkled it against the altar on all sides. They handed him the burnt offering piece by piece, including the head, and he burned them on the altar. He washed the inner parts and the legs and burned them on top of the burnt offering on the altar (Leviticus 9:2–14).

So Aaron went to the altar and killed the calf of the sin offering, which was offered for himself and his sins. Then he killed the burnt offering, which was offered for himself and his sins. Here we see, once again, the strange prominence of sacrifices and blood which dominates the book of Leviticus. Why does God insist on all of this blood? Why could God's people not be purified apart from a sacrificial death?

God is telling us something important. No, He is not merely telling us—He's shouting to us! He is trying to get through to us! He wants us to understand a fundamental truth about our condition and about our need for a priesthood. He is trying to tell us that the resurrection power of the living God can never be exercised apart from a sacrificial death.

When the Israelites brought their offerings, the blood of innocent animals had to be shed. These sacrifices were not intended, as many people suppose, to appease the anger of a tribal God. They were intended to teach the people of Israel an important lesson: Sin has a cost. When a person sins and offers a sacrifice for that sin, the sinner cannot simply slay an animal and then go on sinning as if nothing is changed. Something within that sinner must die. The offering means that the sinner is identified with the sacrifice. If the sinner does not identify with the sacrifice, then the sacrifice is meaningless and without effect.

That is what God is trying to tell us through these sacrifices in Leviticus. That is what Jesus was telling us when He said, "I tell you the truth, unless a kernel of wheat falls to the ground and dies, it remains only a single seed. But if it dies, it produces many seeds" (John 12:24). That is what Jesus was telling us when He said, "For whoever wants to save his life will lose it, but whoever loses his life for me and for the gospel will save it" (Mark 8:35).

Death precedes life. The only life worth living comes from death. We don't like to hear that, but it's true: The only way we can truly live is to let go of our lives, to identify with our Lord's death, and to die to ourselves. The world says, "Look out for number one!" Our media culture encourages us to give ourselves over to greed, arrogance, ego, and selfishness. But Jesus tells us that all those who live for self will see their lives slip through their fingers like grains of sand. If you live for self, you will lose your soul. If you grasp your self tightly, you will throw your soul away.

And that is what God teaches us in picture form through these sacrifices. The Old Testament and the New Testament agree: Out of death comes life. Out of sacrifice comes resurrection. When we surrender our dependence on our own resources and wisdom, we are able to lay hold of the supernatural life and power of our resurrected Lord. This is the power that enables us not only to live but also to minister to others as a priesthood of believers.

## THE GLORY AND THE FIRE

Next, we see what takes place as a result of the sacrifices that are offered on behalf of Aaron the high priest, his priestly sons, and the people of Israel.

Aaron then brought the offering that was for the people. He took the goat for the people's sin offering and slaughtered it and offered it for a sin offering as he did with the first one.

He brought the burnt offering and offered it in the prescribed way. He also brought the grain offering, took a handful of it and burned it on the altar in addition to the morning's burnt offering.

He slaughtered the ox and the ram as the [peace] offering for the people. His sons handed him the blood, and he sprinkled it against the altar on all sides. But the fat portions of the ox and the ram— the fat tail, the layer of fat, the kidneys and the covering of the liver—these they laid on the breasts, and then Aaron burned the fat on the altar. Aaron waved the breasts and the right thigh before the LORD as a wave offering, as Moses commanded.

Then Aaron lifted his hands toward the people and blessed them. And having sacrificed the sin offering, the burnt offering and the [peace] offering, he stepped down.

Moses and Aaron then went into the Tent of Meeting. When they came out, they blessed the people; and the glory of the LORD appeared to all the people. Fire came out from the presence of the LORD and consumed the burnt offering and the fat portions on the altar. And when all the people saw it, they shouted for joy and fell facedown (Leviticus 9:15–24).

What a dramatic scene! The whole camp of Israel gathered at vantage points where they could observe what happened in the open space before the door of the tabernacle, where the brazen altar was located. They watched Aaron and his sons kill these animals, put them on the altar, and sprinkle the blood and pour it out.

When everything was completed exactly as the Lord had commanded, Moses and Aaron went together into the tabernacle. A hush fell upon the whole assembly—no one knew what would happen next. Then Moses and Aaron come out again and they blessed the people—

And suddenly the glory of the Lord appeared!

What was this manifestation? The Scriptures indicate that it was a shining cloud of light called the Shekinah—a radiance that suddenly appeared and filled the whole area. A supernatural fire proceeded from the Shekinah. In a flash, that supernatural fire consumed the rest of the offerings upon the altar.

This was a powerful, astonishing scene! The shining radiance of God Himself appeared right before their eyes! No wonder the people fell on their faces and shouted. Notice, too, that they did not shout with fear but with joy. This was a scene of triumph, and the people expressed their awe and wonder over the fact that God, the King of glory and the Creator of the universe, was in their midst. (The Shekinah would later take up residence in the tabernacle, in the holy of holies, where it would hover over the ark of the covenant.)

These sacrifices, symbols, and events were all designed, Paul said, as lessons for our instruction: "Now these things occurred as examples to keep us from setting our hearts on evil things as they did" (1 Corinthians 10:6). This is God's way of teaching us.

What is the lesson? It is that we are to be priests, and the purpose of priesthood is to produce the glory of the Lord. When the priesthood operates as God intended, then the shining presence of the Lord is manifested. The glory and the fire of God appear for all to see. What is this glory and fire of the Lord, and how is it manifested among us today? It is the beautiful, shining character of Jesus, radiating from our lives.

The Spirit of God is at work in our hearts to produce glory. Paul expressed this truth in these words: "For God, who said, 'Let light shine out of darkness,' made his light shine in our hearts to give us the light of the knowledge of the glory of God in the face of Christ" (2 Corinthians 4:6). The character of Jesus, which is the character of God Himself, shines through our lives in our daily encounters with other people.

## GRIEF INTO JOY

I once spoke at a prayer breakfast in Illinois. I noticed a woman in the audience who had a patch covering her right eye and cheek and much of her nose. Though part of her face was obscured, the rest of her face was radiant with joy. In fact, I have rarely seen anyone who was as glowingly joyful as this woman. At the end of the meeting she came to me, took my hand, and thanked me for coming and speaking. It was not easy for her to speak; the condition that had caused her disfigurement had apparently damaged her mouth so that she had trouble forming the words. Even so, her face continued to shine.

I later met this woman's husband, and he told me, "Three or four years ago, my wife was diagnosed with cancer of the eye. The surgeons removed her eye, but the cancer reappeared. So the doctors operated again and removed the bone around her eye. It came back again, and they removed part of her nose and cheekbone. It came back again, and now they have removed practically half of her face. She has struggled with the fear of death, with the pain of the surgeries, and with the horror of having her face taken away from her by these surgeries.

"But this experience has driven her deeper into prayer and into a trusting relationship with God. And in the process, she has become a more joyful and glowing Christian than she ever was before the cancer.

"Years ago, she complained and whined about every little problem. But look at what she's been through—and now she never complains about anything. God has used this disease to transform her personality. He has turned all her complaints and sorrows into joy!"

That is what God seeks to do in your life and mine. He wants to transform our hearts so that our lives will shine into the darkness of this world. He wants our lives to radiate with His glory, just as the glory and fire of the Lord appeared to all the people of Israel. He wants our lives to burn as living sacrifices for Him, so that when all the people around us see that we are on fire for Him, they will shout for joy and fall facedown in worship before the living God.

God wants to send us out into the world as priests, ministering to the needy souls all around us. How will He do that? By turning our present sorrows into joy. Do you remember what Jesus said to His disciples in those last terrible hours before the cross? He told them, "I tell you the truth, you will weep and mourn while the world rejoices. You will grieve, but your grief will turn to joy" (John 16:20). And do you remember the comforting prophecy of Isaiah, in which he foretold the wonderful ministry of Jesus the Messiah? The prophet wrote that Jesus would give those who grieve "a crown of beauty instead of ashes, the oil of gladness instead of mourning, and a garment of praise instead of a spirit of despair."

God is building us into a priesthood—and He is doing so by transforming our sorrows into joy. Because you and I have experienced hurt, sorrow, oppression, and loss, we are better equipped as priests to minister with sensitivity to other suffering and grieving people. God wants to use us as wounded healers who are able to speak authentic words of release to people who are in bondage and despair.

But more than that, the purpose of the priesthood is that the glory of the Lord might be manifest to the world. It should fill us with awe and wonder to know that the Creator of the universe is pleased to ordain you and me as His priests, revealing His glorious light to a dark and hurting world.

So let's stop resisting His work in our lives. Let's stop complaining and whining about our petty problems. Instead, let's die to self so our souls might truly live by the resurrection power of our risen Lord—for it is only by death that we truly experience His glorious, radiant life.

# CHAPTER 10

# STRANGE FIRE

## LEVITICUS 10:1–7

CHRISTIAN FRIEDRICH SCHÖNBEIN was a German chemistry professor at the University of Basel, Switzerland, in the mid-1800s. Soon after Schönbein and his wife were married, Mrs. Schönbein discovered that her husband liked to tinker with chemicals. Sometimes his experiments would fill their home with the stench of rotten eggs or a vapor that stung her eyes. Finally, Mrs. Schönbein put her foot down—no more chemical experiments in the house!

Professor Schönbein reluctantly promised to abide by his wife's rules— but he didn't keep his promise. When he knew that his wife would be out of the house for most of the day, he would sneak bottles of chemicals into the house and conduct his experiments—then, after he was done, he would open the doors and windows and air out the house to avoid getting caught.

One day, while his wife was out, Schönbein was conducting an experiment in his wife's kitchen when he accidentally spilled a mixture of nitric acid and sulfuric acid on the tile counter. Horrified that he would destroy the tile and incur Mrs. Schönbein's wrath, he grabbed his wife's cotton apron from the place where it hung next to the oven. He quickly mopped up the spill with the apron and hung it back on the peg to dry.

When his wife returned, everything was in place just as she had left it. Professor Schönbein had erased all evidence of his forbidden experiments. He was in the study of his home when he heard a scream from the kitchen. He dashed into the kitchen and found out why his wife was screaming: Her apron had spontaneously burst into flames! Fortunately, the apron was still hanging on the peg by the oven—she hadn't put it on yet.

It turned out that when he had mopped up the acid mixture with the cloth apron, Professor Schönbein had accidentally invented a substance now known as nitrocellulose or guncotton—a highly explosive and flammable substance. In disobeying his wife's wishes, he had made a new chemical discovery. His discovery could have had tragic consequences, however, if his wife had been wearing her apron when it exploded.

As we come to Leviticus 10, we meet two sons of Aaron, Abihu and Nadab. These two priests disobey God's commands by experimenting with "strange fire"—and the consequences of their disobedience are tragic indeed!

## SUDDEN FIERY JUDGMENT

In Leviticus 9, we saw the results of priesthood. When everything was done as the Lord commanded, the result was a manifestation of the presence of God, a shining forth of the Lord's radiant glory. We saw Aaron—who is an Old Testament picture of Jesus Christ, our Great High Priest—joined by his sons in the priesthood. The sons' relationship to their father, Aaron, pictured our relationship with Christ. And when Aaron and his sons had done all that God had commanded, then the sacrifice was consumed in a flash of fire, the shining glory of God's presence appeared in their midst, and there was great joy among all the people of Israel. Leviticus 9 ends with a scene of great triumph.

But as we move from Leviticus 9 to Leviticus 10, triumph turns to tragedy. On the day that this tremendous breakthrough occurs in the camp of Israel, tragedy strikes, and the judgment of God appears with a shocking suddenness.

> Aaron's sons Nadab and Abihu took their censers, put fire in them and added incense; and they offered unauthorized fire before the LORD, contrary to his command. So fire came out from the presence of the LORD and consumed them, and they died before the LORD (Leviticus 10:1–2).

The same Shekinah which had consumed the sacrifice now flares up and consumes the two priests, Aaron's sons, as they minister. Imagine the shock this must have been to Aaron and his two remaining sons. Imagine the horror and amazement throughout the camp of Israel.

I picture Aaron watching with justifiable pride as his two sons carry out their priestly duties before the Lord. The young men fill their censers with glowing coals, place incense upon the coals, and go before the presence of the Lord. Suddenly, to Aaron's horror, a billow of fire blazes up out of the Shekinah glory and envelops his sons, killing them right before his eyes! How would you have reacted if you had seen such a terrible sight? The people of Israel were stunned, sobered, and shaken. Aaron was grief-stricken.

Why did this happen?

In the King James Version, this passage tells us that Nadab and Abihu "offered strange fire before the LORD, which he commanded them not." The NIV tells us that they "offered unauthorized fire before the LORD, contrary to his command." The passage does not explain in detail what is meant by "strange fire" or "unauthorized fire." But as nearly as we can determine, it appears that these sons of Aaron substituted a different incense from that which God had commanded.

This might seem like a minor offense to us—yet it triggered immediate judgment from God, an instantaneous and terrible death sentence. Why did Aaron's sons substitute "strange fire" for the fire that God had specifically commanded? We don't know. But we do know that God dealt with their disobedience in the most severe way imaginable.

How do you feel when you read this passage? I suspect that at the very least, you feel uneasy about this episode. Perhaps it bothers you, or even angers you, that God would react so harshly over what seems to be such a trivial act of disobedience on the part of these two priests. You may think, "God is unfair," or even, "God is cruel." Perhaps Aaron and his sons felt this way as they watched Nadab and Abihu die.

## A SIN OF PRESUMPTION

There are other stories in the Old Testament that speak of the swift and terrible judgment of God. For example, Miriam, the sister of Aaron, did nothing more than criticize Moses, yet God judged her and struck her with leprosy (Numbers 12). There is the story of Uzzah, who reached out to steady the ark of the covenant as David was returning it to Jerusalem—and for merely touching the ark, he dropped dead (2 Samuel 6). In the New Testament, there is the story of Ananias and Sapphira, who were slain for lying to the Holy Spirit and pretending to be more generous donors than they were (Acts 5).

We look at these incidents, and we think that God is being unreasonably harsh. Many people find it hard to reconcile this God of judgment with the fact that God is love, so they mentally create two Gods—the vengeful and tyrannical God of the Old Testament and the gracious and forgiving God of the New Testament.

But the God of the Old Testament and the God of the New are one and the same. There is no inconsistency between the Old Testament and New Testament depictions of God. The only reason we think there is an inconsistency is because we read our Bibles so superficially. God's judgment and His love are completely consistent. They flow from the same source. God is just, and God is loving. He never deviates from what He has revealed Himself to be. When He acts in judgment, He is also acting in love.

This passage contains a number of facts that will better enable us to understand the full range of God's personality. The first of these facts: The two priests, Nadab and Abihu, did not act in ignorance. They acted in presumption. They knew that they were violating God's commandment, yet they presumed to have a better plan than the one that God had already given them. In the book of Exodus, we see that God had given the priests clear instructions for the burning of incense:

> "Aaron must burn fragrant incense on the altar every morning when he tends the lamps. He must burn incense again when he lights the lamps at twilight so incense will burn regularly before the LORD for the generations to come. Do not offer on this altar any other incense or any burnt offering or grain offering, and do not pour a drink offering on it" (Exodus 30:7–9).

God makes Himself abundantly clear in this passage. He warns the priests against using the wrong kind of incense. So the actions of Nadab and Abihu are in clear violation of a direct command from God. They were forewarned, and they ignored God's warning. God never judges anyone for actions done in ignorance. As Isaiah 42:3 tells us, "A bruised reed he will not break, and a smoldering wick he will not snuff out. In faithfulness he will bring forth justice." In other words, God understands the heart of someone who is trying to find Him, who is trying to do what is right but lacks knowledge or understanding. God is patient, tender, compassionate, and understanding.

But the sin of these two priests was not committed in ignorance. It was an act of willful presumption. They took it for granted that they could offer "strange fire" and that God wouldn't care, even though He had said He would. They insisted on their own way instead of God's way.

The second fact we notice in this passage is that God dealt severely with the sin of Nadab and Abihu because their sin distorted God's revelation of Himself. In all of these priestly sacrifices and rituals, God was explaining something about Himself so that we might learn what kind of God He is. But by their disobedience, these priests conveyed a false impression of God's nature, and that is why God judged them.

We saw this same principle at work in the life of Moses. When he was leading the people of Israel through the wilderness, on the way to the land of Canaan, the people needed water. In obedience to God's command, Moses struck a rock, and water flowed forth. Later, when the need for water arose again, God told Moses to speak to the rock, and not to strike it. But Moses, in his anger against the people, struck the rock.

Though God, in His grace and mercy, allowed the water to come forth, He told Moses, "Because you did not trust in me enough to honor me as holy in the sight of the Israelites, you will not bring this community into the land I give them" (Numbers 20:12). In other words, Moses had misrepresented God's nature, so even though God continued to use Moses in a great way, Moses paid a heavy price: God did not permit him to enter the land of promise.

Here, in Leviticus 10, we have a similar situation. The priests operate as instruments of God, and one of their functions is to reveal the true nature of God to the people. If they disobey God's commandments, then they mislead the people about the reality of God. That is what we discover next in this passage:

> Moses then said to Aaron, "This is what the LORD spoke of when he said:
>
>> "'Among those who approach me
>> I will show myself holy;

in the sight of all the people
   I will be honored.'"
Aaron remained silent (Leviticus 10:3).

It is evident that Aaron was in shock and grief. Perhaps he was angry toward God. It appears that he was about to cry out against what God had done in taking the lives of two of his sons. But Moses spoke to Aaron and said, in effect, "This is what God meant when He said that those who approach me as priests must present an accurate image of me to the people. They must show me as holy, so that the people will understand who I truly am and honor me as a holy God."

When Moses said this, Aaron went silent. Whatever he had planned to say died instantly on his lips. Aaron knew that God was righteous and that his sons had sinned by presenting a false picture of God. They had approached God as if His commandments had no effect. Even in his pain and sorrow, Aaron understood that God's judgment was righteous.

## WORSHIP THAT DELIGHTS THE HEART OF GOD

Why did God insist on this one kind of incense? Elsewhere in Scripture, we see that the incense used was frankincense, a dried resin extracted from the sap of the boswellia tree. As it burns, clouds of fragrant smoke rise into the air. What does this image remind you of?

In Scripture, incense is always a picture of prayer—the prayers of God's people, prayers of praise and thanksgiving, rising up to God in glorious, fragrant clouds. The symbol of incense, then, is intended to help us to understand how God views our prayers and our praise, which rise up to Him from our obedient and thankful hearts. Furthermore, I believe that frankincense pictures for us not merely prayers of praise and thankfulness for the blessing of life but also our prayers in the midst of hardships and trials.

Frankincense never yields its fragrance until it is burned. You and I must sometimes go through fiery trials, but if we do so with hearts filled with prayer and praise, then we give off a fragrance that is sweet and delightful to God. Why? Because those are the times when we manifest the character of God, and we show that we are learning the lessons of this life which are designed to make us more like God.

But the lesson that God wants to teach us through the picture of the clouds of fragrant incense becomes distorted if His priests substitute some other kind of perfume, if they offer God a "strange fire." A mere perfume would present a false image of the kind of prayers God desires from us. Perfume suggests happiness, so a perfumed fire would indicate to the people that God is concerned only with our happiness and with making us feel good. It would imply that our temporary times of happiness come from God but that God is not equally present with us in our times of sorrow and pain. That is a philosophy which, in many forms, is with us today.

One form of this philosophy is hedonism, the belief that anything that makes you happy is the reason for life. If it is pleasurable, it is right (or, as it is sometimes expressed, "If it feels good, do it!"). One variation on this philosophy is what we might call Christian hedonism, the belief that God exists to serve us and make us happy. According to this philosophy, God wants us to be healthy and wealthy and happy all the time, and if we are not, then it must be because we don't have enough faith. This philosophy, which has permeated much of the church today, is a "strange fire" that is consuming many lives. People who fall prey to this misleading impression of God often find their faith shattered when they go through suffering, because they have not learned to experience joy, praise, and thanksgiving in the fiery trials of life.

When people are taught an illusion about God, they will surely be disillusioned by the harsh realities of life. That is why God's judgment is so swift and terrible against those who would distort His truth. He loves His people, and He does not want them to be misled by disobedient and presumptuous priests. Those who mislead God's people by offering the "strange fire" of false doctrines and lying worship are calling down His judgment upon themselves.

God wants us to know that true, lasting joy does not come from momentary pleasures but from a relationship with God. It comes from losing our lives and sacrificing ourselves so that we can find the resurrection life that Jesus came to bring us. Only by yielding ourselves and our wills to God can we find our true humanity and our true joy.

Perhaps the most graphic demonstration in the Bible of what it means to offer "strange fire" to God is the prayer Jesus recounted for us—the prayer of the proud Pharisee. Remember how he stood and prayed: "God, I thank you that I am not like other men—robbers, evildoers, adulterers—or even like this tax collector. I fast twice a week and give a tenth of all I get" (Luke18:11–12). This Pharisee recited all he had done for God, and he suggested that God was lucky to have this man on His side!

That is what is meant by offering "strange fire" before the Lord. Whenever we try to offer God our self-righteousness and our self-will, whenever we stop relying on the life He gives us as a free gift and start relying on our resources, we are offering "strange fire." And God does not receive "strange fire"—He rejects it instantly.

How can we offer Him worship that truly delights His heart? By learning to rejoice and praise Him in times of trial and testing as well as in good times. Whenever we go through pain and problems, we have an opportunity to manifest the character of God the Father and the resurrection life of His Son, Jesus. We should never waste those opportunities. Instead, we should offer our lives and our suffering to Him as a fragrant sacrifice, as sweet as incense, that is precious and pleasing to Him.

Any pagan can be happy and thankful when all of his bills are paid and he has money in the bank, when he is living in luxury, when he has no health problems, no relationship problems, no career problems, when all is smooth sailing. But it takes a person of godly, Christlike character to be joyful and grateful when his circumstances have turned against him, when he is sick and in distress, when people are persecuting him, when he has lost his job, his savings, and all his worldly goods. God is looking for hearts which have genuinely learned to rejoice in the trials of life.

How will we ever show God's forgiving character if we do not experience hurt and the opportunity to forgive others? How will we show the world how Christlike character responds to persecution unless we ourselves are persecuted? How will we show the world that God returns good for evil unless someone does evil to us? How will we demonstrate to the world God's limitless resources unless we ourselves are pushed far beyond our resources and into total, abject reliance upon Him?

Whenever we manifest the life of Jesus, we delight the heart of God. And the most vivid way that we can manifest the life of Jesus is through times of trial and testing. That is when the incense of our lives is heated to the burning point, so that it gives off a pleasing fragrance. That is why Paul tells us, "But thanks be to God, who always leads us in triumphal procession in Christ and through us spreads everywhere the fragrance of the knowledge of him. For we are to God the aroma of Christ among those who are being saved and those who are perishing" (2 Corinthians 2:14–15). This is the great lesson that God is seeking to impart to us.

Again and again, throughout the New Testament, we hear this message: "Consider it pure joy, my brothers, whenever you face trials of many kinds" (James 1:2). And: "In this you greatly rejoice, though now for a little while you may have had to suffer grief in all kinds of trials. These have come so that your faith—of greater worth than gold, which perishes even though refined by fire—may be proved genuine and may result in praise, glory and honor when Jesus Christ is revealed" (1 Peter 1:6–7). When we experience joy in our trials, we accurately express the character of God to the world, and we delight the heart of our loving Father.

Annie Johnson Flint was born on Christmas Eve 1866 in Vineland, New Jersey. When Annie was three, her mother died; her father died a few years later, leaving Annie and her sister as orphans. The two girls were reared by Christian foster parents, and Annie came to know Jesus Christ as her Lord and Savior.

During Annie's teen years, both of her foster parents died, leaving Annie and her sister orphaned a second time. Two years after she completed high school, she began to develop symptoms of painful, crippling arthritis. She saw a number of doctors, but the arthritis grew steadily worse until it became almost impossible for her to walk—even though she was only in her early twenties. She spent the rest of her life in constant pain, supporting herself by writing inspirational poetry. Her earnings were meager, and she often found it difficult to pay her extensive medical bills.

At the same time, Annie had a number of Christian friends who told her that God intended that every Christian should be healthy. Since she was suffering so much, they reasoned, Annie must either lack faith in God's ability to heal or she must have some hidden sin in her life. Annie, of course, found this counsel troubling, and she wondered if her friends where right.

So she prayed to God and searched the Scriptures. After weeks of seeking to understand God's will for her life, she came to the conclusion that while God does heal some Christians in a dramatic and miraculous way, He chooses not to heal other Christians of their afflictions. She became convinced that

God intended to use her pain to bring glory to Himself. She was able to say, along with the apostle Paul, "Therefore I will boast all the more gladly about my weaknesses, so that Christ's power may rest on me" (2 Corinthians 12:9). Out of this experience, Annie Johnson Flint wrote a poem that has blessed and comforted millions of people since she penned it in 1919:

> God hath not promised skies always blue,
>   Flower-strewn pathways all our lives through;
> God hath not promised sun without rain,
>   Joy without sorrow, peace without pain.
> But God hath promised strength for the day,
>   Rest for the labor, light for the way,
> Grace for the trials, help from above,
>   Unfailing sympathy, undying love.

So the question that confronts you and me is this: When we bow our heads to give thanks to God, what shall we thank Him for? Our food and clothing, the roof over our heads, the family times we enjoy, the blessings of life? Or can we go deeper into our relationship with God and offer Him the fragrant incense of a heart that rejoices even in suffering? Can we say, "Thank you, God, for the deep truths you are teaching me through my painful circumstances"? Can we say, "Thank you, Lord, for the way you are revealing yourself to me even amid these hardships and crushing disappointments"?

When we learn to lean upon God and draw upon His abundant resources in times of loss, pain, and stress, then we are able to offer Him the sweet-smelling clouds of frankincense in which He delights. There is no substitute for frankincense, which releases its fragrance only when it is burned. We cannot offer Him perfume or cologne or potpourri—that is "strange fire," and unacceptable to God. We must not distort God's image, as Nadab and Abihu did when they offered "strange fire" to God. We must worship Him in spirit and in truth.

## HOW WE OFFER "STRANGE FIRE" TO GOD

The third fact we notice in this passage is that God's judgment is exemplary. God makes an example of Nadab and Abihu but never acts in the same way again. God judged and punished these priests for their violation of His command, but He did this only once, at the beginning of the priesthood. In a similar way, God judged the sin of Ananias and Sapphira once (Acts 5). Even though their sin was probably not unique among Christians in the early church, and though it is undoubtedly common today, God has never judged violators with sudden physical death as He did Ananias and Sapphira. God takes action to teach His people a lesson, but He does so only once.

As you read through the rest of the Old Testament and on into the New Testament, you will find that the later priests of Israel violated God's commandments regarding worship and sacrifice, yet God did not kill them for it. In the days of the Maccabees, the priests even offered pig's blood—the blood of an unclean animal—and this was a horrendous violation of God's commandment, yet there is no record of God's sudden judgment in that case.

But God thought that it was important to show the seriousness of His commandments at least one time. Though His judgment seems harsh to our limited understanding, this is a manifestation of God's love and concern. He is trying to prevent this kind of desecration from happening again, and He is giving us fair warning of the serious consequences of deliberate sin.

It is also important to understand that the fact that Nadab and Abihu were killed and consumed does not mean that they were eternally lost and condemned. I am personally convinced that these two young priests were with God in glory at the instant of their deaths. God took them home—not because He had condemned them to hell but because they had violated their ministry. He called them home as an example so that other priests would take their ministry seriously and not violate it in the same way.

What are some ways you and I may violate our priestly ministry and offer "strange fire" before the Lord? We do so whenever we depart from the Word of God while counseling others who are in need of a priest. When we listen to hurting people or counsel people who are struggling with guilt and sin, we must do so prayerfully and in a way that is consistent with the full counsel of the Word of God.

Suppose, for example, that someone comes to you who has been mistreated and insulted. This person describes the offense that has been committed, and says, "What should I do? How should I respond?" In our flesh, you and I might be tempted to respond, "Why, I would punch that guy in the nose!" But that is not how God's Word tells us to respond, is it? There are many passages in Scripture that clearly tell Christians how to respond when they are mistreated—as, for example, this counsel from the pen of the apostle Paul:

> Do not repay anyone evil for evil. Be careful to do what is right in the eyes of everybody. If it is possible, as far as it depends on you, live at peace with everyone. Do not take revenge, my friends, but leave room for God's wrath, for it is written: "It is mine to avenge; I will repay," says the Lord. On the contrary:
>    "If your enemy is hungry, feed him;
>        if he is thirsty, give him something to drink.
>    In doing this, you will heap burning coals on his head."
>    Do not be overcome by evil, but overcome evil with good (Romans 12:17–21).

So if, in our role as God's priest, we give advice or counsel to another person that violates God's Word and God's character, then we are offering "strange fire" before God. We are guilty of the sin of Nadab and Abihu. We are all, as Christians, members of the priesthood of all believers, so we must offer to God and to the people around us a priestly service that is consistent with God's Word.

## THE TEMPTATION TO QUIT

The next few verses reveal an understandable and human reaction on the part of Aaron and his two remaining sons.

> Moses summoned Mishael and Elzaphan, sons of Aaron's uncle Uzziel, and said to them, "Come here; carry your cousins outside the camp, away from the front of the sanctuary." So they came and carried them, still in their tunics, outside the camp, as Moses ordered.
>    Then Moses said to Aaron and his sons Eleazar and Ithamar, "Do not let your hair become unkempt, and do not tear your clothes, or you will die and the LORD will be angry with the whole community. But your relatives, all the house of Israel, may mourn for those the LORD has destroyed by fire. Do not leave the entrance to the

Tent of Meeting or you will die, because the LORD's anointing oil is on you." So they did as Moses said (Leviticus 10:4–7).

You can imagine how hard it must have been for Aaron and his sons Eleazar and Ithamar to stand by and watch their relatives carry off the two charred bodies and take them for burial. Aaron and his sons were in shock, and their hearts were shattered with grief. Their natural inclination would be to collapse in grief, to fall down in the dust and mourn, to take the day—perhaps many days—to weep and remember and wallow in sorrow.

But Moses told them, in effect, "Don't leave the entrance of the tabernacle. You are still priests of God, and His anointing oil is on you. Don't neglect your priestly duties. Stay on the job or you, too, will die."

God understood what these young men needed. He knew that out of the shock and pain and anguish of their grief would come a new power and a new sense of purpose. So, speaking through His servant Moses, God told them, "Let the rest of Israel mourn Nadab and Abihu. You are my priests. You do not have the privilege of quitting. You have a job to do."

Have you ever felt like quitting? I have, many times. Sometimes the stress, the heartache, the sorrow, and the weariness of life become so great that we feel we don't have the strength to take another step for God, to do another act of ministry for God. Many times I have thought, I never expected my ministry for God to be this difficult! I just want to quit!

But God tells us the same thing He told Aaron and his two sons: "Don't quit! Be strong! Stay on the job!" That is why we read in the New Testament letter to the Hebrews:

> And you have forgotten that word of encouragement that addresses you as sons:
>> "My son, do not make light of the Lord's discipline,
>>     and do not lose heart when he rebukes you" (Hebrews 12:5).

Don't shrink from the Lord's discipline. Don't complain that God is giving you more than you can bear. Out of the pain of your heart will come a clearer understanding, a deeper compassion, and a stronger, more realistic word of counsel to people who need a priest.

God is the ultimate realist. Nobody understands reality more completely than He does—for, after all, He created reality! God deals with life the way it is. We are the ones who are so easily victimized by illusions and fantasies. We sometimes think that we can toss off a word of advice according to our opinions, or our feelings of the moment, or the philosophies of this godless world. But God wants us to understand that we are priests. We are anointed by the Holy Spirit to minister to one another in the body of Christ. This is a solemn responsibility, and we dare not take it lightly.

You cannot shut your eyes and ears and say, "I don't want to be a priest! I don't want the responsibility!" You don't have that option. If you are a follower of Jesus Christ, then you are a priest, and God calls you to faithfully fulfill your priestly office. Don't say, "My pastor can be the priest—after all, he's been to seminary, he's the professional." No, in God's eyes, your pastor is no more a priest than you are. God has called you as surely as He has called anyone, so you need to exercise your priesthood right where you are—in your office, your shop, your school, your neighborhood, your home.

A day is coming when God will call you to account for your ministry as a priest. He will ask you, "How did you respond to this situation? To that person? What kind of counsel did you give? Why weren't you attentive when I sent you this opportunity to minister in my name? Why did you offer 'strange fire' instead of the authentic worship I commanded of you?" What will you say when God asks for an accounting?

God has placed a heavy responsibility on us. He takes this responsibility seriously—and the way He dealt with Nadab and Abihu proves it. Now the question is: Do we? Are we serious about our responsibility as God's priests and as servants of one another?

God is sovereign, He is to be respected, and He is not to be trifled with. But at the same time, He is a God of love. Every action He undertakes toward us is an action of love—even if those actions sometimes seem harsh. When He sees sin in our lives, He seeks to arrest it before it destroys us. He seeks to keep us from hurting ourselves, harming others, and distorting the truth about Himself.

So let us be serious about this very serious matter. Let us not bring Him any false ministry or "strange fire." Instead, let us be priests who bring pleasure to God by offering to Him the incense of pure worship and priestly service.

≫———≪

# CHAPTER 11

# HOW TO BE A PRIEST
## LEVITICUS 10:8–20

ONE OF THE most life-changing truths of the Christian life is the fact that if you are a Christian, you are a priest. I never tire of watching Christians discover the fact of their own priesthood, because that realization always hits home with a sense of excitement and joy. Many people have been church members for years, yet they have never understood this great truth. Once they discover that God wants them to experience far more than coming to church, warming a pew, and placing an envelope in the collection plate, their lives are transformed. They discover that the Holy Spirit has equipped them with gifts that enable them to make a powerful difference in the lives of others, inside and outside of the church.

Without a doubt, the fact that all Christians are called to be a priesthood of believers is one of the most electrifying and radical truths in all of Scripture. And that is why it is so important that we study the book of Leviticus, the book of the priesthood. Here in this ancient and often-neglected book, God teaches us by pictures and symbols what our priesthood truly means today.

I wonder if we have any idea how important this principle of our priesthood is in the world today. We look around us at the despair and violence in our inner cities, the moral decay in our entertainment media, the corruption in our government, the epidemics of alcoholism, drug abuse, and suicide in our culture, and the threats of war and terrorism. We think, *The world is coming apart at the seams. What hope is there for this fallen and dying world?*

Yet there is hope for this world. And you might think, *Well, of course, Jesus Christ is the only hope for the world.* And that's true—but how does Jesus choose to work and minister to the world? Through you and me. That's right, the only hope for this world is Christ, ministering and loving the world through us, His church. We are His priests, and the world is dying because we are not doing the job God has ordained us to do. The world is ripping apart at the seams for the lack of a priesthood. The church has not been what God has called it to be.

Both as individual Christians and as a collective church, we have neglected the priesthood which was committed to us. We have failed to be salt and light in this dying world, as Jesus said we should (see Matthew 5:13–16). Without priestly salt as a preservative, there is nothing to keep our world from putrefying and corrupting at a fearful rate. Without priestly light, there is nothing to keep our world from sinking into a spiritual and moral darkness that is deeper than night.

A friend of mine and I once spoke at a public high school in the Deep South in the early 1970s. We spoke to the student body about how God was changing lives and hearts through the Jesus Movement in California. Many of the white students at that school were excited about our report. But we noticed that after our talk at the school assembly, many of the African-American students who lined the halls that we walked through were visibly hostile and sullen. They glowered at us with undisguised resentment. The air in those halls crackled with tension.

I knew instantly what was wrong in that school. These African-American students had been subjected to racism and mistreatment, and the white Christians in that school had not been a priesthood to them, reaching out with love and understanding. So when my friend and I came to speak at the school, they didn't see us as Christians or as priests of God or as bearers of the good news of Christ. They saw us as two more members of the white race, keeping them in social and economic bondage.

We also saw that the white students and the white adults in that school were largely blind to the racial tensions that were all around them. I tried to point out some of the danger signs to the white Christian adults in that community. I told them that the African-American students at the school needed Christians to stop ignoring them and to start reaching out to them in love. It was hard to convince these people that a problem even existed.

Before we hasten to judge these white Christians, we should ask ourselves: Are we equally blind to the needs, hurts, anger, tensions, and injustices that surround us? God calls us to open our eyes and see our world clearly. He calls us to break down walls of indifference and apathy and to truly become His priests in a suffering and hate-torn world. He calls not only preachers and missionaries but common, ordinary Christians like you and me. This world is dying for lack of a priest, and you and I are the ones God has called to fill that gap and meet that need.

As we continue our study in Leviticus 10, we will look at God's instructions for our lives. We will discover how to be priests.

## WE ARE UTTER REALISTS

Following the account of the death of Nadab and Abihu, we come to an instructive passage.

> Then the LORD said to Aaron, "You and your sons are not to drink wine or other fermented drink whenever you go into the Tent of Meeting, or you will die. This is a lasting ordinance for the generations to come. You must distinguish between the holy and the common, between the unclean and the clean, and you must teach the Israelites all the decrees the LORD has given them through Moses" (Leviticus 10:8–11).

Here, God tells us of two great privileges of ministry that priests enjoy.

First, priests are privileged to discriminate between the holy and the common, between the clean and the unclean. In the Old Testament priesthood, this meant distinguishing between clean and unclean animals, holy and common vessels, and so forth.

In our priesthood, the New Testament priesthood of all believers, this means distinguishing between that which merely feeds the natural life and that which improves a person's spiritual relationship with God. It means distinguishing between that which is harmful in our lives and that which is wholesome and healthful to our lives. This is not easy to do! It takes a discriminating eye and a discerning mind to tell the difference between right and wrong, good and evil.

Second, priests are privileged to teach God's truth and unveil His reality.

Priests are to tear down the illusions and lies that keep people in spiritual bondage, so that they can be free to see life as it really is. The Old Testament priests were responsible to teach the people of Israel all the statutes which the Lord had spoken to them through Moses. In much the same way, we are responsible to study and know the revealed truth of God's Word and to unveil and explain God's truth to the people around us.

Notice how these two ministries of the priesthood complement each other. The first ministry corrects what is wrong and untrue. The second ministry replaces untruth with what is right and true. This is a twofold ministry that our world desperately needs today.

In Paul's first letter to the Corinthians, he closes a section about the spiritual equipment of the believer by saying, "The spiritual man makes judgments about all things, but he himself is not subject to any man's judgment: For who has known the mind of the Lord that he may instruct him? But we have the mind of Christ" (1 Corinthians 2:15–16). In other words, God has enabled us to see the world as Christ sees it, as it really is, and thus we are utter realists. That is the job of a priest—your job, my job—to take God's truth and to set it before people in such a way that they can see the truth about themselves and about life.

I was once working on my Sunday sermon while traveling on an airplane when a flight attendant leaned over and said, "Sir, what are you working on?" I said, "I'm studying the Bible." She said, "Oh, that's interesting. What do you learn about in the Bible?" I said, "Well, I learn about life—and I learn about you and your life, too."

That surprised and intrigued her. "What do you mean?" she asked. "Tell me a little about yourself, and I'll tell you," I said. "Well," she said, "to begin with, I'm married." I said, "Well, that's what I mean. The Bible has a lot to say about married people and how they should live. Let me give you something." I reached into my briefcase and took out a copy of one of my printed messages entitled "What Every Husband Should Know." I gave it to her and said, "Why don't you give this to your husband? There is also one for wives. I don't have it with me, but I can mail it to you if you'll give me your address."

She took the printed message and went about her work. After a while, I looked up from my studies and there she stood—with two other flight attendants. She said, "I read a few pages from your pamphlet, and it's great! I want my husband to read this, too! And my friends also want copies for themselves and their husbands!"

That is the work of a priest. I was ministering to human needs at an altitude of forty thousand feet—not because I am a pastor of a church but because I'm a follower of Christ, just as you are. God wants you and me to minister for Him wherever we live, work, and travel. The world needs to hear the truth of God's Word, and how will the world ever hear if we don't go out as priests and talk about it?

Think of how many people are confused in the area of materialism and values. So many people today are discovering that material things never bring true satisfaction. A generation of empty, seeking people desperately needs a priesthood of all believers who will point the way to true peace and satisfaction.

Think of how many people today have a twisted view of their sexuality. For good or ill, our sexual urges drive a great deal of our behavior. Human sexuality affects every aspect of our society, from our politics to our entertainment—yet as a culture we have so little true understanding of this powerful force in our lives. Sex is one of God's greatest gifts to the human race, and it is a thing of beauty and significance when it is expressed as God intended, within the safe enclosure of marriage. Yet sex becomes one of the most destructive forces in human lives, human relationships, and human society when it is expressed outside of God's plan. The world desperately needs a priesthood of all believers who will teach the truth about sex from God's Word.

## WINE AND STRONG DRINK

Next, notice that there is one thing the priests must not do. In Leviticus 10:8–9, we read: "Then the LORD said to Aaron, 'You and your sons are not to drink wine or other fermented drink whenever you go into the Tent of Meeting, or you will die. This is a lasting ordinance for the generations to come.'"

Now, don't misunderstand that. The Bible never says that anything is wrong with wine except the abuse of it—that is, in drinking to excess. The Bible does say, with complete consistency all the way through, that drunkenness (and this principle applies equally to getting high on other drugs, such as cocaine, marijuana, and so forth) produces a lack of control. Being out of control because of substance abuse is wrong in God's eyes because it diminishes our humanity and it destroys lives and families.

God warned His priests that they should be sober when entering the tabernacle for ministry. Some people try to apply these Old Testament injunctions,
which were given to the Old Testament priesthood, to our lives today. But
in order to be completely consistent, we would also have to sacrifice animals
today as the priests of Leviticus did. We know that animal sacrifice is a symbolic picture of the death of Christ on our behalf, and now that we have the
reality of Christ's death to look back upon, we no longer need the symbolic
picture. Similarly, when God forbade the priests to drink wine or strong drink,
He was picturing something on the spiritual level in our lives. It signifies that
we should avoid on the spiritual level that which wine and strong drink do on
the physical level.

What does wine do to us physically? It diminishes our discernment and
distorts our judgment. It makes it much more difficult for us to discriminate
between that which is harmful and that which is wholesome and healthy. So
God has forbidden us to do anything that would destroy our ability to make
wise judgments for ourselves and for others with whom we may be ministering.

This is a warning we should urgently heed! For example, I have seen many
incidences in which Christians, with the best of intentions, have gotten involved
in shady financial deals, trying to make a lot of money quickly while justify-
ing it on the grounds that they could use that money to contribute more to
the church or to missionaries. Sometimes, they have used that rationalization
to justify cutting ethical and legal corners—sometimes even committing acts
that would trouble the conscience of a pagan! They allowed their greed and
covetousness to blind their minds to moral and spiritual reality, so that they
couldn't tell right from wrong. That is an example of what God seeks to warn
us against here.

Another example: I have seen Christians who have tried to counsel someone
who is caught in sexual sin. In the process of spending time trying to counsel
that straying person and perhaps talking frankly about intimate issues with
that person, they have seduced themselves into sexual sin. Our sexual urges are
more powerful than we imagine, and those who try to help others in this area
must have strong moral and spiritual boundaries. They should also have other
Christians praying for them and holding them accountable for the purity of
their lives. It is easy for even strong Christians to have their passions aroused, so
that they begin to rationalize and blur the distinction between right and wrong.

## THE STRENGTH OF A PRIEST
The next section deals with the source of the priests' strength.

> Moses said to Aaron and his remaining sons, Eleazar and Ithamar,
> "Take the grain offering left over from the offerings made to the
> LORD by fire and eat it prepared without yeast beside the altar, for it
> is most holy. Eat it in a holy place, because it is your share and your
> sons' share of the offerings made to the LORD by fire; for so I have
> been commanded" (Leviticus 10:12–13).

The grain offering, as we have already seen, is a picture of the perfect humanity of Jesus—a human being as God created humanity and intended humanity
to be. Through His Son Jesus, God has identified with us. What's more, we
can identify with Jesus, because He was tempted in every point as we are. He
knows exactly what we go through. He experienced every pressure, sorrow, and
temptation that we undergo.

Now notice where the priests are to eat the grain offering: beside the altar.
God commanded that the priests eat the symbol of humanity (the grain) in the
shadow of the symbol of sacrificial death (the altar, where the sacrificial animals
were killed). Why? So that the priests would be reminded of a fundamental principle that runs throughout Scripture: "For whoever wants to save his life will lose
it, but whoever loses his life for me and for the gospel will save it" (Mark 8:35).

This is the basic law of human existence. If you try to cling selfishly to your
existence, you will lose your life. It will wither and die, and you will be left
desolate. But if you give yourself away to others, if you die to self and live for
God as living sacrifice, then you will save your life and you will be left with joy,
peace, and a satisfied heart.

Through these symbols, the priests are being instructed as to the source
of their strength for carrying out their duties as priests. They are being told,
through symbolic pictures, that they are to live selflessly, sacrificing their
humanity for the sake of others. Only by dying to self can they have the objec-
tivity they need to dispense God's Word and God's wisdom to those who are
in need of a priest.

Next, God uses two more symbolic pictures to suggest two other sources of
strength that the priests are to draw upon.

"But you and your sons and your daughters may eat the breast that was waved and the thigh that was presented. Eat them in a ceremonially clean place; they have been given to you and your children as your share of the Israelites' [peace] offerings. The thigh that was presented and the breast that was waved must be brought with the fat portions of the offerings made by fire, to be waved before the LORD as a wave offering. This will be the regular share for you and your children, as the LORD has commanded" (Leviticus 10:14–15).

Notice the emphasis on the continuity of this provision: "This will be the regular share for you and your children." This provision shall be available all the time, forever.

We have already studied the meaning of these two portions of the sacrificial animals. The breast is a symbol of the love of Christ for us. The thigh symbolizes His strength and power on our behalf.

So this passage tells us, in effect, "When you feel discouraged and beaten down by life, remind yourself of the love the Lord Jesus has for you. Remember how He cares for you and accepts you, and that His love never changes." That is what it means to feed upon the breast portion of the sacrificed animal.

This passage also tells us, "When you feel so weak and powerless that you cannot serve God and others, when you feel the demands that are placed upon you are too great, then remind yourself that Christ's life is in you and that His strength is yours to draw upon." That is what it means to feed upon the thigh. Notice that these portions of the animal may be eaten anywhere—not just at the altar, but anywhere you need them. God wants us to know that the love and strength of Jesus are available to us anywhere, anytime.

## BEYOND THE LETTER OF THE LAW

The final section of this passage deals with a problem that arose. In this passage, Moses learns an important lesson from Aaron.

When Moses inquired about the goat of the sin offering and found that it had been burned up, he was angry with Eleazar and Ithamar, Aaron's remaining sons, and asked, "Why didn't you eat the sin offering in the sanctuary area? It is most holy; it was given to you to take away the guilt of the community by making atonement for them before the LORD. Since its blood was not taken into the Holy Place, you should have eaten the goat in the sanctuary area, as I commanded."

Aaron replied to Moses, "Today they sacrificed their sin offering and their burnt offering before the LORD, but such things as this have happened to me. [Note: Aaron refers here to the death of his two sons.] Would the LORD have been pleased if I had eaten the sin offering today?" When Moses heard this, he was satisfied (Leviticus 10:16–20).

Do you see the problem here? There were two kinds of sin offering, as explained in the law of the sin offering, Leviticus 6. One of these offerings specified that the blood of the sacrifice was to be carried into the inner sanctuary, into the Holy Place, and there it was to be sprinkled on the horns of the golden altar of fragrant incense. This procedure was required as a picture of human depravity and evil. Because of that depravity, no part of the animal was to be eaten, but it was all to be taken outside the camp and burned. The symbolic message of this offering is that human evil is so deep that only God may consume it.

But there was another kind of sin offering in which the blood was sprinkled on the horns of the brazen altar in the outer court. There the flesh of the animal was to be eaten by the priests as a picture of their understanding of the nature of their evil and as a token of their acceptance of the forgiveness of God.

The offering that takes place in these verses is of the second kind. The blood had not been brought into the sanctuary, so Moses said, in effect, "You should have eaten this meat! Why didn't you do it?" Moses feared that the judgment of God which consumed Nadab and Abihu would now consume the rest of the priests.

But Aaron explained his action to Moses, saying, in effect, "Two of my sons have sinned. And even though a sin offering was offered this very morning, my two sons died. There is evidently some depth of depravity here that we don't understand but which has taken their lives. Therefore it seemed to me that the Lord would not be pleased if I ate the sin offering. So we have treated it as though the blood were sprinkled before the golden altar, and the body of this animal has been burned in its entirety."

When Moses heard Aaron's explanation, he understood and approved of Aaron's action. He realized then that Aaron had gone deeper than the letter of the law; he had understood the intent of it. Aaron had understood what God wanted to accomplish through these sacrifices and ceremonies. God, in His mercy, did not exercise judgment here because Aaron had pressed beyond the letter to the deep intent of the Law. And Moses was content with that.

The attitude displayed by Aaron always pleases God. Contrary to what many people think, God is not interested in our rituals. Ultimately, God is not impressed by the fact that we come to church every Sunday, or that we use certain lofty-sounding words when we pray, or that we observe this liturgy or recite that creed. There is only one thing that matters to God: Is our heart right with Him? Rituals and activities do not make us more acceptable in His sight. He wants to know if we sincerely love Him, if we have sincerely, obediently placed our trust in Him.

David the psalmist wrote these words after repenting from his terrible double sin of adultery and murder:

> O Lord, open my lips,
>     and my mouth will declare your praise.
> You do not delight in sacrifice, or I would bring it;
>     you do not take pleasure in burnt offerings.
> The sacrifices of God are a broken spirit;
>     a broken and contrite heart,
>     O God, you will not despise (Psalm 51:15–17).

Those words express the attitude of Aaron as he brought his sacrifice. When Moses understood the heart of the high priest, he was content to permit the letter of the Law to be violated because the intent of the Law was so beautifully fulfilled.

That is what God seeks in your life and mine. That is what God expects from His priests. He doesn't want our religious folderol. Rituals and ceremonies are just pictures to reveal spiritual truth. The ceremonies are for our benefit and instruction, not God's. What He truly seeks in our lives is a heart that is open, responsive, and obedient before Him.

That—and that alone—is what truly delights the heart of God.

※———————※

# CHAPTER 12

# GOD'S STANDARD FOR OUR LIVES

## LEVITICUS 11

IT WOULD AMAZE us if we totaled up all the time we spend each week eating, thinking about eating, planning and preparing what we are going to eat next, and shopping for food. Sometimes it seems that our whole lives revolve around food! Someone once assembled a set of seven "scientifically proven" diet tips, which I now pass along to you, though I confess that I cannot vouch for their validity.

Diet Tip No. 1: Snacks consumed in a movie theater are not fattening, because they are considered entertainment, not food. Diet Tip No. 2: Though whole cookies are fattening, *pieces* of cookies contain no calories. This is because the calories leak out when the cookies are broken. Diet Tip No. 3: If you drink a diet soft drink with a candy bar, the soft drink and candy bar cancel each other out. Diet Tip No. 4: Snacks consumed after midnight have no calories. Diet Tip No. 5: A rule of thumb for any food is that if no one sees you eat it, it has no calories. Diet Tip No. 6: Calories don't count if you eat with someone else *and* you both eat the same amount. Diet Tip No. 7: Food taken for medicinal purposes does not contain calories. "Medicinal" foods include Ghirardelli chocolates, Ben & Jerry's ice cream, and Sara Lee cheesecake.

As we come to Leviticus 11, we find God's dietary advice, as given through

Moses to the people of Israel. On the surface of this passage, we see that God was so concerned for His people and involved in their lives that He instructed them in all the details of their lives, even in what they ate, what they wore, where they went, and what they did. But as we look beneath the surface of this passage, we will see that God has an equal concern for us that goes beyond our physical well-being, all the way to the care and feeding of our eternal spirit and soul.

## GUIDELINES FOR HEALTHY LIVING

In this section of Leviticus, we come face to face with our need for a standard, a measuring stick by which we can distinguish between things that are harmful and ones that are wholesome and healthy—between right and wrong, good and evil. This is not easy to do, as you well know. Here we see the realism and reliability of Scripture in action. Here we discover how God's Word deals practically and realistically with the day-to-day issues of our lives.

Certain secular opinion leaders today would have us believe that there is nothing in life that is truly harmful or immoral. According to them, it is only our distorted thinking that makes certain things right or wrong, good or bad. They would have us believe that the Bible, with its narrow and judgmental focus on so-called sin, makes people feel guilty for following their natural urges. If a person seeks fulfillment and pleasure by abandoning his or her family and having a sexual relationship (or many relationships) outside of marriage, who are we to judge? This secularist amoral attitude is rapidly becoming the dominant view in our culture today.

The teaching of the Bible stands in stark contrast to the teaching of our secular culture. The Bible tells us that there is objective truth, absolute good, and absolute evil. God's Word tells us that it is vitally important that we be able to discern right from wrong, wholesome from harmful, lest we be destroyed by our lusts and fallen appetites. There are snares and traps all around us, and God wants to make us aware of them so that we can live the kind of healthy, effective, satisfying life He created us to live.

People continually rebel against God's view of reality. They say, "Why shouldn't I use drugs if drugs make me feel good? Why shouldn't I have sex in any form that I want, with whomever I want? Why does God impose so many rules on our lives? Doesn't He just want to prevent us from having fun and enjoying life?" Yet these same people are the first to complain of God's unfairness when they wakeup to find themselves addicted to drugs or infected with a sexually transmitted disease.

God wants us to live healthy, whole, satisfying lives—but to live that way, we must be able to tell the difference between good and evil, healthful and harmful. In every choice that confronts us in life, He wants us to learn to distinguish between the equivalent of a tasty, wholesome mushroom— and a poisonous toadstool. That is why He has given us His guidelines for healthy living in the dietary realm and in the moral and spiritual realm.

Turning to Leviticus 11, we see that God is concerned about what people eat. He regulated the diet of the people of Israel. In this passage, He sets forth laws for distinguishing clean animals from unclean, as well as various sanitary practices. These laws were not in any way capricious or arbitrary. God's laws helped preserve Israel from the many diseases and epidemics that were rife in the nations around them. God kept His people physically clean and healthy through these regulations.

In his excellent book *None of These Diseases*, medical missionary and college physician Dr. S. I. McMillen explains how many of the illnesses and ailments of our present life could be avoided if we would follow the practical, common-sense regulations which God taught His people in the Old Testament. [Editor's note: *None of These Diseases* has been revised and updated by Dr. McMillen's grandson, Dr. David E. Stern; it is published by Fleming H. Revell (third edition, 2000).] It is important to realize, however, that not all of God's regulations in Leviticus were given for reasons of health and hygiene.

Many of the animals that were prohibited to the Israelites as food were not harmful in any way. They were prohibited only to teach a symbolic lesson to the people of Israel. This fact is made clear in the book of Acts, in the story of Peter's dream on the housetop before his visit to the Gentile, Cornelius, in Caesarea (see Acts 10:9–16). In his dream, Peter sees a sheet let down from heaven with various kinds of animals on it, clean and unclean. Peter, steeped in the Jewish law, has never even considered eating such animals. Many are creeping and crawling things forbidden in Leviticus 11.

But in the dream, God commands, "Get up, Peter. Kill and eat." Peter is shocked and replies, "Surely not, Lord! I have never eaten anything impure or unclean." Then God corrects Peter, saying, "Do not call anything impure that God has made clean." Many of these animals which were prohibited in Leviticus make decent, healthy, nourishing food. They were prohibited solely in order to teach a symbolic lesson. It is this symbolism that we are interested in.

## HOW TO MEDITATE ON GOD'S WORD

God distinguished four different types of animals as either clean or unclean. First, the animals which walk on the earth—the normal and natural food of humankind. Some of these were declared clean, and others were considered unclean. Second, the animals which come from the sea. Third, there was food from the heavens—the birds and winged insects. Fourth and finally, animals that crawl or creep along upon the ground.

These four divisions directly correspond to four spheres of human life. They correspond to four areas from which we draw nourishment for our inner life. What the Israelites were forbidden to eat on the physical level, we are also forbidden to take into ourselves on the spiritual and emotional level, the level of our inner life. There are clean and unclean ideas and concepts and spheres of knowledge that we need to distinguish today. These dietary laws help us greatly, because the same basic principles apply in the physical level of life and the spiritual and emotional level.

First, let's look at the normal and natural food of humanity—animals that walk upon the ground—and see what those animals symbolize for our inner life.

> The LORD said to Moses and Aaron, "Say to the Israelites: 'Of all the animals that live on land, these are the ones you may eat: You may eat any animal that has a split hoof completely divided and that chews the cud.
>
> "'There are some that only chew the cud or only have a split hoof, but you must not eat them. The camel, though it chews the cud, does not have a split hoof; it is ceremonially unclean for you. The coney, though it chews the cud, does not have a split hoof; it is unclean for you. The rabbit, though it chews the cud, does not have a split hoof; it is unclean for you. And the pig, though it has a split hoof completely divided, does not chew the cud; it is unclean for

you. You must not eat their meat or touch their carcasses; they are unclean for you'" (Leviticus 11:1–6).

This passage has been widely ridiculed by the skeptics of the Bible who say that this shows that the Bible doesn't know anything about natural science, because rabbits and coneys (hares) do not chew the cud. It is true that they don't ruminate like cows and other ruminants. But it has recently been discovered that they do have another process, somewhat similar, by which food is redigested, called refection. And so the Bible is right, after all.

Why did God impose these dietary restrictions on the people of Israel? Notice that animals that were approved had two characteristics: They had to chew the cud, and they had to divide the hoof. If an animal had one of these characteristics but not both, they were prohibited.

The animals which God permitted Israel to eat were taken from the normal range of food animals, such as cattle and sheep. These animals correspond to the normal area of feeding for the believer. They symbolically represent the normal body of knowledge, insight, and understanding that we, as believers, are to feed ourselves upon. And what is that normal body of knowledge? The Word of God.

Over and over in Scripture, we are told that God's Word is our food. Jesus Himself said, "Man does not live on bread alone, but on every word that comes from the mouth of God" (Matthew 4:4). Elsewhere in Scripture, God's Word is likened to milk, to meat, and to bread. The Word of God is knowledge and food.

We are to feed our mind, soul, and spirit on knowledge—but only that knowledge which has been tested by two processes that are described here in the symbols of the chewing of the cud and the dividing of the hoof. What do these symbols mean? What is the chewing of the cud a picture of? If you have ever watched an animal that chews its cud, you know that it is a beautiful picture of the art of meditation. We take in knowledge and concepts, and we tentatively swallow them undigested—then we bring them up again to chew on them, to rethink them and reexamine them and redigest them.

Many people treat the Word of God lightly and casually. They read a verse of Scripture one time and believe they know all there is to know about it. They consume a verse, swallow it, and forget it. But one superficial reading of God's

Word does not even begin to extract all the richness and meaning that is at the heart of each verse of Scripture, each kernel of God's truth. In order to truly feed on God's Word, we need to chew on it again and again, we need to adopt the practice of meditating on His truth. When we learn to do that, God's Word will truly come alive in our minds and in our lives. We only begin to taste the richness of Scripture when we learn to chew it again and again.

We can all make better use of our time by meditating on Scripture while waiting for a red light or tied up in a traffic jam, or sitting in the dentist's chair, or washing the dishes, or mowing the lawn, or raking the leaves. We can memorize Scripture, then meditate on it, think deeply about it, and discover its hidden truths and secrets. God has designed Scripture to contain many layers of truth. That is why a verse of Scripture we thought we understood many years ago continues to yield fresh insights every time we study it.

## How to Separate Right from Wrong

However, it is not only the chewing of the cud but also the dividing of the hoof that is important. What does God mean by this symbol? It is a picture of the principle of separation, discrimination, and discernment. We need to learn how to distinguish between right and wrong, between the truth of God and the lies of Satan, between the clarity of godly thinking and the confused and twisted ideas of humanity.

Two attorneys, a prosecutor, and a defense attorney, once opposed each other in a courtroom. The prosecutor thought he would make a great impression on the jury by quoting from the Bible. So he said, concerning the defendant, "We have it on the highest authority that it has been said, 'Skin for skin! A man will give all he has for his own life.'" Then he sat down, smirking at the defense attorney.

But the defense attorney knew the Bible better than the prosecutor. He stood and addressed the jury, saying, "I'm very much impressed by the fact that my distinguished colleague regards as the highest authority the one who said, 'Skin for skin! A man will give all he has for his own life.' You will find that this saying comes from the book of Job, the second chapter, the fourth verse—and the one who utters those words is the devil himself! That is who the prosecutor regards as the highest authority!"

We should not quote the Bible indiscriminately. We should understand what the Bible says and what it means in context. Many cults have arisen because of the failure of people to use God's Word as it was intended to be used.

The book of Ecclesiastes, for instance, has given rise to many false ideas which have been widely disseminated and attributed to the Bible. These ideas are found in the Bible, but they are not the ideas of God. They are human ideas, reflecting a human perspective, not the viewpoint of God. The existential despair that is expressed throughout the book of Ecclesiastes is God's reflection to us of the meaninglessness of a life that is lived only to accumulate wealth, fame, knowledge, or power. So we need to learn how to discern right from wrong, truth from error, even when we read God's Word.

## LIVING AS FISH

The next realm from which the Israelites were to take food was the realm of the sea. We read:

> "Of all the creatures living in the water of the seas and the streams, you may eat any that have fins and scales. But all creatures in the seas or streams that do not have fins and scales—whether among all the swarming things or among all the other living creatures in the water—you are to detest. And since you are to detest them, you must not eat their meat and you must detest their carcasses. Anything living in the water that does not have fins and scales is to be detestable to you" (Leviticus 11:9–12).

The sea is used throughout Scripture as a symbol of human society. Isaiah, for example, describes the wicked human race as "like the tossing sea, which cannot rest, whose waves cast up mire and mud." The symbolism of the humanity as a sea encompasses the whole realm of the business world, academia, the political world, the entertainment industry, the broadcast industry, the music industry, the publishing world. This is the human sea, and when we feed on the animals of the sea, we are to be discriminating. Just as God told Israel to distinguish edible food by its fins and scales—not one or the other, but both—He tells us to be discriminating when we consider taking into our inner selves the ideas and isms and ideologies of the human sea.

In this passage, God gives us clues by which we are to discern what is good and bad in the human sea. What are these clues? First, fins give a fish the capacity to penetrate the water and move through its element, the sea. Second, scales protect the fish against harm. So when we translate these clues to the human sea of our society, we see that we need to have the capacity to penetrate ideas and ideologies. We do not want to be tossed to and fro by the sea; we want to be able to move volitionally and intentionally through the sea of ideas as God directs.

God teaches us His truth with uncanny accuracy in these symbolic pictures. As the Israelites observed the dietary restrictions of Leviticus, they found that they couldn't eat shellfish, such as clams or oysters, nor could they eat crustaceans, such as shrimp, lobsters, or crabs. They also could not eat catfish, which have fins but no scales. There is nothing unhealthy about these foods—you and I eat them all the time with no ill effects. But those sea creatures did not teach the symbolic lesson God wanted His people to learn, so they were prohibited.

The Christian is to handle the knowledge of the world in the same way a finned sea creature plies the water: We are to keep moving forward all the time. We are to ask penetrating questions of every idea that confronts us: Where does this idea lead? Where is it going to take me? We are not to be content with superficial knowledge of a subject, but we are to go straight to the heart of the matter and understand the implications of every idea for our inner lives—for our heart, mind, soul, and spirit. We are to resist being captured, swayed, or tossed to and fro by any human idea or ideology.

Jesus told us that we are to be in the world but not of it (see John 15:19). What does this mean in practical terms? It means that we are to live as Jesus lived—right in the midst of life, shoulder to shoulder with people who are involved in all sorts of wrong ideas and bad behavior, living among them but not living as they live, engaging them in conversation but not engaging in their way of life. We are to move through the crowds, penetrating their false ideas, not being swayed by them but swaying them toward Christ as we continue making progress through life.

## TRUTH AND FALSEHOOD IN THE SPIRITUAL REALM

The third realm from which the Israelites could take their food was from the heavens, from the sky.

> "These are the birds you are to detest and not eat because they are
> detestable: the eagle, the vulture, the black vulture, the red kite, any
> kind of black kite, any kind of raven, the horned owl, the screech
> owl, the gull, any kind of hawk, the little owl, the cormorant, the
> great owl, the white owl, the desert owl, the osprey, the stork, any
> kind of heron, the hoopoe and the bat" (Leviticus 11:13–19).

These specific birds and the flying mammal, the bat, were all forbidden. If
you look through the list, you can see why. For the most part, these were either
carnivorous birds, which feed on live or freshly killed animals, or carrion eaters,
such as vultures and buzzards, that feed on dead animals they find, or omni-
vores—scavengers that eat anything. This is instructive, as we shall soon see.

Linked with these animals are the winged insects.

> "All flying insects that walk on all fours are to be detestable to you.
> There are, however, some winged creatures that walk on all fours
> that you may eat: those that have jointed legs for hopping on the
> ground. Of these you may eat any kind of locust, katydid, cricket or
> grasshopper. But all other winged creatures that have four legs you
> are to detest" (Leviticus 11:20–23).

You may think all insects are detestable, no exceptions! But in many parts
of the world, insects are a delicacy and are served in many interesting ways.
When I was in Asia, I was offered roasted grasshoppers, covered in chocolate.
I declined on the grounds that I shouldn't have chocolate. Locusts, you may
recall, were the dietary staple of John the Baptist (along with wild honey).
These were permitted under the dietary restrictions of Leviticus 11, but almost
every other insect was forbidden to the Jews. Why would some insects be considered edible and others forbidden? And what does this tell us in a symbolic
way about the realm of ideas and knowledge?

Here we are dealing with food from the heavens. In Scripture, the heavens are always the realm of the spirit. The function of the human spirit is that
it enables us to relate to God. This is the realm of faith and religion. Human
beings are made to worship. The urge to worship is wired into our inner being.
So food from the realm of the heavens involves all forms of our need to worship.

It includes authentic biblical faith—but it also includes the false doctrines of worldly metaphysics, the occult and witchcraft, UFOs, and extrasensory perception. When we are dealing with this realm, we need to carefully test what we take into our inner being, to make sure that we are not poisoning ourselves with spiritual falsehood.

First, we are to reject all food that is obviously carnivorous—that is, those ideas and notions that are related to the flesh, that are carnal in nature. These are the self-indulgent, self-gratifying, self-focused ideas that often pass themselves off as spiritual, but are sensual and hedonistic.

Next, we are to reject all food that is carrion-like—that is, those ideas and ideologies that are focused on death. Examples include spiritualism and mediums (those who channel the dead through séances and other occult practices), as well as spiritual practices that demonstrate a fascination with death (from murderous religious cults like the Manson family to the devotees of gothic religion, with their unholy obsession with vampirism and other death-oriented fantasies and beliefs).

Then we are to reject all food that is eclectic and omnivorous—that is, those philosophies and ideologies which attempt to take a little from here, a little from there, then blend it all together to create a religion that is supposedly the best from all the religions. This, God tells us, is forbidden. Our faith is to be the pure, unadulterated faith that we have received through His Word, not some hodgepodge of the most agreeable parts of many religions.

In the physical realm, those who touched the carcasses of prohibited animals were to be considered ceremonially unclean and must take certain actions to cleanse themselves.

> "You will make yourselves unclean by these; whoever touches their carcasses will be unclean till evening. Whoever picks up one of their carcasses must wash his clothes, and he will be unclean till evening.
>
> "Every animal that has a split hoof not completely divided or that does not chew the cud is unclean for you; whoever touches the carcass of any of them will be unclean. Of all the animals that walk on all fours, those that walk on their paws are unclean for you; whoever touches their carcasses will be unclean till evening. Anyone who picks up their carcasses must wash his clothes, and he

will be unclean till evening. They are unclean for you" (Leviticus 11:24–28).

As we extend the symbolism of this passage to its logical conclusion, we realize that we are contaminated whenever we touch unclean ideas and ideologies. The only way to cleanse our minds and spirits from the contamination of the world is by the washing of God's Word (see John 15:3; Ephesians 5:26).

## CREATURES THAT CREEP ALONG THE GROUND

Finally, this passage addresses the realm of creatures that were in full contact with the ground.

"Of the animals that move about on the ground, these are unclean for you: the weasel, the rat, any kind of great lizard, the gecko, the monitor lizard, the wall lizard, the skink and the chameleon. Of all those that move along the ground, these are unclean for you. Whoever touches them when they are dead will be unclean till evening. When one of them dies and falls on something, that article, whatever its use, will be unclean, whether it is made of wood, cloth, hide or sackcloth. Put it in water; it will be unclean till evening, and then it will be clean. If one of them falls into a clay pot, everything in it will be unclean, and you must break the pot. Any food that could be eaten but has water on it from such a pot is unclean, and any liquid that could be drunk from it is unclean. Anything that one of their carcasses falls on becomes unclean; an oven or cooking pot must be broken up. They are unclean, and you are to regard them as unclean. A spring, however, or a cistern for collecting water remains clean, but anyone who touches one of these carcasses is unclean. If a carcass falls on any seeds that are to be planted, they remain clean. But if water has been put on the seed and a carcass falls on it, it is unclean for you.

"If an animal that you are allowed to eat dies, anyone who touches the carcass will be unclean till evening. Anyone who eats some of the carcass must wash his clothes, and he will be unclean till evening. Anyone who picks up the carcass must wash his clothes, and he will be unclean till evening.

"Every creature that moves about on the ground is detestable; it is not to be eaten. You are not to eat any creature that moves about on the ground, whether it moves on its belly or walks on all fours or on many feet; it is detestable. Do not defile yourselves by any of these creatures. Do not make yourselves unclean by means of them or be made unclean by them" (Leviticus 11:29–43).

Here we have the entire category of animals that crawl or creep on their bellies along the ground. What does this category of creatures suggest to your mind? The fall of humanity in the Garden of Eden. After seducing Adam and Eve into disobeying their Creator, the serpent in the Garden was cursed by God to crawl on his belly for the rest of his existence. Crawling upon the belly, then, is a symbol of a curse.

God gives us great freedom to explore the realm of human ideas and knowledge. But once we discover an idea or practice or realm of knowledge that is satanic and under God's curse, then we are to go no further. We are to reject it. Such ideas are seductive; they seem harmless at first, but they draw human beings into error, pride, self-deification, and self-glorification. The end of such ideas is hate, rebellion against God, and death, physical and spiritual. We are not to take these ideas into our inner being. They contaminate and stain the soul.

This is why Christians are forbidden to explore the realms of satanic thought. This is why God warns us, as He warned ancient Israel, "Let no one be found among you who sacrifices his son or daughter in the fire, who practices divination or sorcery, interprets omens, engages in witchcraft, or casts spells, or who is a medium or spiritist or who consults the dead" (Deuteronomy 18:10–11). These are practices and ideas which crawl upon the ground, which are under the curse of God, and which Satan still uses to seduce the souls of men and women—and yes, even children.

God concludes His declaration of His standards for the nation of Israel with these words:

"I am the LORD your God; consecrate yourselves and be holy, because I am holy. Do not make yourselves unclean by any creature that moves about on the ground. I am the LORD who brought you up out of Egypt to be your God; therefore be holy, because I am holy.

"These are the regulations concerning animals, birds, every living thing that moves in the water and every creature that moves about on the ground. You must distinguish between the unclean and the clean, between living creatures that may be eaten and those that may not be eaten" (Leviticus 11:44–47).

At the outset of this book, we observed that the key to the book of Leviticus is found in Leviticus 20:26, which reads, "You are to be holy to me because I, the LORD, am holy, and I have set you apart from the nations to be my own." Here, at the end of Leviticus 11, we see that same statement: "I am the LORD your God; consecrate yourselves and be holy, because I am holy." To be holy is to be whole—a complete person, fulfilling one's God-given potential as a human being.

A whole person is one who performs the function for which he or she was originally designed. A whole and holy person is one who belongs to God and fully reflects God's image, in which that person was created.

Let's look at some other uses for that word *holy*. The Holy Land is the land that belongs to God. It is His. We call the Bible the Holy Book because it is God's Book. It belongs to Him, it originated with Him, and it exists for His glory. In the same sense, we are God's holy people, because God is holy. He made us, we belong to Him, we originated with Him, and we exist for Him. He created us and loves us, and He is working through us to bring glory to Himself.

God is love, God is holy, and God is a whole and wholly integrated Being. In His love for us, He wants us to be holy and whole as well, and He wants us to fulfill our humanity. That is why God lovingly sets limits and restrictions on our lives. That is why He says, "Don't get involved with these things. Don't take them into your inner being. Don't fool around with these dangerous ideas and practices! You will be trapped if you do. You will be defiled and contaminated; your humanity will be compromised and destroyed. You will not be able to fulfill the purpose I lovingly planned for you." So He limits us out of love.

God is not really interested in our religious activities, our religious busyness, our religious fervor or emotionalism. He is interested in the kind of character we display. He wants us to be whole and holy. In our homes, in our businesses, in our schools, in our neighborhoods, He wants people to see His holy character shining through our lives, expressed through the qualities of love, joy, peace, forgiveness, patience, and understanding we show to the people around us. That is the character of a whole person.

So God says to you and me, just as He said to the people of Israel so long ago, "Be holy because I am holy. Shun the things that would defile you and contaminate you and fragment you. Be whole. Be holy. This is my standard for your lives."

# CHAPTER 13

# THE CURE FOR LEPROSY

## LEVITICUS 12:1–13:46

DR. PAUL BRANDT, in *Where Is God When It Hurts?* described his work among people afflicted with leprosy (or Hansen's disease), one of the most feared and disfiguring diseases in human history. One of the effects of leprosy is that it destroys the nerves so that sufferers of the disease are unable to feel sensations such as pain.

On one occasion while he was on the grounds of the leprosy clinic where he worked, Dr. Brandt attempted to open a rusted padlock, without success. A young man who was infected with the disease came over and said, "Here, Dr. Brandt, let me help you." The young man wrestled with the key and lock for a moment, then the lock clicked open. As the patient took his hand away from the lock, Dr. Brandt noticed that the fellow's hand was bleeding—he had cut his finger all the way to the bone and hadn't even noticed.

Leprosy is a horrible disease with a long history of tormenting the human race. As we come to Leviticus 12 and Leviticus 13, we are confronted with the problem of leprosy, as well as a number of other afflictions. Yet, as we look beneath the surface of this passage, we see that these verses symbolically deal with the reality of our relationship to God and to others. We find that it is easy to do damage to our most important relationships without even being aware of the harm we are causing.

The afflictions of the body that are described in this passage symbolize the troubling and hurtful things we often do and say to one another without even being aware of the harm we cause. Just as physical leprosy blocks nerve impulses that signal bodily damage, our spiritual leprosy blocks our awareness of the damage we cause to ourselves and others. God wants us to be physically healthy, but He even more urgently desires that we be healthy in our relationships and our innermost being.

## CHILDBIRTH, PURIFICATION, AND SACRIFICE

As we examine this passage, we will see that many modern sanitary and hygienic procedures are anticipated by the regulations laid down by Moses for the people of God. If these health and sanitation guidelines had been followed through the course of the centuries, many outbreaks of plague and epidemic would have been avoided. In this passage, for example, we see that God tells His people how to practice early detection of serious diseases, how to care for the sick, and how to quarantine contagious cases. He also instructs His people that bed rest is one of the most important keys to recovery when people are sick. This passage opens with a short chapter about childbirth.

> The LORD said to Moses, "Say to the Israelites: 'A woman who becomes pregnant and gives birth to a son will be ceremonially unclean for seven days, just as she is unclean during her monthly period. On the eighth day the boy is to be circumcised. Then the woman must wait thirty-three days to be purified from her bleeding. She must not touch anything sacred or go to the sanctuary until the days of her purification are over. If she gives birth to a daughter, for two weeks the woman will be unclean, as during her period. Then she must wait sixty-six days to be purified from her bleeding'" (Leviticus 12:1–5).

At first glance, you might think that this passage teaches that childbirth is an inherently unclean event. That is not what this passage teaches. There is nothing wrong with childbirth, or with the sexual activity that preceded it, or with women and their bodies. The entire context of the Bible makes it clear that the act of procreation, the process of conception, the act of childbirth, and the female body are all beautiful and glorious, for they are designed and created by God.

Why, then, did God give the people of Israel these requirements for a woman to be purified from her uncleanness following childbirth? These requirements were given so that God's people would remember a basic and fundamental fact: Since the fall of Adam, every human being born into this world is born into a fallen race. We are born into a sinful race.

There is no way that we, in our natural condition, can permanently solve the fundamental problems of human relationships. Though we were made in God's image, that image has been marred by sin. As a result, we human beings do not function as we were created to function. Our understanding is limited. Our motives are tainted. Our relationships are distorted. God impresses this truth upon His people by imposing a restriction on women in childbirth.

The restriction is this: A mother was to be considered ceremonially unclean for a week after the birth of a male child, then undergo thirty-three days of purification. In the case of the birth of a female child, she was to be considered unclean for two weeks, followed by sixty-six days of purification. All of this was intended to remind the woman and her family that a baby is always born with a tainted nature.

Many people today teach that children are born in complete innocence. Some pretend that babies come into the world in a state of complete innocence, and if you just leave them alone and give them the opportunity to express themselves, they will grow into whole, fulfilled persons. That destructive philosophy has caused chaos in many homes, in our educational system, and in society as a whole. If you are a parent, you probably know this philosophy is not true. Children are clearly born with a sin nature, and they need a great deal of guidance and training in order to learn responsibility, character, self-control, discipline, values, and faith. That is one reason why God teaches His people from the beginning that there is a problem in human nature—the sin nature that we are born with.

The circumcision of the male baby was another reminder that something needs to be removed from the life inherited from Adam. The circumcision rite was followed by thirty-three days of purification for the mother. This time of purification was doubled after the birth of a female child. We can't be sure why this is so. We know, however, that the purification period was partly a compassionate consideration. During the purification period, the mother was relieved from certain obligations to work around the house. The longer period of purification after the birth of a girl is probably a reminder of the fact that the temptation to sin entered the human race through the weakness of the woman, who was deceived by Satan. The human race fell in Adam, the man, who sinned knowingly; but temptation entered the human race through Eve, who was deceived.

Next, a sacrifice is commanded. Why? Because God is teaching Israel that purification ultimately requires a death. Even when a new life is born, death must be acknowledged—the substitutionary death of Jesus our Great High Priest, as represented by the sacrifice.

> "When the days of her purification for a son or daughter are over, she is to bring to the priest at the entrance to the Tent of Meeting a year-old lamb for a burnt offering and a young pigeon or a dove for a sin offering. He shall offer them before the LORD to make atonement for her, and then she will be ceremonially clean from her flow of blood.
>
> "These are the regulations for the woman who gives birth to a boy or a girl. If she cannot afford a lamb, she is to bring two doves or two young pigeons, one for a burnt offering and the other for a sin offering. In this way the priest will make atonement for her, and she will be clean" (Leviticus 12:6–8).

The sacrifice cleanses. It pictures for us the sacrifice of Jesus upon the cross, which cleanses us from sin. In the New Testament, we have this account of the circumcision of Jesus and Mary's purification and sacrifice.

> On the eighth day, when it was time to circumcise him, he was named Jesus, the name the angel had given him before he had been conceived. When the time of their purification according to the Law of Moses had been completed, Joseph and Mary took him to Jerusalem to present him to the Lord (as it is written in the Law of the Lord, "Every firstborn male is to be consecrated to the Lord"), and to offer a sacrifice in keeping with what is said in the Law of the Lord: "a pair of doves or two young pigeons" (Luke 2:21–24).

The phrase from the Law that is quoted in this passage is from Leviticus

12:8. Mary and Joseph followed the Levitical law to the letter. Even though Jesus was born without sin, He was circumcised, and Mary underwent the time of purification and made the sacrifice of a pair of doves. This was so that Jesus would be fully identified with sinful humanity.

It is significant that God commanded circumcision to take place on the eighth day. Doctors tell us that the eighth day is the first day that a baby's blood contains enough blood-clotting factors to make such an operation safe. In fact, the blood-clotting factors skyrocket on the eighth day to a level higher than normal, then rapidly level off to normal. So the eighth day is the safest day of all for circumcision to be performed.

## THE DETECTION OF DISEASE

Leviticus 13 deals with the problem of diseases and hygiene. The fact that it is linked with Leviticus 12 suggests that the taint of sin is not removed at the moment we are born again by faith in Christ. Though we have moved from death to life, the sinful flesh is still there. Christians can and do sin. Many people seem to forget this obvious fact, and they expect instant perfection from Christians at the moment of their conversion. That's simply not possible. We need help in dealing with the sin problem. The flesh needs to be recognized and controlled—and that isn't easy.

Take, for example, the issue of anger. Temperaments differ from person to person. One may have a quiet, calm temperament while another may be fiery and explosive by nature. There is nothing wrong with these personality differences; God made each of us unique. We can't all be cool and dispassionate; some are more volatile and quick to react—and that is not wrong. There is sinful anger, and there is righteous anger. But we all know that righteous anger—for example, anger that is directed at oppression and injustice—can turn to a sinful and hateful rage, or to malice, bitterness, and grudge-bearing. How do we learn to respond to difficult situations in a righteous and godly manner instead of responding in our sinful flesh?

You might be surprised to discover that this is, in fact, the underlying theme of Leviticus 13, which opens with these words:

> The LORD said to Moses and Aaron, "When anyone has a swelling
> or a rash or a bright spot on his skin that may become an infectious

skin disease, he must be brought to Aaron the priest or to one of his
sons who is a priest. The priest is to examine the sore on his skin,
and if the hair in the sore has turned white and the sore appears to
be more than skin deep, it is an infectious skin disease. When the
priest examines him, he shall pronounce him ceremonially unclean.
If the spot on his skin is white but does not appear to be more than
skin deep and the hair in it has not turned white, the priest is to
put the infected person in isolation for seven days. On the seventh
day the priest is to examine him, and if he sees that the sore is
unchanged and has not spread in the skin, he is to keep him in isolation another seven days. On the seventh day the priest is to examine him again, and if the sore has faded and has not spread in the
skin, the priest shall pronounce him clean; it is only a rash. The man
must wash his clothes, and he will be clean. But if the rash does
spread in his skin after he has shown himself to the priest to be pronounced clean, he must appear before the priest again. The priest is
to examine him, and if the rash has spread in the skin, he shall pronounce him unclean; it is an infectious disease" (Leviticus 13:1–8).

The obvious and overriding focus of this chapter is the detection of an infectious disease. The King James Version uses the word "leprosy," but the New
International Version, which is quoted above, wisely uses the term "infectious
disease." In the original language, the Hebrew word translated "leprosy" in the
KJV and "infectious disease" in the NIV does not merely refer to the disease
we now call Hansen's disease. The Hebrew word includes other contagious and
infectious skin diseases in addition to leprosy.

These diseases were regarded as a serious threat not only to the sick individual but also to the whole camp of Israel. It was important that these diseases
be detected early. So the Levitical law established a process of inspection and
detection. The priest would examine the symptoms of the sufferer, then quarantine that person for seven days, examine again, then (if necessary) quarantine
the sufferer again. At the end of that time, the priest would determine whether
the disease was contagious or not.

These procedures and instructions have a counterpart in our spiritual lives.
This passage doesn't just talk about afflictions and diseases of the body, but of

the spirit as well. These afflictions of the spirit are the hurtful attitudes and burning resentments we harbor, the grudges we carry around in our hearts. These dangerous spiritual diseases are to be detected by the priest. And who is our priest today?

Remember that, according to the New Testament pattern, all believers are priests. So we, as believers, should be helping each other to see ourselves more clearly, detect emotional and spiritual diseases, and help each other to be cleansed of that spiritual uncleanness.

Unfortunately, we are all blind to ourselves. Most of us tend to see ourselves as better and more spiritually healthy people than we really are. But when we look around at other people, we can spot all kinds of flaws that they themselves don't seem to see! We wonder why everyone around us can't be as genial, gracious, and inoffensive as we ourselves are!

The truth is that we are blind to our failings. We can't detect our flaws because they hide in our blind spots. That is why we need one another in the church, the body of Christ. As priests to one another, we can hold up a mirror and help each other to see and correct those flaws. So when the Israelites were required to be inspected by the priest, it was not only a matter of good hygiene in ancient Israel but a matter of good spiritual, emotional, and relational health for us today. We need to have our priests, our fellow believers, inspect our lives, watch our behavior, monitor our attitudes, and help us to grow more and more like Jesus Christ.

The procedure that the priest of Israel was to use was a careful examination, not a hasty, impulsive judgment. The priest didn't merely glance at a skin lesion, snap his fingers, and say, "Oh, I know what you have! You've got measles—or mosquito bites—or leprosy." No, he carefully watched the development of the case for seven days (notice that the number seven is the number of perfection in the Bible). He gave the matter time to see if the case worsened. He allowed his understanding of the situation to grow and clarify. Only when he could speak with certainty and confidence did he make his pronouncement.

The procedure that is outlined for a priest of Israel is instructive for our lives as we seek to be wise and caring priests to one another in the body of Christ. When someone comes to us confessing a sin or asking for guidance and counsel with a spiritual crisis or a relationship problem, we should always be quick to listen and slow to speak. A priest should never render a hasty, impulsive

judgment. We should never leap to conclusions or prescribe superficial reme-
dies for spiritual, moral, emotional, or relational problems.

## FOUR SYMPTOMS OF SPIRITUAL LEPROSY

Although the priest was concerned with detecting the threat of any infectious disease, he was especially concerned about the threat of leprosy. There
are four characteristics of leprosy, and each is important and instructive. The
priests looked for these four manifestations. If the afflicted person had them,
then a diagnosis of leprosy was made. If not, then the illness was probably of
short duration and relatively harmless. The next passage gives us the four characteristics by which leprosy was recognized.

> "When anyone has an infectious skin disease, he must be brought
> to the priest. The priest is to examine him, and if there is a white
> swelling in the skin that has turned the hair white and if there is
> raw flesh in the swelling, it is a chronic skin disease and the priest
> shall pronounce him unclean. He is not to put him in isolation,
> because he is already unclean" (Leviticus 13:9–11).

The priest was to first examine any spot, outbreak, or eruption on the skin
to see what it was. It could be just a harmless pimple, or it might be more serious. Anyone with an outbreak brought it to the priest, just as we are to bring
to one another the blemishes and eruptions in our soul, spirit, emotions, or
relationships.

The first symptom the priest would look for was swelling, a sign that the
lesion or spot on the flesh went deeper than the skin. A temporary pimple was
only a superficial, skin-deep problem. But swelling suggested a symptom of a
deeper, more dangerous, and seriously infectious condition.

Transposing this to the spiritual realm, we see the same principle at work.
When people swell up in pride, it often indicates a deep-seated arrogance and
conceit within the heart. When people swell up in anger, it often indicates a
soul filled with bitterness and resentment—not always, but sometimes. The
swelling we observe may be no more than the manifestation of a passing mood,
a minor irritation of spirit.

But if the swelling doesn't subside, and if we see other symptoms as well, then it may be a sign of a more permanent, deeply rooted, and dangerous sin problem within that individual. As Jesus said, "What comes out of a man is what makes him 'unclean.' For from within, out of men's hearts, come evil thoughts, sexual immorality, theft, murder, adultery, greed, malice, deceit, lewdness, envy, slander, arrogance and folly" (Mark 7:20–22).

The second symptom the priest would look for was white hair. The priest would check to see if the hair at the site of the eruption had turned white. White hair is always a sign of approaching death—relatively speaking. Whenever I look at the clippings that have fallen from my head to the floor around the barber chair, I try to tell myself otherwise, but I can't deny it: With advancing age and approaching death comes white hair.

White hair is always a sign that the aging process is at work. "When the snow appears on the mountain," goes the old saying, "winter is at hand." So it was with the infectious disease that is here called leprosy. The disease would accelerate the process of approaching death, causing the hair at the site of the infection to turn white. (We should note, however, that white hair is not a standard symptom of what we call leprosy today—that is, Hansen's disease.)

In our spiritual and emotional lives there are also certain signs to watch for. There are emotional reactions and attitudes that we all have. Some are momentary and benign; others are long-lasting and poisonous. If, for example, a person flashes with momentary anger, it is nothing more than the equivalent of a rash or skin irritation. But if a person stews for months or years, brooding over bitterness, malice, hatred, and thoughts of self-pity or revenge, then that person is showing signs of a malignant infection, a leprosy of the soul.

The third symptom the priest would look for was raw flesh—a lesion that was open and ugly and which stubbornly refused to heal. An eruption that was healing on its own was nothing to worry about. But the presence of raw flesh was a strong indication of infectious disease.

In his letter to the Galatians, Paul describes what raw flesh means in spiritual terms. In the original Greek, Paul speaks of "the acts of the flesh," or, as the New American Standard Bible renders it, "the deeds of the flesh." The NIV changes it to "the acts of the sinful nature"—and, of course, when Paul speaks of "the flesh" he does mean our sinful nature, the fallenness of our human flesh. So I will insert the bracketed phrase "[the flesh]" into the NIV text from Galatians so that you can clearly see what Paul is saying to us.

> The acts of [*the flesh*] are obvious: sexual immorality, impurity and debauchery; idolatry and witchcraft; hatred, discord, jealousy, fits of rage, selfish ambition, dissensions, factions and envy; drunkenness, orgies, and the like. I warn you, as I did before, that those who live like this will not inherit the kingdom of God (Galatians 5:19–21).

Here is the raw flesh of our humanity, the symptoms of a person infected with a leprosy of the soul: Sexual immorality, impurity, and debauchery—the sinful misuse of our sexuality. Idolatry—worshiping anything other than God. Witchcraft—allying oneself with the forces of Satan and his demons. Hatred, discord, jealousy, fits of rage, selfish ambition, dissensions, factions and envy—acts that harm other people and which divide and disrupt the body of Christ. Drunkenness and orgies—giving oneself over to a substance abuse (involving not just alcohol, but any mood-altering drug), wild partying, and engaging in debased and immoral behavior with other people.

Just to make sure we can't say, "Well, my particular vice isn't on this list," Paul adds the phrase "and the like," a reference to any related behavior that he might not have listed but which results from our fallen flesh. Twenty-first century society has invented many new ways to indulge in the acts of the flesh, such as viewing pornography on computers, engaging in phone sex, developing illicit relationships with other people over the Internet, and on and on. The fact that Paul didn't specifically list our chosen vice twenty centuries ago does not let us off the hook! Such acts are leprous and deadly to our souls.

## WHEN THE INFECTION HAS SPREAD

The fourth symptom the priest would look for was that the infection was spreading—this symptom is mentioned in Leviticus 13:12. But God makes a curious pronouncement in connection with this symptom, as we are about to see. This fourth symptom requires careful examination.

> "If the disease breaks out all over his skin and, so far as the priest can see, it covers all the skin of the infected person from head to foot, the priest is to examine him, and if the disease has covered his whole body, he shall pronounce that person clean. Since it has all

turned white, he is clean. But whenever raw flesh appears on him, he will be unclean. When the priest sees the raw flesh, he shall pronounce him unclean. The raw flesh is unclean; he has an infectious disease. Should the raw flesh change and turn white, he must go to the priest. The priest is to examine him, and if the sores have turned white, the priest shall pronounce the infected person clean; then he will be clean" (Leviticus 13:12–17).

Here is the fourth mark of leprosy: it has spread. We see this same principle in the spiritual realm, when the infection of sin, malice, immorality, or dissension spreads from one person and affects others in the body of believers. A bitter spirit can be as contagious as smallpox. A rebellious attitude can spread like an epidemic. When this occurs, the person with the leprous disease of the soul is unclean in God's sight. The infection of sin is dangerous and harmful to the individual and to the body of Christ in which He lives. As the book of Hebrews tells us, a spirit of bitterness and dissension easily "grows up to cause trouble and defile many" (Hebrews 12:15).

In Luke 17 there is the account of ten lepers who came to Jesus and asked for help and healing. Jesus told them to go and show themselves to the priests, according to the law of Moses. As they went, their leprosy turned white, and they knew that they were cleansed. This is a beautiful picture for us of how to cure the leprosy in our lives. When what had been leprous turns white, then, even though the whole body was infected from head to foot, the priest pronounced the person clean. When the leprosy turns white, the evil has been arrested, the infection has been stopped, and the sufferer has been cleansed.

Transposing this principle to the spiritual realm, we realize that the evil we have done must be brought under the judgment of the Word of God in order for us to be cleansed. We must face our sin, name it for what it is, see it as God sees it, and repent of it. All of our defenses and denials have to be broken down, and we must go to God, fully confessing our sin. Then God can cleanse us and turn the leprosy of our sin pure white.

This does not mean we will not suffer the aftereffects of our sin. The scars may remain, perhaps for the rest of our lives. We may have to deal with health problems, damaged relationships, financial problems, or the humiliation of having our secret sin exposed before others. Those are our scars. But the action of the sin has been arrested, and we no longer need to fear it.

This is a beautiful illustration of the truth of 1 John 1:8–9—"If we claim to be without sin, we deceive ourselves and the truth is not in us. If we confess our sins, he is faithful and just and will forgive us our sins and purify us from all unrighteousness." What a gracious provision God has made for the healing of our spiritual leprosy!

What prevents us from being healed? Our defenses and excuses. We say, "Oh, I can't help being prone to infidelity. I just can't get enough of the opposite sex!" Or, "Our family has had a problem with alcohol for generations. It's in my genes." Or, "I can't help getting mad and lashing out at people. It's just because I'm Irish [or Italian or Latin or whatever ethnic component we wish to blame]. Don't expect me to change—it's just who I am."

We use these excuses to avoid the hard work and painful self-examination required to find the cure for our spiritual leprosy. Our desire to clutch these hurtful, injurious attitudes is proof of the fallen, distorted, Adamic nature within us. Isn't it strange that we cling so tenaciously to the very things that cause pain to ourselves and the ones we love? The pride of our hearts drives us to resist God's attempt to bring us healing and wholeness. When someone comes to us as a priest, trying to help us see our sin, we respond by lashing out and acting spitefully. This resistance to God's way of helping and healing us reveals the fact that a potent spiritual leprosy is at work in our lives.

## OTHER TYPES OF AFFLICTIONS AND DISEASES

The rest of Leviticus 13 deals with other types of afflictions and diseases, and the same basic treatment is administered. There were boils, burns, itches, scabs, and other problems that appear to be what we would today call psoriasis and eczema. We read:

> "When someone has a boil on his skin and it heals, and in the place where the boil was, a white swelling or reddish-white spot appears, he must present himself to the priest. The priest is to examine it, and if it appears to be more than skin deep and the hair in it has turned white, the priest shall pronounce him unclean. It is an infectious skin disease that has broken out where the boil was. But if,

when the priest examines it, there is no white hair in it and it is not more than skin deep and has faded, then the priest is to put him in isolation for seven days. If it is spreading in the skin, the priest shall pronounce him unclean; it is infectious. But if the spot is unchanged and has not spread, it is only a scar from the boil, and the priest shall pronounce him clean.

"When someone has a burn on his skin and a reddish-white or white spot appears in the raw flesh of the burn, the priest is to examine the spot, and if the hair in it has turned white, and it appears to be more than skin deep, it is an infectious disease that has broken out in the burn. The priest shall pronounce him unclean; it is an infectious skin disease. But if the priest examines it and there is no white hair in the spot and if it is not more than skin deep and has faded, then the priest is to put him in isolation for seven days. On the seventh day the priest is to examine him, and if it is spreading in the skin, the priest shall pronounce him unclean; it is an infectious skin disease. If, however, the spot is unchanged and has not spread in the skin but has faded, it is a swelling from the burn, and the priest shall pronounce him clean; it is only a scar from the burn.

"If a man or woman has a sore on the head or on the chin, the priest is to examine the sore, and if it appears to be more than skin deep and the hair in it is yellow and thin, the priest shall pronounce that person unclean; it is an itch, an infectious disease of the head or chin. But if, when the priest examines this kind of sore, it does not seem to be more than skin deep and there is no black hair in it, then the priest is to put the infected person in isolation for seven days. On the seventh day the priest is to examine the sore, and if the itch has not spread and there is no yellow hair in it and it does not appear to be more than skin deep, he must be shaved except for the diseased area, and the priest is to keep him in isolation another seven days. On the seventh day the priest is to examine the itch, and if it has not spread in the skin and appears to be no more than skin deep, the priest shall pronounce him clean. He must wash his clothes, and he will be clean. But if the itch does spread in the skin after he is pronounced clean, the priest is to examine him, and if the itch has spread in the skin, the priest does not need to look for yellow hair; the person is unclean. If, however, in his judgment it is unchanged and black hair has grown in it, the itch is healed. He is clean, and the priest shall pronounce him clean.

"When a man or woman has white spots on the skin, the priest is to examine them, and if the spots are dull white, it is a harmless rash that has broken out on the skin; that person is clean" (Leviticus 13:18–39).

If we venture to interpret these various afflictions, we can see their counterparts in the spiritual realm. Boils are always painful infections which finally come to a head, much like the crises of our attitudes and our negative dispositions. You know what it feels like when someone says some sharp, hurtful word to you; it wounds you and angers you, and that hurt can quickly fester into a growing resentment. You try to set it aside, but it keeps growing and growing until it finally comes to a head, much like a boil that grows and becomes more painful until it ruptures and the pressure is relieved.

Burns are injuries caused by circumstances outside of ourselves. We can be burned emotionally and spiritually as well as physically. Sometimes, when we are hurt by other people, we actually express it in those terms: "I really got burned by that person!" When we get burned in an emotional sense, we need to treat that wound with the healing grace of God. We should turn to our family of faith and allow them to be priests to us, and minister God's healing touch to our stinging emotions, our wounded spirit.

Itches are maddening irritations—they are not painful, but they are insistent, and the more you scratch them, the worse they become. Scabs are the crusty residue of wounds and lesions—not quite healed but not yet a scar. If they are not allowed to heal properly, scabs can become reinfected and worse than before.

This entire catalog of afflictions and diseases is focused on one question: Are your leprous spots being properly dealt with in the light of God's Word? Are they being brought to the One who can heal our leprosy with a touch? Or are we hiding our wounds and diseases from our fellow priests and our Great High Priest, Jesus Himself? What are you and I doing to be healed of our foul moods, our temperamental outbursts, our bitterness and resentment, our self-centeredness, our depression?

Next, God offers a word of reassurance for those (like myself) whose hair is thinning.

> "When a man has lost his hair and is bald, he is clean. If he has lost his hair from the front of his scalp and has a bald forehead, he is clean. But if he has a reddish-white sore on his bald head or forehead, it is an infectious disease breaking out on his head or forehead. The priest is to examine him, and if the swollen sore on his head or forehead is reddish white like an infectious skin disease, the man is diseased and is unclean. The priest shall pronounce him unclean because of the sore on his head" (Leviticus 13:40–42).

Leprosy could hide beneath a full, youthful head of hair, but age and thinning hair make leprosy harder to hide. The same is often true in the spiritual realm. Everyone expects young people to behave in an immature or unwise way from time to time. But if we fail to build Christlike character and wisdom into our lives as we grow older, a time eventually comes when our defects of character begin to show. The leprosy in our spirit becomes obvious for everyone to see, like a splotch of leprosy on the head of a bald man. We should deal with our spiritual leprosy early in life, so that when we reach a ripe old age, people will be able to say, "There is a person who has spent a lifetime building a whole, healthy, Christlike personality."

Finally, God's guidelines for health and hygiene close with these words, which describe the fate of those whose leprosy goes uncured.

> "The person with such an infectious disease must wear torn clothes, let his hair be unkempt, cover the lower part of his face and cry out, 'Unclean! Unclean!' As long as he has the infection he remains unclean. He must live alone; he must live outside the camp" (Leviticus 13:45–46).

In ancient times, lepers were a common sight on the edge of town, begging beside the road. They sometimes lived alone in caves or together with other lepers, and they looked exactly as this passage describes: torn clothes, unkempt hair, the lower part of their faces masked. They called out "Unclean!" as a warning to the uninfected people to keep their distance so that they would avoid becoming victims of the disease.

Here again, God teaches us with a powerful visual symbol. What the law of Moses demanded is what God allows to take place in the lives of those who fail to deal with the leprosy in their inner being. These issues cannot be avoided. This is what will happen to those who do not deal with their leprous souls, as taught by these symbols.

The first symbol is the torn clothes. Throughout Scripture, clothes symbolize human behavior, the outward actions of an individual. Torn clothes are a picture of behavior that has no sense, no unity, no wholeness. A person who does not seek healing in the leprous areas of his or her inner being will manifest a poorly integrated, fragmented personality. That person's walk and talk will not match. He or she will get tripped up in lies, cover-ups, secret sins, and shame. That is what the leper's torn clothes tell us.

The second symbol is unkempt hair. In Scripture, hair is always a mark of beauty. A woman's hair, especially, is regarded as her crown of glory. Unkempt hair, then, is beauty disarrayed, beauty lost. The potential is there, but the inherent beauty of the personality is lost. A life that is marked by an inner leprosy is one in which so much potential beauty has been squandered, twisted, and made ugly by sin.

The third symbol is a masked face. There is shame in having a leprosy-ridden soul. Such people must continually hide who they truly are. They shrink back from discovery. They are afraid to let others know them. It is a terrible way to live.

The fourth symbol is the cry of "Unclean! Unclean!" This is a vivid picture of what happens when leprosy of the soul goes unhealed. The individual announces his or her uncleanness to the world. Leprosy—whether physical or spiritual—can be hidden in the early stages. Eventually, however, it shows, it announces itself, and it leaves the individual feeling conspicuously shamed and condemned. People who are unclean with a leprosy of the soul are spotted and avoided by other people. Leprosy produces revulsion, and that revulsion makes outcasts of lepers.

Lepers dwell alone. They might wish to be close to other people, but they cannot. They long for love like anyone else, but they find themselves rejected and shunned. Ultimately, they are friendless and alone.

The message of this passage is that now is the time to face our leprous attitudes and behavior, our selfish motivations, our destructive habits, and our broken relationships. Now is the time to take our diseased souls to the Great High Priest, the Great Physician, so that He can reach out and heal us. With just the touch of His Word, He can arrest the infection of our sin, turn our leprosy white, and set us free.

# CHAPTER 14

# SICK GARMENTS AND DISEASED HOUSES

## LEVITICUS 13:47–14:57

IN RECENT YEARS we have been hearing about something called Sick House Syndrome. Since the late 1970s, people living in modern, well-constructed, well-insulated homes noticed that they were experiencing such symptoms as itchy skin, headaches, watery eyes, nasal congestion, coughing, wheezing, dizziness, and fatigue. At first, sufferers were told that the problem was simply hay fever, or even that the symptoms were all in their minds.

But then a discovery was made: After the energy crisis of the late 1970s, when energy costs for heating and air conditioning rose dramatically, people began insulating, weather-stripping, and otherwise sealing up their homes to make them more energy-efficient. The result was that these modern, well-constructed, well-insulated homes no longer had the ventilation that homes once had. These homes could no longer breathe.

Once these homes were tightly sealed, they became unhealthy. They trapped humidity and moisture, becoming a breeding ground for molds and mildew. Tightly sealed homes concentrated dust mites in the air, triggering a higher rate of asthma attacks. They also trapped dangerous gases such as carbon monoxide from furnaces and stoves and radioactive radon gas from the rocks beneath the home. Remodeling efforts to make older homes more energy-efficient had caused the airborne release of dangerous particles of leaded paint, asbestos, and formaldehyde.

In an effort to make homes more efficient, people were making their homes sick—and these contaminated homes were making people sick. As we continue moving through Leviticus 13 and on into Leviticus 14, we find that God was concerned with the problem of contamination in the homes and garments of the people of Israel. In those ancient times, there were problems of contamination and mildew which could bring disease into the camp.

## The Problem of Contaminated and Infectious Garments

Here is how God addresses the problem of contamination and infection, beginning with the issue of contaminated clothing:

> "If any clothing is contaminated with mildew—any woolen or linen clothing, any woven or knitted material of linen or wool, any leather or anything made of leather—and if the contamination in the clothing, or leather, or woven or knitted material, or any leather article, is greenish or reddish, it is a spreading mildew and must be shown to the priest" (Leviticus 13:47–49).

Here we see God's concern about certain molds, mildews, and bacterial and fungal growths which could attach themselves to garments and spread infection to the whole camp. Long before human science understood the operation of bacteria and fungal spores, the people of Israel were taught that some spots that they might find on clothing or in their houses were not necessarily harmless stains but could be symptoms of contamination that could grow and spread.

As we apply these hygienic guidelines to the level of life on which we live today—the spiritual, social, emotional, and relational levels of our lives—we need to determine what these garments and infections symbolize. In Scripture, garments are used as a picture of character, especially as expressed in behavior. In Leviticus 8, we saw how the garments of the high priest revealed how our Great High Priest, the Lord Jesus Christ, is equipped to deal with our problems. His garments reveal His character. Garments are used this way throughout Scripture and are associated closely with the individual who wears them.

"Clothe yourselves with the Lord Jesus Christ," Paul writes in Romans 13:14, "and do not think about how to gratify the desires of the sinful nature." And in Colossians 3:12, he adds, "Therefore, as God's chosen people, holy and dearly loved, clothe yourselves with compassion, kindness, humility, gentleness and patience." Peter uses the same symbolism in 1 Peter 5:5—"Clothe yourselves with humility toward one another."

Today, we still identify ourselves with our garments. The way we dress is a statement about who we are and what matters to us. Have you noticed how good you feel when someone compliments your attire? You take it as a reference to you as a person—to your style, your taste, your values, your character, and even your position in life. We are identified by the clothes we wear, and we identify with them.

We change our garments to suit the various roles we play in life. We wear one set of clothes to the gym or out jogging; we wear another set of clothes to putter around the house; we wear another set of clothes to a wedding or to the symphony. We dress in a way that is suitable for our task, our setting, our role. Our garments symbolize not only who we are but also what we do. So garments are used in Scripture as a symbol of our character, our roles, our behavior, our relationships with others.

Here in Leviticus 13, God is teaching us that our lives—our personality and character, our roles and relationships—can be contaminated by a disease-like infection. Certain aspects of our relationships with one another can have spots in them which are dangerous. Certain behaviors and attitudes can be virulent and destructive to others, even to our entire church, spreading contagion and infection to everyone they touch.

## AVOID HASTY JUDGMENT

Just as a garment may be beautifully designed and skillfully made but ruined by a spot of contamination, a personality or a relationship may be beautiful except for one area, one attitude, one bad habit that lurks and contaminates all that it touches. God wants us to deal with these contaminating forces in our own personality, attitudes, behavior, and relationships. In symbolic language, He tells us how to do it. The passage continues:

"The priest is to examine the mildew and isolate the affected article for seven days. On the seventh day he is to examine it, and if the mildew has spread in the clothing, or the woven or knitted material, or the leather, whatever its use, it is a destructive mildew; the article is unclean. He must burn up the clothing, or the woven or knitted material of wool or linen, or any leather article that has the contamination in it, because the mildew is destructive; the article must be burned up" (Leviticus 13:50–52).

Earlier in Leviticus 13, we saw that the priest was not to apply a hasty, impulsive judgment to problems of human illness, such as leprosy. When a person had a disease in his or her flesh, God prescribed a careful process of examination, quarantine, and reexamination before judgment should be rendered. Here, in the case of a contaminated garment, God outlines a similar procedure. There is to be no hasty, impulsive judgment regarding a garment that is suspected of contamination. Transposing this from the symbolic realm to our everyday world of behavior and relationships, we realize that we frequently transgress this command of God.

We see people going into a certain place, or talking to a certain person, or engaged in a certain activity, and we immediately jump to the worst possible conclusion. This person is sinning! This person is carrying on a sinful relationship or engaged in scandalous behavior! Only after we have made judgments and spread rumors do we find out that this person did nothing wrong—but by that time, it's too late. The damage is done, the feelings are hurt, the reputation is destroyed, the lives are ruined. God does not want us to make hasty judgments that hurt other people.

Notice that, in our own lives, we tend to be slow to judge our behavior. We linger in wrongful relationships because we enjoy the emotional thrill it brings. We wallow in sinful habits because we like our sin and don't want to give it up. We don't want to examine our sinful behavior—and we surely don't want others to question what we are doing! It's none of their business! How dare they judge me? We are slow to judge ourselves, yet quick to judge others.

So, through this passage in Leviticus, God tells us, in effect, "Take your time. Be careful. Do not be too quick to condemn the spotted garment of another person's life. Take time to examine the behavior or relationships. Take time to understand, so that you don't make a terrible mistake and bring suffering and embarrassment upon an innocent person." God calls us to investigate anything that is hurtful, sinful, and infectious in our lives and relationships—but He also calls us to be careful, patient, and slow to pass judgment.

So the garment must be inspected and then reinspected on the seventh day. If, at that point, it is clear that the contamination is spreading, then the garment must be destroyed. The clothing is unclean and the priest "must burn up the clothing, or the woven or knitted material of wool or linen, or any leather article that has the contamination in it, because the mildew is destructive; the article must be burned up." What does this mean in symbolic terms for our lives today?

It means that if a pattern of behavior or a relationship is found to be harmful and infectious, if it is contrary to God's Word, then it must be stopped. Contaminating habits and relationships can spread to other people and infect a church. They can take over our lives and cause us to neglect our most important priorities and responsibilities. That is why drastic action must be taken. That is why unwholesome relationships, destructive habits, and sinful behavior must be confronted and ended. The infected garment must be destroyed, or it will spread that infection throughout the household.

## THE WASHING OF THE WORD OF GOD

Not all spotted garments need to be burned and destroyed. As we go on to read, some spotted clothing can be made clean by washing.

> "But if, when the priest examines it, the mildew has not spread in the clothing, or the woven or knitted material, or the leather article, he shall order that the contaminated article be washed. Then he is to isolate it for another seven days. After the affected article has been washed, the priest is to examine it, and if the mildew has not changed its appearance, even though it has not spread, it is unclean. Burn it with fire, whether the mildew has affected one side or the other" (Leviticus 13:53–55).

In other words, there were spots which, if they didn't spread, were not necessarily an infectious contamination, and they could be remedied by washing the garment. Washing, in Scripture, is a symbol of the action of the Word of God. Jesus said to His disciples, "You are already clean because of the word I have spoken to you" (John 15:3). Sometimes, our lives, behavior, and relationships have problems that can be solved by the cleansing of the Word of God.

We often become involved in behavior or a relationship that is not sinful per se, but we have allowed it to create an imbalance in our lives. For example, eating is a good thing, because food is pleasurable and keeps us healthy; overeating, however, is destructive to our health. So if our problem is overeating, God would not want us to burn our behavior of consuming food and stop eating. Rather, He would have us wash our behavior in God's Word (which condemns the sin of gluttony), so that we can eat in a moderate and healthy fashion.

Young people will sometimes form a romantic relationship involving behavior that is immoral and relationally unhealthy. Often, the relationship itself is not wrong—that is, there is no reason why these two Christian young people shouldn't court each other and possibly marry someday. But if their behavior toward each other has been unchaste, then their relationship needs to be brought under the authority of God's Word. It needs to be washed and cleansed. The couple needs to make a commitment to remain chaste and virtuous from this day forward, and should be held accountable to do so. Then their relationship can continue in a healthy and godly way. Leviticus 13 concludes:

> "If, when the priest examines it, the mildew has faded after the article has been washed, he is to tear the contaminated part out of the clothing, or the leather, or the woven or knitted material. But if it reappears in the clothing, or in the woven or knitted material, or in the leather article, it is spreading, and whatever has the mildew must be burned with fire. The clothing, or the woven or knitted material, or any leather article that has been washed and is rid of the mildew, must be washed again, and it will be clean."
>
> These are the regulations concerning contamination by mildew in woolen or linen clothing, woven or knitted material, or any leather article, for pronouncing them clean or unclean (Leviticus 13:56–59).

Here, beneath the surface of what appears to be merely advice for the care and cleaning of clothing, is practical advice for daily living. Perhaps you have a spot in your relationship with your spouse or children, an area where you tend to be harsh, judgmental, or quick to criticize. Perhaps you have been toying with the idea of divorcing your mate or ordering your teenager out of the house—in essence, burning the relationship.

God says, in effect, "Be careful! Don't be too quick to destroy an important relationship! Don't be too quick to put people out of your life! That which is merely spotted can be washed by the Word and made clean and good again." These are wise words and helpful principles that will spare us much grief if we will heed what God is telling us through the symbolism of spotted garments.

## THE CLEANSING OF LEPERS

In Leviticus 14, God continues to speak to Moses—and to us—about the issue of contamination. Once again, there is a deeper truth to be discerned here than mere physical infection.

> The LORD said to Moses, "These are the regulations for the diseased person at the time of his ceremonial cleansing, when he is brought to the priest: The priest is to go outside the camp and examine him. If the person has been healed of his infectious skin disease, the priest shall order that two live clean birds and some cedar wood, scarlet yarn and hyssop be brought for the one to be cleansed. Then the priest shall order that one of the birds be killed over fresh water in a clay pot. He is then to take the live bird and dip it, together with the cedar wood, the scarlet yarn and the hyssop, into the blood of the bird that was killed over the fresh water. Seven times he shall sprinkle the one to be cleansed of the infectious disease and pronounce him clean. Then he is to release the live bird in the open fields" (Leviticus 14:1–7).

Here, God begins by addressing the issue of people who have apparently been healed of leprosy. He lays out a beautifully symbolic ritual that is not intended to heal a person but to cleanse a person who has already been healed. Only God can heal. The act of healing is a sovereign act of God that takes place in the inner life of a human being. Cleansing is a symbolic act that enables us to understand that God's basis for healing is nothing less than a blood sacrifice. That is the picture which is drawn for us here.

We need to understand that all of us, as human beings, have hearts that are infected with spiritual leprosy. We are full of sin, envy, covetousness, lust, resentment, hatred, and malice. We have a hard time seeing the true sickness of our hearts unless God draws it out for us with symbols such as these. When we truly see the sinfulness and leprosy of our hearts, we can do nothing but fall before God and plead, "Lord, heal me!"

And God does! The moment we let down our defenses and admit our sickness and sinfulness, He reaches into our hearts with His touch of grace and heals our inner leprosy. The leprosy is arrested, and we are healed.

But after we are healed, we still need cleansing. We need to understand the basis on which our inward healing occurred so that our outward behavior can be adjusted to a new pattern. That is what is brought out here in this symbolic cleansing of the leper. The ceremony is not ritual for ritual's sake. It is a vivid and visual representation of what God does in the life of a sinner who is cleansed from sin. It is clear that God has thought through every detail in order to teach us profound truths.

The first thing we learn is that the basis for our healing is always the shedding of blood. God never heals, never blesses, never arrests the action of evil apart from the shedding of blood. The meaning of the symbols is obvious for anyone to see.

The priest takes two live birds, some cedar wood, some blood-colored scarlet yarn, and hyssop (a tiny, moss-like plant that grows in nooks and crannies of the rocks). The priest has one of the birds killed over fresh water in a clay pot. Then the other bird is dipped into the bloody water, along with the wood, yarn, and hyssop. Then the healed leper is sprinkled seven times, and the living bird is released and allowed to go free.

The blood, of course, pictures for us the blood of the Lord Jesus. Throughout Leviticus, the sacrifices continually picture for us the sacrificial death of Christ, which puts the old nature to death and brings us new life. God never puts a bandage on cancer; He strikes at the root of the cancer, destroys it, and gives us a whole new life. He doesn't just salve our symptoms; He heals our disease. The shed blood of this innocent bird is a beautiful picture of the Lord Jesus and His death for us.

The clay pot is a picture of the humanity of Jesus. Paul spoke of our humanity this way: "But we have this treasure in jars of clay to show that this all-surpassing power is from God and not from us" (2 Corinthians 4:7). Fresh water, newly drawn from a spring or stream, always pictures the Holy Spirit in His refreshing, life-giving quality. Jesus spoke of the Spirit in these words: "Whoever believes in me, as the Scripture has said, streams of living water will flow from within him." In other words, the Spirit of God flows from the hearts of those who believe in Jesus.

The cedar tree was regarded in Israel as the acme of beauty and symbolized the glory of God. The moss-like hyssop, by contrast, was regarded as a symbol of the lowliness of humanity. So here we have a picture of the two extreme opposites that were embodied in Jesus Christ—His divine glory and His lowly humanity. The scarlet yarn symbolized His kingliness. All of these items were dipped in the shed blood, baptized in death. The living bird, too, was dipped in the shed blood and released—a picture of the resurrection of the Lord Jesus and of our identification with Him in His death and resurrection. By our identification with Him, we are set free from death and sin and released to the heavens, just like that bird. Through His sacrifice, Jesus sets us free to be new creatures in Him.

It is amazing how meaningful these Old Testament symbols are. They demonstrate that the Old and New Testaments tell us one consistent story, from Genesis to Revelation. As Jesus told the Pharisees, "You diligently study the Scriptures because you think that by them you possess eternal life. These are the Scriptures that testify about me" (John 5:38). Clearly, the rich symbolism of Leviticus speaks volumes about Jesus.

The next step in the ritual involved the personal cleansing of the healed leper, followed by a seven-day waiting period to make sure that the leper's healing and cleansing was genuine.

> "The person to be cleansed must wash his clothes, shave off all his hair and bathe with water; then he will be ceremonially clean. After this he may come into the camp, but he must stay outside his tent for seven days. On the seventh day he must shave off all his hair; he must shave his head, his beard, his eyebrows and the rest of his hair. He must wash his clothes and bathe himself with water, and he will be clean" (Leviticus 14:8–9).

After this, the leper was to bring four offerings. The importance of the exact order of the four offerings should not be overlooked.

"On the eighth day he must bring two male lambs and one ewe lamb a year old, each without defect, along with three-tenths of an ephah of fine flour mixed with oil for a grain offering, and one log of oil. The priest who pronounces him clean shall present both the one to be cleansed and his offerings before the LORD at the entrance to the Tent of Meeting.

"Then the priest is to take one of the male lambs and offer it as a guilt [trespass] offering, along with the log of oil; he shall wave them before the LORD as a wave offering. He is to slaughter the lamb in the holy place where the sin offering and the burnt offering are slaughtered. Like the sin offering, the guilt offering belongs to the priest; it is most holy.

"The priest is to take some of the blood of the guilt offering and put it on the lobe of the right ear of the one to be cleansed, on the thumb of his right hand and on the big toe of his right foot. The priest shall then take some of the log of oil, pour it in the palm of his own left hand, dip his right forefinger into the oil in his palm, and with his finger sprinkle some of it before the LORD seven times. The priest is to put some of the oil remaining in his palm on the lobe of the right ear of the one to be cleansed, on the thumb of his right hand and on the big toe of his right foot, on top of the blood of the guilt offering. The rest of the oil in his palm the priest shall put on the head of the one to be cleansed and make atonement for him before the LORD.

"Then the priest is to sacrifice the sin offering and make atonement for the one to be cleansed from his uncleanness. After that, the priest shall slaughter the burnt offering and offer it on the altar, together with the grain offering, and make atonement for him, and he will be clean" (Leviticus 14:10–20).

The trespass offering was first. Leprosy in a garment symbolizes the harm and injury that our sin causes to others or that they cause to us. A trespass has occurred, a relationship has been hurt or broken, and that needs to be dealt with first. So the trespass offering (or, in the NIV, guilt offering) comes first. Jesus offered Himself as the sacrifice for our trespasses.

Next came the sin offering. This offering goes deeper, to our fallen sin nature. This offering teaches us that through the death of Christ, God has dealt with the source of evil within us—the sinfulness that is woven into our fallen flesh. Because Jesus dealt with our sin nature, we don't have to follow the urges to sin anymore. We still feel them, but we are not bound to them as we once were. We are freed from the dominion of sin.

Next was the burnt offering, which recognized the devotion of a heart that has been cleansed and is now open, accepting, and dedicated to God.

Finally came the grain offering, which represents the presentation of our humanity to God. All of this renders the leper clean from his leprous disease, and even his relationships are cleansed, and so he is free to enter normal life once again.

What do these offerings mean? They are all symbolically significant, and all of them except the grain offering involve the shedding of blood. The blood in these sacrifices is always a picture of guilt removed, of evil ended. The blood is applied to remove the offense of the ear, the hand, and the foot. Those who are infected with the leprosy within have listened to false philosophies, so the ear must be cleansed. They have manipulated and maneuvered and committed other evil deeds, so the hand must be cleansed. Their feet have gone down sinful paths, so their walk must be cleansed.

The great teaching of this passage is that the blood of the guilt offering cleanses the sinner. When there is a spot of sin in your life and you confess it and its action has been halted by the repentance of your heart, then God applies the blood of His Son to you so that your sin is cleansed away. All of the members of your flesh that have engaged in sin are cleansed—your ear, your hand, your walk. You are forgiven.

Notice, next, that in addition to the blood, oil is also applied to those same members of the body—the ear, hand, and toe. Oil is the symbol of the Holy Spirit. The blood is only the first step—the step that leads to our salvation from sin. The next step is that we must apply the oil; we must yield ourselves to the Spirit of God. The oil is placed on the ear and the thumb and the foot in order that the mind may now be devoted to hearing the things of the Spirit, that the hand may be offered to the service of God, and that the walk may follow the leading of the Spirit.

Once the blood has cleansed and the oil has been applied, symbolizing yieldedness to the Spirit, the leper is ready to return to society. These symbols are beautiful and instructive for our lives.

A young woman, a college student, once approached me for help with a personal problem. "My roommate has the most annoying habits," she said. "She does these irritating things, and I feel resentful toward her. But I know it's wrong to feel that way, so I keep confessing my feelings to God. Yet those feelings of resentment keep coming back. How can I be freed from this?"

I said, "The problem is that you are doing only part of what the Lord tells us to do in situations like this. Yes, we are to confess our sin and ask forgiveness; you are doing the first step. But God also wants us to turn around and make the members of our bodies available to God for His work. We are to offer them to Him for righteous purposes. You are confessing your sinful resentment, but you are not turning around and actively loving your roommate in the power of God. The negative is not enough; we must also do what God requires of us in a positive and proactive way."

In other words, we need not only the blood of Christ to cleanse the sin of the ear, hand, and foot, but we also need the oil of the Holy Spirit to lead the ear, hand, and foot in a new and positive direction. We need to yield ourselves to the Spirit so that He can take over and enable us to reach out to others in love.

The next section shows that God is concerned with the meaning of the sacrifice, not how expensive the sacrifice is. God wants the message and rich symbolism of the cleansing ritual to be available to all, including the poor.

> "If, however, he is poor and cannot afford these, he must take one male lamb as a guilt offering to be waved to make atonement for him, together with a tenth of an ephah of fine flour mixed with oil for a grain offering, a log of oil, and two doves or two young pigeons, which he can afford, one for a sin offering and the other for a burnt offering.
>
> "On the eighth day he must bring them for his cleansing to the priest at the entrance to the Tent of Meeting, before the LORD. The priest is to take the lamb for the guilt offering, together with the log

of oil, and wave them before the LORD as a wave offering. He shall
slaughter the lamb for the guilt offering and take some of its blood
and put it on the lobe of the right ear of the one to be cleansed, on
the thumb of his right hand and on the big toe of his right foot. The
priest is to pour some of the oil into the palm of his own left hand,
and with his right forefinger sprinkle some of the oil from his palm
seven times before the LORD. Some of the oil in his palm he is to put
on the same places he put the blood of the guilt offering—on the
lobe of the right ear of the one to be cleansed, on the thumb of his
right hand and on the big toe of his right foot. The rest of the oil in
his palm the priest shall put on the head of the one to be cleansed,
to make atonement for him before the LORD. Then he shall sacrifice
the doves or the young pigeons, which the person can afford, one
as a sin offering and the other as a burnt offering, together with the
grain offering. In this way the priest will make atonement before the
LORD on behalf of the one to be cleansed."

These are the regulations for anyone who has an infectious skin
disease and who cannot afford the regular offerings for his cleansing
(Leviticus 14:21–32).

The symbolism in this section yields the same rich Christ-centered message
as the previous section—but it does so in a way that is within reach of even the
poorest people of Israel.

## THE SOLUTION FOR SICK HOUSES

The final section of Leviticus 14 deals with the issue of contamination in the
houses of the people of Israel. We read:

The LORD said to Moses and Aaron, "When you enter the land
of Canaan, which I am giving you as your possession, and I put a
spreading mildew in a house in that land, the owner of the house
must go and tell the priest, 'I have seen something that looks like
mildew in my house.' The priest is to order the house to be emptied
before he goes in to examine the mildew, so that nothing in the
house will be pronounced unclean. After this the priest is to go in

and inspect the house. He is to examine the mildew on the walls, and if it has greenish or reddish depressions that appear to be deeper than the surface of the wall, the priest shall go out the doorway of the house and close it up for seven days. On the seventh day the priest shall return to inspect the house. If the mildew has spread on the walls, he is to order that the contaminated stones be torn out and thrown into an unclean place outside the town. He must have all the inside walls of the house scraped and the material that is scraped off dumped into an unclean place outside the town. Then they are to take other stones to replace these and take new clay and plaster the house.

"If the mildew reappears in the house after the stones have been torn out and the house scraped and plastered, the priest is to go and examine it and, if the mildew has spread in the house, it is a destructive mildew; the house is unclean. It must be torn down— its stones, timbers and all the plaster—and taken out of the town to an unclean place.

"Anyone who goes into the house while it is closed up will be unclean till evening. Anyone who sleeps or eats in the house must wash his clothes.

"But if the priest comes to examine it and the mildew has not spread after the house has been plastered, he shall pronounce the house clean, because the mildew is gone. To purify the house he is to take two birds and some cedar wood, scarlet yarn and hyssop. He shall kill one of the birds over fresh water in a clay pot. Then he is to take the cedar wood, the hyssop, the scarlet yarn and the live bird, dip them into the blood of the dead bird and the fresh water, and sprinkle the house seven times. He shall purify the house with the bird's blood, the fresh water, the live bird, the cedar wood, the hyssop and the scarlet yarn. Then he is to release the live bird in the open fields outside the town. In this way he will make atonement for the house, and it will be clean" (Leviticus 14:33–53).

Here, God instructs the people of Israel to use the same procedure to cleanse a house as to cleanse a human leper. Though we are dealing with mildews and molds and fungi, the kinds of things which can appear on the walls of a house, these growing infections are symbolically identical to the infection of leprosy in a human being. I have been in the tropics and have seen plaster walls that were covered with green mold, and I can tell you that it truly does appear is if the house has a disease such as leprosy.

We have seen that these instructions for dealing with infected people and contaminated objects all have symbolic meaning for our lives. What, then, does a mildew-infected house symbolize for us today?

Remember that the New Testament calls the church "God's household" or "the house of God" (see 1 Timothy 3:15; Hebrews 10:21). This, of course is not a reference to a church building but to the true dwelling place of God—His people. So when we see a house used in Leviticus, what does it symbolize? Clearly, it is an assembly of God's people. Today, we know that assembly as the church. And the church, like a house, can become contaminated and infected in such a way that it resembles leprosy. When God's church becomes infected, it must be cleansed. This sometimes requires drastic treatment.

God lays out a process of dealing with a house that has a stubborn mildew contamination. The contaminated stones must be torn out and discarded in a trash dump outside of town; then the walls must be scraped clean and new stones and plaster must be used to repair the house and replace the discarded material. And if the mildew reappears even after these measures have been undertaken, then the house must be declared unclean, and it must be dismantled and the stones and timbers must be sent to the trash dump.

We see this principle at work in the New Testament where Paul writes to the Corinthian church about an infection of immorality in the church. There was a man in the church who was living incestuously with his father's wife, his step-mother (see 1 Corinthians 5:1–5). The situation was so scandalous that even the pagans in the city were offended. Yet many of the Corinthian Christians were boasting about how broad-minded they were!

Paul replied, "And you are proud! Shouldn't you rather have been filled with grief and have put out of your fellowship the man who did this?" In other words, Paul told them they should remove the offender from their midst, just as God had told the people of Israel to remove contaminated stones from their homes. Paul went on to reprove the Corinthian Christians for other wrongs they had allowed to arise—so he was scraping their contaminated plaster, too!

When Paul wrote his second letter to the Corinthians, he used a different tone. The severe treatment had its desired effect—a cleansing effect. The house—the church in Corinth—was preserved. In fact, God graciously restored the lost stone; the man who had sinned with his father's wife repented and was reinstated in the house of God.

What God pictures for us in this section of Leviticus is church discipline. Sometimes, disciplinary action must be exercised in the church in order to arrest a contagious infection and prevent it from spreading to the other members of the church. If the infection is not halted, a day will come when the entire house must be destroyed. This is pictured for us by the house with the infection that will not go away and which must be torn down, every stone and every timber, and disposed of outside of town.

In the opening chapters of Revelation are seven letters from the Lord Jesus to seven churches in Asia. In those letters, the Lord, as the Great High Priest, examines seven of His houses. In each one He sees certain things that are wrong and need to be corrected. He gives careful directions as to what must take place in order to resolve the problem. In each case He says that a failure to heed His warning will result in judgment—the uncleansed house will be broken down and will cease to have a testimony in the community where it lives.

This is what God does when Christians fail to remove the contamination of sin in their midst. The house is broken down, and the testimony disappears. If the people in the church will not clean their house, God will clean it for them—and leave nothing standing.

The chapter goes on to make provision for the ceremonial cleansing of a house in which the contamination has been arrested. Once again, God uses the symbol of two birds—one slain, the other dipped in the blood then released to the heavens. This ritual depicts the death and resurrection of the Lord Jesus Christ as the only basis upon which the church, the house of God, can be cleansed.

The final lines of Leviticus 14 reveal once more God's tender concern and compassion for His people.

> These are the regulations for any infectious skin disease, for an itch,
> for mildew in clothing or in a house, and for a swelling, a rash or
> a bright spot, to determine when something is clean or unclean.

These are the regulations for infectious skin diseases and mildew (Leviticus 14:54–57).

God wants every spot to be examined, because it could be harmful to the individual or to the community. This is true whether we are speaking of a spot of leprosy on the body, a spot of mildew on a garment or the wall of a house, or a spot of immorality in a human life or in the church. God loves His people, and He instructs us so that we may be protected from the things that corrupt and destroy.

Once again, we see that God desires our wholeness and our holiness, which are truly one and the same thing. He wants us to be able to clearly distinguish between that which is harmful and that which is wholesome and holy. As the key verse of Leviticus tells us, God tells us: "You are to be holy to me because I, the LORD, am holy, and I have set you apart from the nations to be my own" (Leviticus 20:26).

God calls us to be whole people, for He is a whole Person. He calls us to look at our attitudes, our habits, our relationships, and our behavior. Where we see unhealthiness and contamination, He calls us to healing and cleansing. So let us heed His call on our lives. Let us examine ourselves and invite others in the priesthood of all believers to examine our lives. Let us be healed and restored, cleansed and renewed, whole and holy, for we serve a whole and holy God.

※————————※

# CHAPTER 15

# THE MOST FEARED CHAPTER IN LEVITICUS

## LEVITICUS 15

TODAY WE COME to the famous fifteenth chapter of Leviticus. One Sunday, while I was in the middle of a series of messages on Leviticus, a member of the congregation came to me after church and said, "Pastor, I'm fearful."

I said, "Fearful of what?"

He said, "I am a little afraid of what you're going to say when you come to the fifteenth chapter of Leviticus!"

What is it about Leviticus 15 that makes some Christians feel anxious and concerned? Answer: Bodily functions. Even in this anything-goes media age in which we live, when almost every taboo has been broken on television, radio, and in the movies, people still feel uncomfortable to find these matters discussed in their Bibles. Many Christians feel these matters are so personal and private that it is not proper to refer to them in public. My reply is this: If God didn't intend Leviticus 15 to be read, He would not have written it.

The book of Proverbs assures us that "every word of God is pure" (Proverbs 30:5 KJV). There is nothing immoral, indecent, or unclean about any portion of Scripture, even though it often deals with the immorality, indecency, and uncleanness of human beings and the human condition. If the Holy Spirit of

God, who inspired the Bible, is guilty of poor taste, then what is the measure of good taste?

When it comes to Leviticus 15, our attitudes need to be corrected. It is the Word of God that judges and corrects our lives; it is not we who judge and correct the Word of God. If the Bible offends us, then we should reexamine our prudishness and hypersensitivity. The Bible looks at the human body with a wonderful frankness, and its treatment of the functions of the body is candid but never vulgar.

Like many Christians, I was raised under a Victorian morality which assumed that the human body ended at the waist—nothing below that point should ever be mentioned. Today, of course, that Victorian morality has almost vanished, to be replaced by an extreme and shocking permissiveness in matters of sexual and bodily functions. I suspect that much of that permissiveness is the direct result of an overreaction to the old Victorian prudery.

The human race seems incapable of ever finding a balanced approach toward the human body. Throughout history, the pendulum has swung from one extreme to the other but has never really settled at that balanced view that God expresses in His Word. God, of course, created our bodies and our sex drive, and He pronounced it good. There is nothing sinful or shameful about the way we are constructed, the way our bodies function, or with a frank discussion of such matters. When we read in Leviticus 15 of such matters as menstruation, seminal emissions, or the normal discharges of elimination, there is no need for us to blush or feel embarrassed. If we do, it is a sign that we need to adjust to reality.

## Sound Sanitary Precautions

I am reminded of the time I was discharged from the United States Navy at the end of World War II. Every soldier and sailor leaving military service had to undergo a physical examination. There were over two hundred men gathered in one building, all stripped naked. We stood in line and passed by a series of doctors who gave us an extremely thorough examination. At one point, as we approached a particularly humbling and embarrassing part of the examination, the man next in line to me remarked, "I just can't get over how many things the United States Navy is interested in!"

As we come to this chapter, we marvel at how many aspects of our lives God is interested in. You can't read Leviticus without seeing how intimately God is concerned with His people. He regulates their food, clothing, and activities for the sake of their health and happiness. He gives advice on every matter of life. Those who accuse God of being remote and unconcerned about the human race need only to read Leviticus to get a very different impression. No wonder the Lord Jesus said to His disciples, "Indeed, the very hairs of your head are all numbered" (Luke 12:7). Everything about us is of great concern to our heavenly Father.

We will also see, as we look at these various bodily functions from God's perspective, that there are still more symbols and pictures that relate to spiritual realities in our lives today. The chapter divides into sections. Leviticus 15:1–18 deals with bodily functions concerning men; Leviticus 15:19–30 deal with bodily functions of women; Leviticus 15:31–33 forms a brief summary. The first problem addressed in this passage deals with bodily discharges associated with certain diseases.

> The LORD said to Moses and Aaron, "Speak to the Israelites and say to them: 'When any man has a bodily discharge, the discharge is unclean. Whether it continues flowing from his body or is blocked, it will make him unclean. This is how his discharge will bring about uncleanness'" (Leviticus 15:1–3).

When people get sick, they experience bodily discharges such as diarrhea and runny noses. God is concerned for His people, and He wants them to avoid spreading these illnesses from person to person, so He set up rules of cleanliness and quarantine to prevent the spread of disease throughout His people.

> "'Any bed the man with a discharge lies on will be unclean, and anything he sits on will be unclean. Anyone who touches his bed must wash his clothes and bathe with water, and he will be unclean till evening. Whoever sits on anything that the man with a discharge sat on must wash his clothes and bathe with water, and he will be unclean till evening.
>
> "'Whoever touches the man who has a discharge must wash his clothes and bathe with water, and he will be unclean till evening.

"'If the man with the discharge spits on someone who is clean, that person must wash his clothes and bathe with water, and he will be unclean till evening.

"'Everything the man sits on when riding will be unclean, and whoever touches any of the things that were under him will be unclean till evening; whoever picks up those things must wash his clothes and bathe with water, and he will be unclean till evening.

"'Anyone the man with a discharge touches without rinsing his hands with water must wash his clothes and bathe with water, and he will be unclean till evening.

"'A clay pot that the man touches must be broken, and any wooden article is to be rinsed with water'" (Leviticus 15:4–12).

It is important for us to remember the people of that day had no understanding of such matters as bacteria and viruses and the transmission of infectious diseases. When they heard and followed these instructions, it was all a matter of ritual to them. They followed these practices as a matter of religious ceremony, not as a matter of scientific understanding or sanitary precaution.

So it is all the more amazing that the procedures described in these chapters are almost exactly the same procedures used in hospitals today to prevent the spread of contagious diseases. In today's health care environment, the objects touched by a sick person are considered unclean and need to be sterilized or disposed of before they can be used by other people. Those who come in contact with a sick person must wash and remove the contamination that could spread the disease. These practices were anticipated in a book written some seventeen or eighteen centuries before Christ and were imposed upon God's people by their heavenly Father in order to safeguard them from plagues and epidemics that were rampant in the ancient world.

When God called His people out of Egypt, He promised them, "If you listen carefully to the voice of the LORD your God and do what is right in his eyes, if you pay attention to his commands and keep all his decrees, I will not bring on you any of the diseases I brought on the Egyptians, for I am the LORD, who heals you" (Exodus 15:26). This is the way God fulfilled His promise. He instructed them in procedures of sanitizing and quarantining, to prevent the spread of contagious disease.

These restrictions and regulations saved the nation of Israel from many dangerous plagues which decimated the pagan populations around them. I suspect that these health guidelines from God are a major reason that Israel has been preserved as a nation throughout the centuries.

## SEX AND SYMBOLISM

Once a person was relieved of these discharges and cleansed, he was to offer a sacrificial offering, as we have seen in earlier instances in Leviticus.

"'When a man is cleansed from his discharge, he is to count off seven days for his ceremonial cleansing; he must wash his clothes and bathe himself with fresh water, and he will be clean. On the eighth day he must take two doves or two young pigeons and come before the LORD to the entrance to the Tent of Meeting and give them to the priest. The priest is to sacrifice them, the one for a sin offering and the other for a burnt offering. In this way he will make atonement before the LORD for the man because of his discharge'" (Leviticus 15:13–15).

The illnesses referred to here were of a much less serious nature than the disease of leprosy which was addressed in Leviticus 12 and Leviticus 13. The healed leper had to undergo a much more rigorous cleansing ceremony than we see here, involving a series of offerings. In Leviticus 15, however, the simplest of the offerings is prescribed: two turtledoves or two young pigeons, one for a sin offering, one for a burnt offering. This is the least expensive and most readily available of the offerings.

Notice, however, that God never sets aside the requirement for the blood of an innocent substitute. By this means, God underscores the fact that human nature needs to be dealt with by blood, by a life being poured out. Our defilement and contamination is a deep and complicated problem. Throughout Leviticus, God constantly underscores the need for a blood sacrifice, because He continually points His people toward the sacrifice of Jesus.

Next, God deals with a second type of bodily discharge which involves male sexuality.

"'When a man has an emission of semen, he must bathe his whole body with water, and he will be unclean till evening. Any clothing or leather that has semen on it must be washed with water, and it will be unclean till evening. When a man lies with a woman and there is an emission of semen, both must bathe with water, and they will be unclean till evening'" (Leviticus 15:16–18).

Here, God deals with the emission of semen in the context of married sex. It is important to understand that this passage does not suggest in any way that sex in marriage is immoral or dirty. Why, then, does God require the man and woman to bathe? Why are they to be considered "unclean till evening"?

This is simply God's reminder of the fact that human nature is fallen and polluted by sin and that our fallen nature is passed on even as a man passes his semen to a woman and a child is conceived. The child that is the product of that sex act will have the same fallen and sinful nature that the parents were born with. The symbolism of the washing and ceremonial uncleanness speak of our desperate need for a Savior—yet the marital sex act itself is holy, moral, and good.

## What Makes Us "Unclean"

Next, God deals with the intimate issues of a woman's body. Leviticus 15:19–30 deals with the monthly menstrual flow of women and with problems caused by diseases.

> "When a woman has her regular flow of blood, the impurity of her monthly period will last seven days, and anyone who touches her will be unclean till evening.
>
> "Anything she lies on during her period will be unclean, and anything she sits on will be unclean. Whoever touches her bed must wash his clothes and bathe with water, and he will be unclean till evening. Whoever touches anything she sits on must wash his clothes and bathe with water, and he will be unclean till evening. Whether it is the bed or anything she was sitting on, when anyone touches it, he will be unclean till evening.
>
> "If a man lies with her and her monthly flow touches him, he will be unclean for seven days; any bed he lies on will be unclean.
>
> "When a woman has a discharge of blood for many days at a time other than her monthly period or has a discharge that

continues beyond her period, she will be unclean as long as she has the discharge, just as in the days of her period. Any bed she lies on while her discharge continues will be unclean, as is her bed during her monthly period, and anything she sits on will be unclean, as during her period. Whoever touches them will be unclean; he must wash his clothes and bathe with water, and he will be unclean till evening.

"'When she is cleansed from her discharge, she must count off seven days, and after that she will be ceremonially clean. On the eighth day she must take two doves or two young pigeons and bring them to the priest at the entrance to the Tent of Meeting. The priest is to sacrifice one for a sin offering and the other for a burnt offering. In this way he will make atonement for her before the LORD for the uncleanness of her discharge.'"

Again, in these references to ceremonial uncleanness, to bathing and cleansing and sacrifices, God is not suggesting that there is anything morally wrong or dirty about this female function. The symbolic significance and the offerings are exactly the same as when a man has an emission of semen. Here again, God uses this regular monthly function as a reminder of our human need for a sacrifice that cleanses us and removes our defilement. God continually points the attention of His people toward Jesus, who was offered for our sins.

The primary significance of this section of Leviticus is not the issue of physical hygiene but the spiritual and symbolic meaning of these issues. God gave us these pictures in the Old Testament to remind us of our spiritual need for God and for a Savior. This is what Paul meant when he wrote to the Christians in Rome, "For everything that was written in the past was written to teach us, so that through endurance and the encouragement of the Scriptures we might have hope" (Romans 15:4).

We don't have to guess at the spiritual application God intended for this passage, because Jesus Himself made those applications clear. He said, "Listen to me, everyone, and understand this. Nothing outside a man can make him 'unclean' by going into him. Rather, it is what comes out of a man that makes him 'unclean'" (Mark 7:14–15). Mark added a parenthetical comment: "(In saying this, Jesus declared all foods 'clean')." Jesus is telling us that nothing we eat or drink can defile us, either ceremonially and morally. There are no unclean foods. There may be dangerous food, even poisonous food, but it is not unclean in a moral sense. It is what comes out of us that defiles us.

Jesus makes it clear that He is speaking in a moral and spiritual sense; He is not referring to physical, bodily discharges. He goes on to say, "What comes out of a man is what makes him 'unclean.' For from within, out of men's hearts, come evil thoughts, sexual immorality, theft, murder, adultery, greed, malice, deceit, lewdness, envy, slander, arrogance and folly. All these evils come from inside and make a man 'unclean'" (Mark 7:20–23). That is the Lord's commentary on Leviticus 15. He is lifting our eyes from the merely physical level to the level of the soul and spirit, the level on which we are to live before God.

Jesus tells us that it is our sins that defile the human spirit, the human tabernacle in which the Spirit of God has taken up residence. Some of these sins, such as murder, adultery, and theft, are acts that decent people generally find unthinkable. But Jesus also lists sins that are common to us all, even Christians: evil thoughts, greed, malice, deceit, lewdness, envy, slander, arrogance, and folly. Even the most devoted and spiritual-minded of believers wrestles with these sins. They come out of us without planning or premeditation. They flow from our fallen nature, even though we are believers and have a new relationship with Christ.

What are we to do about these sins? Are we to merely ignore them? No, for our sins will add up against us and stack up in our subconscious if we do not deal with them. Our guilt will increase, and a sense of shame and restlessness will enter our spirits. Eventually a coldness will settle over our hearts, extinguishing the fire of our passion for God and the warmth of our love for others. That is what happens when we repeatedly defile the sanctuary of this human tabernacle in which we dwell.

So God has provided a remedy. First, a person who is defiled shall bathe. As we have already seen, washing is always a picture of the action of the Word of God. The individual shall consult God's Word and see what God has to say about each defiling deed, thought, statement, tone of voice, and attitude of heart. The washing of the Word is the beginning of cleansing.

What does God mean when He says, "and he will be unclean till evening"? We have seen this phrase all through Leviticus, and we need to know what it conforms to in our spiritual experience. In the Old Testament, we see that there were two ways that people could be rejected, by God and by the nation of Israel, as a result of their sin. First, they could be called "unclean" by God. Second, they could be "cut off" from the people and be called an "abomination" before the Lord.

To put this in New Testament terms, to be unclean would correspond to what we call being out of fellowship. It means to pull back from dependence upon the Spirit of God and to choose to live, in a momentary sense, according to the flesh and the old nature. There is a break in communion with the Spirit of God so that the flow of the life of Christ in the believer is temporarily arrested. Although Christ doesn't forsake that individual for even a moment, that individual has lost something—the joy that comes from being in fellowship with Jesus Christ. That is what it means to be unclean.

To be cut off from the people corresponds to what the New Testament calls apostasy. Apostasy is the state of having moved so far from the core principles of one's faith that one must be set aside by God and the church. This is sometimes expressed as being "handed over to Satan." In 1 Corinthians 5:5, Paul speaks of a man living an openly immoral lifestyle, and he says, "Hand this man over to Satan, so that the sinful nature may be destroyed and his spirit saved on the day of the Lord." And in 1 Timothy 1:20, Paul refers to "Hymenaeus and Alexander, whom I have handed over to Satan to be taught not to blaspheme." If he or she is allowed to continue on the path of apostasy, a person will ultimately become an enemy of the faith and of Jesus Christ.

Uncleanness, being less serious, is a condition that lasts until evening and then is considered to be ended. The words "and he will be unclean till evening" are instructive for us because, among the Hebrews, the day began at sunset. When evening comes, a new day begins. So the uncleanness continued until a new beginning, until the sun set and a new day began. There is a spiritual counterpart of this new beginning at sunset. In the spiritual life, we experience a new beginning when we repent of our fleshly way of life and return to a place of trust in God and obedience to the Holy Spirit. The Spirit is the Lord of creation, so restored fellowship with Him results in a new beginning.

This new beginning takes place whenever we repent, change our minds, and stop defending and excusing our sinful thoughts, words, and actions. Until we repent and become renewed in our trust and obedience to God, we remain unclean. That is how contamination gradually creeps into our soul and spirit, defiling the sanctuary in which God chooses to dwell. In this passage in Leviticus, God teaches that we must deal with the uncleanness that occasionally defiles our lives, and we must continually renew our relationship with Him.

## THE WATER AND THE BLOOD

It is important for us to notice that cleansing comes through the offering of blood. All through Leviticus, we find that God's cleansing agents are water and blood. The apostle John tells us, "This is the one who came by water and blood—Jesus Christ. He did not come by water only, but by water and blood" (1 John 5:6). Jesus came to cleanse us in this twofold way.

The blood speaks of the death of Jesus on our behalf, which frees God to love us without any restraint whatsoever. The blood is what God really sees. The blood of the innocent Substitute pays the debt of our guilt and thus God is vindicated in His justice. God has poured out upon Another all the horrible wrath which He has in His holy nature against sin, so that the world can see that God means it when He says that He hates sin.

The water speaks of the washing of the Word. God's Word cleanses our conscience. You can say, "Yes, God has forgiven me," yet many people who say that fail to go on and forgive themselves. They don't allow their conscience to be cleansed. But when we read in the Word of God that Jesus has washed away our sins and cleansed us from all unrighteousness (see Acts 22:16; 1 John 1:9), and when we believe what God's Word tells us, then our conscience is cleansed, and we are clean indeed.

We often quote 1 John 1:9 while failing to truly apply its meaning to our lives: "If we confess our sins, he is faithful and just and will forgive us our sins and purify us from all unrighteousness." When we read those words, we need to experience God's cleansing by saying to ourselves, "If God said that, He must mean it. So I have to stop beating myself up over sins that God has forgiven and forgotten. God has cleansed me, so I am clean indeed." That is the effect of the water, the washing of God's Word.

The water and the blood work together, cleansing the conscience and freeing us from guilt before the justice of God. He has designed this process to keep us free from contamination, so that we can truly live for Him.

"'You must keep the Israelites separate from things that make them unclean, so they will not die in their uncleanness for defiling my dwelling place, which is among them.'" These are the regulations for a man with a discharge, for anyone made unclean by an emission of semen, for a woman in her monthly period, for a man or a woman with a discharge, and for a man who lies with a woman who is ceremonially unclean (Leviticus 15:31–33).

God is careful to ensure that we walk in a way that will allow Him to pour out to us the fullness of His glory, joy, and peace. When we fail to experience these qualities in our lives, it is often because we have allowed contamination into our lives and remain uncleansed. We didn't intend to rebel against God or sin against God. But we allowed unclean thoughts, attitudes, words, and actions to creep into our lifestyle, and we failed to cleanse ourselves.

If we are to truly live for God and enjoy His presence in our lives, we must be cleansed. We must deal regularly with the sins that so easily sneak into our lives and contaminate us. Many young Christians, in particular, struggle in this area. They start their Christian adventure filled with joy and enthusiasm. After a while, however, their Christian experience seems to go stale, and they don't know why. They have not yet learned to deal with the unavoidable discharges and unclean emissions of their lives—the hurtful things they think, say, and do.

As we learn to apply God's remedy, the sanctuary of our lives will be cleansed. Our humanity—body, soul, and spirit—will be transformed into a clean and fitting dwelling place for the Spirit of God.

# CHAPTER 16

# THE DAY OF ATONEMENT
## LEVITICUS 16

WHEN AN EARTHLY father sits down to figure out the family budget, he usually puts aside so much for rent, so much for food and clothing, so much for recreation, and the like. Our heavenly Father, however, works in a very different way. When He determines the essentials for our lives and makes provision for them, He sets aside so much for love, so much for joy, so much for peace, forgiveness, companionship, understanding, and guidance. These are the essentials as God sees them.

Remember that in the Sermon on the Mount, when our Lord Jesus set forth the secrets of life, He listed all the things people seek in life. Then He added, "So do not worry, saying, 'What shall we eat?' or 'What shall we drink?' or 'What shall we wear?' For the pagans run after all these things, and your heavenly Father knows that you need them. But seek first his kingdom and his righteousness, and all these things will be given to you as well" (Matthew 6:31–33).

We are so quick to reverse God's priorities! We spend most of our time and energy thinking about how to get money to provide food and clothing and so on, and we leave hardly any time for what God considers the essentials. No wonder our lives are frequently out of order. In Leviticus 16, God calls us to put our lives back in balance. He calls us to place a priority on our relationships with one another and on experiencing the love, joy, and peace He offers us. If that is our focus, then all the other things we need will come to us through the normal processes of living this life.

Leviticus 16 is the concluding chapter of the first great section of this book. We have already seen what a wonderful, caring, compassionate heavenly Father we have. He is intimately concerned with every detail of life, even matters of diet and clothing and how to treat diseases and contamination of our possessions and dwellings. Even more important, these details of our physical life have counterparts and parallels in our spiritual life. So these practical guidelines for healthy living are also a tremendous encouragement for us to walk in faith and to draw upon God's infinite resources.

## OUR LONGING FOR ATONEMENT

As we have studied Leviticus together, we have seen that God wants us to see, first, our need for a substitute. Despite all of our accumulated psychological and scientific knowledge, we cannot handle life by ourselves. So, through the sacrificial offerings, God tells us that He has provided a Substitute who, through the shedding of His blood, can take away the entire weight of our sins. Our substitute is Jesus Christ.

Then, because we don't understand the mysteries of our existence apart from someone who can explain them and apply them to us, we also need a Great High Priest. This need is also met in Christ.

And then we need a standard by which to measure our lives and our actions, so that we can know the difference between wholesome and harmful, between good and bad. We need God's revealed Word in order to understand what confronts us in life, so we can distinguish right from wrong. Discerning that difference is not always easy, but God has provided a standard.

Finally, we come to the event called the Day of Atonement—a day that is called *Yom Kippur* in Israel and which is still the high point of the Jewish year. Within every human being is a hunger and a cry for atonement—for a wonderful sense of reconciliation between ourselves and God. It is the cry of the human spirit for the face of God. It seems that a part of us can never forget that once we humans walked in daily fellowship with God, in the cool of the garden He had made for us. We still long for that special relationship with the One who made us, and no human relationship can quite satisfy that yearning. As the psalmist wrote:

> My heart says of you, "Seek his face!"
>     Your face, LORD, I will seek.
> Do not hide your face from me,
>     do not turn your servant away in anger;
>     you have been my helper.
> Do not reject me or forsake me,
>     O God my Savior (Psalm 27:8–9).

Our sins and shameful secrets are like a dark cloud that hides the shining face of God. Our guilty memories come back to haunt us and disturb our conscience. But God wants to restore in us a clear conscience—a sense that we are forgiven by God, by other people, and by ourselves for anything and everything we have ever done wrong.

I have seen so many Christians struggling over this issue. They say, "I know that God has forgiven me. I know that His Word is true, that Jesus has paid the debt for my sins. Yet I still feel guilty, and I am ashamed to keep coming to God with failure after failure—I feel so unworthy." This is one of Satan's favorite ways of attacking us.

To solve this problem, God has provided a special Day of Atonement. Here, God settles the guilt issue once and for all, so that we never need to feel ashamed or excluded from the presence of God. We read:

> The LORD spoke to Moses after the death of the two sons of Aaron who died when they approached the LORD. The LORD said to Moses: "Tell your brother Aaron not to come whenever he chooses into the Most Holy place behind the curtain in front of the atonement cover on the ark, or else he will die, because I appear in the cloud over the atonement cover" (Leviticus 16:1–2).

No greater privilege was ever given to Aaron the high priest than to go before the presence of God in the Holy of Holies. There he stood in the shining presence of the Shekinah glory of God, which hovered over the mercy seat. Now, however, God says, in effect, "Don't come at all times. Come only once a year." This limitation came as a result of the fear in the hearts of Aaron and the rest of the priests after the death of Aaron's two sons.

As we saw in Leviticus 10, Aaron's sons Nadab and Abihu brought "strange fire" before the Lord and were suddenly consumed by a flash of flame from the Shekinah glory. Understandably, this tragedy filled Aaron and his remaining two sons with fear.

I have often suspected that the priests of old, when they realized that they were dealing with a God of righteousness and justice, were so careful to do all that God prescribed in the Law that they probably had checklists, just like the ones airline pilots use before takeoff! I know that I wouldn't want to go into the presence of God without making sure I had dotted every *i* and crossed every *t* of the Law.

Here, God gives a special once-a-year provision by which the whole nation, represented by the high priest, could come boldly, fearlessly into the presence of God Himself. On one day every year, the high priest could confidently enter the Holy of Holies. As we shall see, this is a picture for us of what we are to do continuously in Christ.

## A GOAT FOR THE LORD, A GOAT FOR SATAN

There were a number of steps the high priest had to follow on the Day of Atonement. The first step deals with the washing of the high priest and the garment he was to wear.

> "This is how Aaron is to enter the sanctuary area: with a young bull for a sin offering and a ram for a burnt offering. He is to put on the sacred linen tunic, with linen undergarments next to his body; he is to tie the linen sash around him and put on the linen turban. These are sacred garments; so he must bathe himself with water before he puts them on" (Leviticus 16:3–4).

The high priest was to bathe himself and put on the linen tunic (we saw what these priestly garments symbolized in Leviticus 8). Normally, the high priest wore a number of symbolic items of clothing: The robe of beauty with bells around the hem went over the linen tunic. On top of the robe was placed the ephod, a sort of vest; over that went the breastplate. But all of the outer garments were laid aside when the priest went in to the Holy of Holies. In that special place, the high priest wore only the linen tunic.

You may have heard preachers describe how, when the high priest entered the Holy of Holies, the people outside listened for the tinkling of bells on the hem of his robe so they would know if the high priest were alive or not. I have heard many sermons describe this scene with great dramatic emphasis. In fact, however, this never happened. The high priest did not wear the robe with the bells on the hem when he entered the Holy of Holies. He wore only the linen tunic. This shows that there are, unfortunately, many preachers who have not read this passage with sufficient care!

As we have already seen, the linen tunic was a picture of the personal, private righteousness of the Lord Jesus—the inner righteousness which only God could see. In the entire life of our Lord upon the earth, there was not one moment when His inner righteousness ever faltered—it was always perfect. He never yielded to temptation. He never gave in to sinful thoughts. He experienced every temptation we do, but never once did He give way to sin. This is God's way of teaching us that as we come before His presence, we are to come clothed with the inner righteousness of Jesus Christ, so that our inner life is as acceptable to God as the outer life. Both have been cleansed by the blood of Christ upon the cross.

Next, the high priest must offer a sacrifice as an atonement for his sins and the sins of his family.

> "From the Israelite community he is to take two male goats for a sin
> offering and a ram for a burnt offering.
> "Aaron is to offer the bull for his own sin offering to make atone-
> ment for himself and his household" (Leviticus 16:5–6).

Aaron, of course, was not like Christ. He was not without sin. As the high priest, he was a symbol of Christ, but in the reality of his life, he was a sinful human being just like you and me. So he had to offer sacrifices for himself. Our Lord, however, needed no sacrifice for Himself. As the writer to the Hebrews tells us:

> Unlike the other high priests, he does not need to offer sacrifices
> day after day, first for his own sins, and then for the sins of the peo-
> ple. He sacrificed for their sins once for all when he offered himself
> (Hebrews 7:27).

Then God issues a requirement regarding the two male goats that were mentioned in Leviticus 16:5.

> "Then he is to take the two goats and present them before the LORD at the entrance to the Tent of Meeting. He is to cast lots for the two goats—one lot for the LORD and the other for the scapegoat" (Leviticus 16:7–8).

The Hebrew word translated "scapegoat" in this verse was *azazel*. Many scholars have debated the meaning of *azazel*. Some say the word literally means "the goat of removal," but others believe that Azazel is one of the names for Satan. If we treat this word as one of the names for Satan, then the text reads, "He is to cast lots for the two goats—one lot for the Lord and the other for Satan." This, I believe, is the correct translation, and we will explore the meaning of this strange statement in a moment.

The fate of the two goats is decided by lot—which is akin to the flip of a coin or the roll of a die. We read:

> "Aaron shall bring the goat whose lot falls to the LORD and sacrifice it for a sin offering. But the goat chosen by lot as the scapegoat shall be presented alive before the LORD to be used for making atonement by sending it into the desert as a scapegoat" (Leviticus 16:9–10).

The American Standard Version renders those verses this way:

> And Aaron shall present the goat upon which the lot fell for Jehovah, and offer him for a sin-offering. But the goat, on which the lot fell for Azazel, shall be set alive before Jehovah, to make atonement for him, to send him away for Azazel into the wilderness.

It is important to note that the goat was not named Azazel. Some cults teach that the goat was named Azazel, and therefore it represents Satan; thus, they claim, Satan is the ultimate sin-bearer. This cultic belief is not true, and has no biblical basis. The goat was sent to Satan, and the sins of the people were symbolically placed upon it. Thus, the sins of the people were sent to Satan.

And what of the other goat, the goat that was for the Lord? This goat speaks to us of the fact that God Himself had a stake, a personal investment, in the crucifixion of Jesus. When we consider the death of Jesus, we think of it as taking place on our behalf. We think of the crucifixion as being for our sakes alone—for the sake of our forgiveness. But the goat for the Lord teaches us that God also had a stake in the crucifixion and that God Himself was blessed and glorified in that death.

You see, forgiveness is not an easy thing for God to display. He can't do as many people seem to think He can—look at our evil and say, "Oh, well, that's all right. Forget about it. I love you anyway. Just go on." If that were how we are forgiven, then God would deny His character as a just God. But God is just and, in a very real sense, His justice struggles with His love.

God's justice says, "Everyone who deliberately commits transgressions must be sent away from my presence." Leviticus teaches us this truth again and again. God's justice excludes us from His presence and sends us away. If God were just, and only just, He would wipe out the human race without exception. Not one of us could stand.

But this is where God's justice struggles with His love. God's love doesn't want to see us destroyed. Yet how can His love be expressed unless His justice is satisfied? That is what the death of Christ does. When God's Son hung on the cross, God did not spare Him a thing! God poured out upon Jesus every bit of His wrath against sin. His justice was completely satisfied in the death of His Son upon the cross. Thus God is vindicated.

The whole world can now look at that event and say, "Yes, God is just— even though He loves us." The death of Jesus freed God to show His love to us. Apart from the death of Jesus upon the cross, you and I would never have known of God's mercy, compassion, and forgiving grace. We would never have seen that He is willing to suffer on our behalf. So God Himself is magnified and His character is glorified before the entire world by the death of Jesus. And this is what is portrayed by the goat that was for the Lord. It was on His behalf that this goat was to be sacrificed.

## CLEANSING THE HIGH PRIEST,
## CLEANSING THE TABERNACLE

Next we see the details of how Aaron, the high priest, should sacrifice the bull for his own sins and the sins of his family.

> "Aaron shall bring the bull for his own sin offering to make atonement for himself and his household, and he is to slaughter the bull for his own sin offering. He is to take a censer full of burning coals from the altar before the LORD and two handfuls of finely ground fragrant incense and take them behind the curtain. He is to put the incense on the fire before the LORD, and the smoke of the incense will conceal the atonement cover above the Testimony, so that he will not die. He is to take some of the bull's blood and with his finger sprinkle it on the front of the atonement cover; then he shall sprinkle some of it with his finger seven times before the atonement cover" (Leviticus 16:11–14).

Why does God command Aaron to sprinkle the blood seven times? Because in the Bible, seven was the number of perfection, completion, and absolute satisfaction. The sprinkling of the blood seven times symbolized that the shed blood of Christ is the perfect sacrifice which absolutely, completely satisfied the justice of God.

The sweet-smelling smoke of the incense is also a symbolic message to the human race. By this symbol, God says to us, "The sacrifice of the life of the Lord Jesus on your behalf has rendered you as though you had about you the sweet fragrance of Jesus Himself." When we come before God's presence, He can smell only the sweetness of Christ; He does not smell the rankness of our sin and failure.

This is a vitally important principle for us to understand when we come before God in prayer. One of Satan's strategies for defeating us is to attack us through a guilty conscience, reminding us and accusing us of sins that God has already forgiven and forgotten. He reminds us of the stink of our sins, and he says, "You can't go into the presence of God after the things you've done! God could never accept the prayers of a stinking sinner like you!"

All of those accusations would be true except for one thing—the stench of our sinfulness has been extinguished by the fragrance of Christ. We could never come into the presence of God on the basis of our own righteousness. We can come into His presence on the sole basis of Christ and His shed blood, which has sprinkled us seven times, satisfying God's holy and just demands completely and absolutely. When Satan accuses us of being unacceptable to God, our answer is, "The blood of Jesus covers me completely. When God looks at me, He sees only Christ, and He accepts me and hears my prayers because of what Christ has done for me."

Next we see that the high priest must cleanse not only himself but also the structure of the tabernacle and the altar.

> "He shall then slaughter the goat for the sin offering for the people and take its blood behind the curtain and do with it as he did with the bull's blood: He shall sprinkle it on the atonement cover and in front of it. In this way he will make atonement for the Most Holy Place because of the uncleanness and rebellion of the Israelites, whatever their sins have been. He is to do the same for the Tent of Meeting, which is among them in the midst of their uncleanness. No one is to be in the Tent of Meeting from the time Aaron goes in to make atonement in the Most Holy Place until he comes out, having made atonement for himself, his household and the whole community of Israel.
>
> "Then he shall come out to the altar that is before the LORD and make atonement for it. He shall take some of the bull's blood and some of the goat's blood and put it on all the horns of the altar. He shall sprinkle some of the blood on it with his finger seven times to cleanse it and to consecrate it from the uncleanness of the Israelites" (Leviticus 16:15–19).

The high priest must ceremonially cleanse the entire tabernacle or Tent of Meeting, which symbolically represents our humanity, God's chosen dwelling place. Notice that the high priest must even cleanse the altar and the Holy of Holies, which represents the inner sanctuary of the human spirit. We are the tabernacle in which God dwells. And our whole being—body, soul, and spirit—is cleansed in God's sight by the sacrifice of Jesus on our behalf.

## THE PROBLEM OF DEFILING THOUGHTS

We have all struggled with the problem of evil thoughts that seem to come to us out of nowhere—thoughts that horrify us even while they defile our minds. They might be lustful thoughts, or thoughts of hatred and revenge, or guilty and accusing thoughts about past sins, or fearful worries about future events that will probably never even happen. How can we respond when evil or hurtful thoughts come to us?

Sometimes these thoughts even come to us when we kneel to pray—that's when Satan seems to enjoy attacking us the most! Just as we are opening our hearts to God in prayer, Satan will sometimes whisper an evil suggestion to our minds. Sometimes these thoughts will come to us when we are reaching out to help another person in the name of Jesus—and as we are seeking to serve God and others, Satan will whisper to us a thought of impatience, anger, lust, greed, or resentment. What do we do at such times?

We are tempted to despair. We think, "What's the use? I'm trying to walk in obedience to the Spirit, I'm trying to serve God and fellowship with Him, and even in the very process of lifting my heart to God, an evil thought crosses my mind and I feel defiled!" In this next section of Leviticus, God shows us the provision He has made for such problems.

> "When Aaron has finished making atonement for the Most Holy Place, the Tent of Meeting and the altar, he shall bring forward the live goat. He is to lay both hands on the head of the live goat and confess over it all the wickedness and rebellion of the Israelites—all their sins—and put them on the goat's head. He shall send the goat away into the desert in the care of a man appointed for the task. The goat will carry on itself all their sins to a solitary place; and the man shall release it in the desert" (Leviticus 16:20–22).

The high priest sends the goat back to a solitary place—a symbolic representation of the dwelling place of Azazel, of Satan. This is significant. All the transgressions and sins of the people were placed upon the head of this goat.

It is important to understand that both of these goats are symbolic pictures of Jesus. The slain goat represents Jesus as He was sacrificed to satisfy God's justice. The scapegoat, the goat who bore the sins of the people into the solitary place, represents Jesus as He bore our weight of sin and guilt—all of the evidence that Satan uses as a basis for his accusations against us. All of our sin and guilt has been carried away into the solitary place and dumped at the feet of Satan, where it can no longer be used against us. When our Lord died on the cross, He went into the solitary wilderness of death like this goat, and He returned to Satan all the accusations of all the sins committed by all believers. Our sins have been completely removed from us, and the justice and love of God have been satisfied.

From this Old Testament picture, we gain a practical insight into how we should deal with the accusations and evil thoughts that come to us from Satan. Paul called these satanic attacks "the flaming arrows of the evil one" (Ephesians 6:16). Satan will try to convince us that we are not truly accepted and loved by God, that He still has reservations about us, that we should shrink from God's presence and not go boldly before Him because of our past sins and shame. Satan tries to make us feel unworthy by insinuating filthy or fearful thoughts into our minds.

What should we do when we are assailed by the flaming arrows of Satan? We should place them on the head of Jesus and pray, "Lord, take these thoughts and accusations back to Satan. They don't belong to me. They are not my thoughts. They didn't originate with me. They may feel like my thoughts, but they are not. They belong to the evil one. That is where they came from, and I am sending them back. I know that these thoughts are not held against me in God's sight."

That is the purpose of the great Day of Atonement. The Day of Atonement means that we are to stand and present ourselves before the Lord of Glory and, as Paul says, "in view of God's mercy, to offer your bodies as living sacrifices, holy and pleasing to God—this is your spiritual act of worship" (Romans 12:1).

## THE SABBATH AND WHAT IT MEANS

In the rest of Leviticus 16, God confirms that He accepts us as we offer ourselves to Him as a living sacrifice. In Scripture, the sacrifice of the burnt offering always symbolizes God's total acceptance of a person for whom Jesus Christ has made atonement.

> "Then Aaron is to go into the Tent of Meeting and take off the linen
> garments he put on before he entered the Most Holy Place, and he

is to leave them there. He shall bathe himself with water in a holy place and put on his regular garments. Then he shall come out and sacrifice the burnt offering for himself and the burnt offering for the people, to make atonement for himself and for the people. He shall also burn the fat of the sin offering on the altar.

"The man who releases the goat as a scapegoat must wash his clothes and bathe himself with water; afterward he may come into the camp. The bull and the goat for the sin offerings, whose blood was brought into the Most Holy Place to make atonement, must be taken outside the camp; their hides, flesh and offal are to be burned up. The man who burns them must wash his clothes and bathe himself with water; afterward he may come into the camp" (Leviticus 16:23–28).

In the final verses of Leviticus 16, God concludes His regulations regarding the Day of Atonement by ordaining a day of Sabbath rest.

"This is to be a lasting ordinance for you: On the tenth day of the seventh month you must deny yourselves and not do any work— whether native-born or an alien living among you—because on this day atonement will be made for you, to cleanse you. Then, before the LORD, you will be clean from all your sins. It is a sabbath of rest, and you must deny yourselves; it is a lasting ordinance. The priest who is anointed and ordained to succeed his father as high priest is to make atonement. He is to put on the sacred linen garments and make atonement for the Most Holy Place, for the Tent of Meeting and the altar, and for the priests and all the people of the community.

"This is to be a lasting ordinance for you: Atonement is to be made once a year for all the sins of the Israelites."

And it was done, as the LORD commanded Moses (Leviticus 16:29–34).

A Sabbath is a day of rest. It symbolizes the rest your spirit experiences when you rely not on your works but on the work of Another on your behalf.

It teaches us to recognize the fact that God has cleansed our conscience and we are to rest in that truth. We can relax and rest in the fact that our sense of worth comes not from our accomplishments but from the work that Jesus accomplished on our behalf. God loves us completely, and He has taken care of everything that would exclude us from His presence, including our sin, our guilt, and the accusations of the evil one.

The Sabbath is the fulfillment of the Day of Atonement. It pictures the truth of that great old hymn which expresses our heartfelt prayer of gratitude to the Lord.

> Jesus, I am resting, resting
> In the joy of what Thou art;
> I am finding out the greatness
> Of Thy loving heart.
> Thou hast bid me gaze upon Thee,
> And Thy beauty fills my soul,
> For, by Thy transforming power,
> Thou hast made me whole.

That is what God is after in our lives. He has made us whole and holy, so that we might rest in Him and live daily for Him as His living sacrifices—whole, holy, and pleasing to Him.

# PART TWO

# BASIC HUMAN BEHAVIOR

# CHAPTER 17

# BLOOD AND SEX
## LEVITICUS 17 AND 18

WE NOW COME to the second major section in Leviticus. The first section of the book, which I titled Basic Human Needs, deals with God's provision for His people. In that section, God teaches us through pictures and symbols the same great truths that He teaches to us in plain language in the New Testament.

Paul, in his letter to the Galatians, tells us that "the law was our schoolmaster to bring us unto Christ, that we might be justified by faith" (Galatians 3:24 KJV). A schoolmaster is a teacher, a tutor, an instructor. So the Law—the Ten Commandments, plus the ceremonial law that we have been looking at in Leviticus—was designed to bring us to an understanding of Jesus Christ, His saving work on our behalf, and how we can have His life lived out through us. All of the beautiful imagery of Leviticus was given so that we can experience the reality of Jesus Christ, who is God's provision of life and power for His people.

Now, in the second part of the book, which I call Basic Human Behavior, we learn about the behavior that God expects us to exhibit on the basis of the provision He has made.

Notice the orderly structure of Leviticus. First, God introduces us to the provision He has made for us—Jesus Christ. We see Him in symbol after symbol, picture after picture. Then God gives us the standard of behavior we are to observe. God never reverses that order. He never talks about behavior without first informing us of His provision.

God is not a legalist, as so many believers are today. Legalism places a heavy demand for morality upon people who do not understand how to meet that demand—and that is a deadly requirement. Legalistic Christians either do not understand the power available to them, or they ignore it and try to live moral lives by reliance upon their own self-effort and will power. That is phony Christianity! It has never worked, and it never will.

Legalism has been a destructive force in the church, producing harshness, rigidity, judgmentalism, and sinful religious pride. It has given the church a reputation as a place where people are expected to live up to an unreasonably high standard of moral behavior—a standard that no one truly practices. This is one reason people often say, "I want nothing to do with church—Christians are nothing but hypocrites. They impose their morality on everyone else, but they don't live up to it themselves."

In the Scriptures, God never talks about our behavior until He has first talked about His provision of the power by which we can meet His demands. Only after He shows us His provision of Jesus Christ as our Substitute and Great High Priest does He talk to us about the standards of behavior He expects from us.

## THE TWIN MYSTERIES OF BLOOD AND SEX

Two areas of life were particularly regulated for the people of Israel—their behavior toward blood and their behavior toward sex. Both are great areas of mystery to fallen humanity. We don't understand either one. Because they are mysteries, we are endlessly fascinated with blood and sex, with death and life. The two great themes of all literature, drama, art, film, and song are blood and sex. These themes are flung at us in every conceivable way because they hold a continual fascination for human beings everywhere.

Leviticus 17 deals with the mystery of blood; Leviticus 18 deals with the mystery of sex. So we begin by examining the behavior God requires of the people of Israel with regard to blood. He is very concerned with the subject of blood, and He expends considerable effort to impart some profound truths about the mystery of blood. The first requirement we find is that, in the Levitical sacrifices, all blood must be offered to the Lord.

> The LORD said to Moses, "Speak to Aaron and his sons and to all the Israelites and say to them: 'This is what the LORD has commanded:

> Any Israelite who sacrifices an ox, a lamb or a goat in the camp
> or outside of it instead of bringing it to the entrance to the Tent
> of Meeting to present it as an offering to the LORD in front of the
> tabernacle of the LORD—that man shall be considered guilty of
> bloodshed; he has shed blood and must be cut off from his people'"
> (Leviticus 17:1–4).

The Lord adds a further requirement later in the text:

> "'Any Israelite or any alien living among you who hunts any animal
> or bird that may be eaten must drain out the blood and cover it with
> earth, because the life of every creature is its blood. That is why I
> have said to the Israelites, "You must not eat the blood of any crea-
> ture, because the life of every creature is its blood; anyone who eats
> it must be cut off"'" (Leviticus 17:13–14).

If anyone killed a domestic animal, the carcass had to be brought and offered
as a peace offering to God, and the blood had to be poured out and collected in
a basin. The priest had to perform certain rituals. Then the meat of the animal
could be eaten by the man's family. If the man was out hunting, the blood of
any animal he killed had to be treated with respect and poured out and covered
over with dirt, lest a ceremonial defilement result.

What is God telling us through these requirements? We don't have to follow
the letter of these regulations anymore, but we do have to obey the principles
that they symbolize for us. Notice that for an Israelite to violate this requirement was a serious offense. He was to be cut off from among his people if he
did not follow it carefully. This tells us that there is a vitally important principle
embedded in these requirements.

Earlier in Leviticus, we studied the various penalties that were assessed for
failures among the people of God. The mildest penalty was to be declared
unclean until evening. We saw that this was the equivalent, in our terms, of
reverting to walking in the flesh instead of in obedience to the Spirit. The
moment you begin depending on yourself—your personality, your background, your training, your heredity, your good works—to accomplish something for God's sake, you are walking in the flesh.

The Bible teaches us that walking in the flesh is unacceptable to God. It doesn't make any difference how good the results may appear to the world; it is unacceptable to God. According to Paul, "the mind of the flesh is enmity against God; for it is not subject to the law of God, neither indeed can it be" (Romans 8:7 ASV). So walking in the flesh is the equivalent of uncleanness in the Old Testament.

The penalty prescribed for mishandling the blood in Leviticus 17 is much more severe than uncleanness, however. Here we see that the violator is to be cut off from among the people. This is equivalent to the ostracism of church discipline that is commanded in the New Testament when someone displays a deliberate intent to continue in sinful behavior.

In Matthew 18, Jesus tells us that if your brother falls into a fault of some kind, you are to go to him and tell him what is wrong, between you and him alone. If he will listen to you and repent, then it is over and done with; you have regained fellowship with your brother. But if he willfully continues to offend against you, then you take two or three others with you and confront him in the presence of witnesses. If he is still unwilling to change his behavior, then you tell it to the entire assembly, the church. If he still will not hear the church, then let him be to you as a Gentile or a tax collector—that is, you treat him as though he were not a Christian. You ostracize him and cut him off from his people. That is the kind of penalty God prescribes here in Leviticus 17.

## LIFE BELONGS TO GOD

This penalty is far more serious than it may at first seem. To be set apart from the community of Israel was to have one's whole relationship to God thrown into doubt. Even the question of the individual's salvation was in jeopardy. That is how serious it was to fail to respect the blood and to recognize that it belongs to God. The reason this is such a serious matter is found in the next few verses.

> "'This is so the Israelites will bring to the LORD the sacrifices they are now making in the open fields. They must bring them to the priest, that is, to the LORD, at the entrance to the Tent of Meeting and sacrifice them as fellowship offerings. The priest is to sprinkle the blood against the altar of the LORD at the entrance to the Tent

of Meeting and burn the fat as an aroma pleasing to the LORD. They must no longer offer any of their sacrifices to the goat idols to whom they prostitute themselves. This is to be a lasting ordinance for them and for the generations to come.'

"Say to them: 'Any Israelite or any alien living among them who offers a burnt offering or sacrifice and does not bring it to the entrance to the Tent of Meeting to sacrifice it to the LORD—that man must be cut off from his people'" (Leviticus 17:5–9).

What is the reason for these requirements regarding the blood of animals? God is teaching Israel—and us—that all life belongs to God and that He alone is capable of handling it rightly. God is the Creator of life, and only He understands life. That is the basis for all proper behavior. If you don't understand that your life comes from God and returns to God, you cannot behave in a whole and holy way. You must understand that your life belongs to God and that all other life around you, even animal life, belongs to God. It is a mystery beyond our comprehension but one that demands our respect.

The respect for life that God demands contrasts with the pagan practice of offering animals to demons, called goat idols. These goat idols are also called satyrs in ancient mythology. They were demonic figures that were pictured as half-goat and half-man. Here, God teaches Israel not to try to placate the spirits, as though man could manipulate the unseen spirit world with chants of "Abracadabra!" and "Hocus-pocus!"

It is amazing what a grip magical thinking has on people's minds! All around us, we see rampant fascination with the occult, astrology, witchcraft, and even Satan worship. All of this is motivated by people's desire to manipulate and control the world of the spirits so that they can manage their lives without having to bend the knee to God. In time, those who dabble in the occult end up ensnared by it, and they discover that they do not control the demons—the demons control them.

I once visited the Philippines as a guest of Wycliffe Bible Translators. We flew to northern Luzon, where missionaries were working among one of the remote tribes there. It was a beautiful place where the famous rice terraces of Luzon are located. Those rice terraces have been there for thousands of years and are sometimes called the eighth wonder of the world. We landed on a tiny airstrip carved from the side of a mountain, and we walked to the village where I was to stay overnight.

When I arrived in the village, I found the tribespeople doing something that was both sad and fascinating. They were offering a pig to the demonic spirits. I arrived just as the sacrifice began. They caught the pig and tied it up. Then the old women of the tribe said incantations over the pig, bowed before it and waved cloths over it, muttering to the spirits. Then a man took a knife and slit the pig's throat. They caught the blood in a basin, offered the blood to the spirits, and sprinkled it around as they uttered more incantations.

Why do people sacrifice animals in this way? Notice that when tribespeople sacrifice animals, the ceremony looks like a distorted form of the sacrifices in Leviticus. There seems to be a deep-seated, vestigial inheritance from the first days of humankind—a mixture of false and true beliefs. It seems that people everywhere intuitively understand that life is involved with blood and that life must be sacrificed for some reason. They understand that life is sacred, and it is not enough to merely offer grain or cloth or trinkets. The spirits are not so easily satisfied. It takes blood, it requires the taking of a life to placate and manipulate an angry demon.

The sacrifices in Leviticus, of course, are very different from the pagan sacrifices. They were not meant to placate or manipulate an angry demon. The sacrifices were pictures that pointed ahead to the perfect sacrifice of Jesus Christ, and they were meant to prod the people into examining their lives and relationships and to lead them to repentance and renewal. In the pagan sacrifices, people seek to gain control over the spirits; in the Levitical sacrifices, people obediently submit to the sovereignty of a loving and holy God.

A basic lie, widespread in primitive and civilized cultures, is that human beings can handle life in their own power and wisdom. It is the lie that people really don't need God in their lives. In our day we are witnessing a resurgence of belief in this ancient lie—the lie that we can control and manipulate spirits to do our bidding. It's true that there are spirits—but it is the height of foolish arrogance to think that you or I could ever control those spirits and make them do our bidding.

That is why God commands His people to cease these practices. God alone is sovereign in life. He runs the world, and He is in control of all things. We live in His universe, and we cannot handle life ourselves. Only a fool would try to live his life apart from God.

## LIFE IS IN THE BLOOD

The next requirement regarding blood was that no one was permitted to eat the blood of animals.

> "'Any Israelite or any alien living among them who eats any blood—I will set my face against that person who eats blood and will cut him off from his people. For the life of a creature is in the blood, and I have given it to you to make atonement for yourselves on the altar; it is the blood that makes atonement for one's life. Therefore I say to the Israelites, "None of you may eat blood, nor may an alien living among you eat blood."
>
> "'Any Israelite or any alien living among you who hunts any animal or bird that may be eaten must drain out the blood and cover it with earth, because the life of every creature is its blood. That is why I have said to the Israelites, "You must not eat the blood of any creature, because the life of every creature is its blood; anyone who eats it must be cut off."
>
> "'Anyone, whether native-born or alien, who eats anything found dead or torn by wild animals must wash his clothes and bathe with water, and he will be ceremonially unclean till evening; then he will be clean. But if he does not wash his clothes and bathe himself, he will be held responsible'" (Leviticus 17:10–16).

As plainly as He possibly can, God teaches His people by means of this visual aid that there is something mysterious and sacred about the blood, for blood is the bearer of life itself. It is only recently that medical science has truly understood the importance of the blood to life. For centuries, people regarded blood as having little to do with maintaining life. Even in our relatively recent history, bloodletting was a common medical practice for curing diseases. Some historians feel that George Washington was accidentally killed by his physicians when they kept bleeding him, which made him too weak to recover from a simple cold. God teaches us that blood is the bearer of life, and He does so by commanding His people not to eat the blood.

If you have ever eaten blood pudding from Great Britain or blood sausage from Bavaria, I don't want you to be disturbed. The Levitical restrictions are only shadows that have now passed away, since the reality has come. There is nothing morally wrong with eating foods made from blood (though, to be candid, you could not coax me to eat any!). If you like to eat such things, feel free to do so. The New Testament teaches that ancient restrictions that forbid certain foods and certain ways of cooking things have been eliminated. We are not subject to the Old Testament restrictions anymore; yet we continue to draw wisdom and insight from the Old Testament pictures of Jesus Christ.

So what is the reality behind God's injunction against eating blood?

## THE BLOOD WE MUST DRINK IN ORDER TO LIVE

Leviticus 17 foreshadows a reality that Jesus declared plainly in words that are recorded by the apostle John. These words have a special meaning to me, because they were spoken at the lakeside town of Capernaum, a site I visited on a tour of Israel. It was a Sunday morning, and I went out on a hillside overlooking the site of ancient Capernaum. I sat down on that hillside and opened my Bible to the various words of Jesus that He spoke in or around Capernaum. The place where I sat, for example, is thought to be the hillside where Jesus preached the Sermon on the Mount. Somewhere nearby, Jesus also spoke the words in this passage from John 5, which I read that morning with a great thrill in my heart.

> Then the Jews began to argue sharply among themselves, "How can this man give us his flesh to eat?"
>
> Jesus said to them, "I tell you the truth, unless you eat the flesh of the Son of Man and drink his blood, you have no life in you. Whoever eats my flesh and drinks my blood has eternal life, and I will raise him up at the last day. For my flesh is real food and my blood is real drink. Whoever eats my flesh and drinks my blood remains in me, and I in him" (John 6:52–56).

Here we see the great reality that Leviticus 17 gives us in the form of shadows and symbols! Again, we see that the Law was our schoolmaster to bring us to Christ. The regulations and sacrifices of Leviticus were designed by God to prepare His people for the proclamation of the truth from the lips of Jesus. If all of His people had understood the real purpose of the Law, they would have received the words of Jesus with gladness and joy.

Tragically, the scribes and Pharisees—the experts in the Law!—completely misunderstood the purpose of the Law. To them, the Law was nothing more than an instrument for controlling human behavior. They did not see the pictures of the promised Messiah that were contained in the ceremonies and sacrifices. They saw only rules and regulations, rituals and rote. So when Jesus came and revealed to them the reality that the Law pointed to, they found His words incomprehensible—and blasphemous.

The scribes and Pharisees had read Leviticus 17 many times, and they could probably recite certain portions by heart, including God's command, "You must not eat the blood of any creature, because the life of every creature is its blood; anyone who eats it must be cut off." They had been taught all their lives that it was an abomination to eat blood. Now, imagine how it must have sounded to their ears when Jesus said, "Unless you eat the flesh of the Son of Man and drink his blood, you have no life in you. Whoever eats my flesh and drinks my blood has eternal life."

In fact, not only were the scribes and Pharisees scandalized, but also many of Jesus' followers were shocked and offended by His teaching. John goes on to record:

> On hearing it, many of his disciples said, "This is a hard teaching. Who can accept it?"
>
> Aware that his disciples were grumbling about this, Jesus said to them, "Does this offend you? What if you see the Son of Man ascend to where he was before! The Spirit gives life; the flesh counts for nothing. The words I have spoken to you are spirit and they are life" (John 6:60–63).

What does this all mean? As Leviticus tells us, blood is life. Jesus now teaches His followers the great truth toward which all the rules and restrictions of Leviticus have pointed—that God has provided humanity with a new life by which to live, the life that flows in the blood of Jesus Himself. God commanded His people not to eat the life of a mere animal, which was part of the fallen creation—that blood is not a proper food for God's people. If you eat the blood of an animal, God was saying, you partake of the life of the fallen creation. Instead, God's people are to feed on the life that is from above, the life of God Himself, flowing from the blood of Jesus.

In Leviticus 17, God is patiently teaching us that we are no longer to depend upon the fallen life, what we call the flesh, the old life. The resources that we lived by and depended upon before we became Christians—our personality, our education, our good works—are no longer to be the resources we live by. We are not to feed on the fallen life, for God has provided a new life, the life of Christ.

Those who eat this new life and drink the blood of Jesus have eternal life. They are feeding on the heavenly provision that God has made available to us. We eat and drink of this life whenever we draw upon the life of Jesus for strength to love an enemy or show patience to annoying people or show kindness to people who are lonely, neglected, or oppressed. These are the evidences that we are feeding on His blood and that His life is flowing in us and working through us. The symbols of the bread and cup that we partake in Communion, in the Lord's Table, are symbolic reminders of the fact that we are to eat His flesh and drink His blood every moment of every day.

## GOD'S TRUTH ABOUT SEX

From blood we move to sex.

Next to the preservation of life, the most powerful human drive is the sex drive. Sex is like a great river which, when it flows between its banks, is a great blessing to humanity and to individual human lives. But when it is raging in full flood, when it overflows its banks, it inundates the landscape with promiscuity and adultery, destroying lives with shame and sexually transmitted diseases, breaking up families, polluting society with pornography, sadism, masochism, and bestiality. Raging, out-of-control sexuality destroys even the lives of children with child sexual abuse and child pornography.

There is a good and protective reason why God's Word carefully regulates human sexual behavior. It continually amazes me that God takes the risk of allowing us to have this much fantastic power in our lives. Though He pleads with us to use this powerful gift as He intended, to keep it channeled within the protective riverbanks that He has outlined, still He doesn't take sex away from us if we misuse it. Here is how God begins the instruction of His people in the use of this beautiful, powerful, dangerous gift called sex.

The LORD said to Moses, "Speak to the Israelites and say to them: 'I am the LORD your God. You must not do as they do in Egypt, where you used to live, and you must not do as they do in the land of Canaan, where I am bringing you. Do not follow their practices. You must obey my laws and be careful to follow my decrees. I am the LORD your God. Keep my decrees and laws, for the man who obeys them will live by them. I am the LORD'" (Leviticus 18:1–5).

Notice how God underscores the purpose of these instructions. They are to make us live, not die. God does not seek to rob us of pleasure or joy. He does not give us these regulations in order to restrict us and prohibit us from expressing ourselves in our sexuality. On the contrary, He wants us to truly live and enjoy life to the fullest.

There have been many popular books that purport to teach us everything about sex—books such as *Everything You Always Wanted to Know About Sex (But Were Afraid to Ask)*. I read that book, and I found it very shallow. The author doesn't know very much about sex. He documents a number of sexual techniques and practices, including a few that I had not previously heard of. But he gives almost no information or context about sex and what it is for. The title is misleading. The very things that people most want to understand about their own sexuality and their sex lives are not even addressed in the book.

Here in Scripture, however, you get the truth about sex. God's Word tells us that sex is to be a total union of a man and his wife, expressing physical, emotional, and spiritual oneness. Marriage, then, is the only possible place of expression for God's gift of sex. The expression of sex outside of the marriage union is always harmful. Sex with the wrong person is always harmful. The most harmful of all, according to Leviticus 18, is sex with those who are closely related.

"'No one is to approach any close relative to have sexual relations. I am the LORD.

"'Do not dishonor your father by having sexual relations with your mother. She is your mother; do not have relations with her.

"'Do not have sexual relations with your father's wife; that would dishonor your father.

"'Do not have sexual relations with your sister, either your father's daughter or your mother's daughter, whether she was born in the same home or elsewhere.

"'Do not have sexual relations with your son's daughter or your daughter's daughter; that would dishonor you.

"'Do not have sexual relations with the daughter of your father's wife, born to your father; she is your sister.

"'Do not have sexual relations with your father's sister; she is your father's close relative.

"'Do not have sexual relations with your mother's sister, because she is your mother's close relative.

"'Do not dishonor your father's brother by approaching his wife to have sexual relations; she is your aunt.

"'Do not have sexual relations with your daughter-in-law. She is your son's wife; do not have relations with her.

"'Do not have sexual relations with your brother's wife; that would dishonor your brother.

"'Do not have sexual relations with both a woman and her daughter. Do not have sexual relations with either her son's daughter or her daughter's daughter; they are her close relatives. That is wickedness.

"'Do not take your wife's sister as a rival wife and have sexual relations with her while your wife is living'" (Leviticus 18:6–18).

In the original Hebrew language, the term here translated "have sexual relations with" was literally "uncover the nakedness of." Today, many people cleverly parse their words when speaking of sexual behavior. They might say, "I didn't have sexual relations with this person," even though they may have been in a state of complete nakedness with that person, engaging in acts which produced sexual arousal, foreplay, and orgasm.

God's Word is uncompromising in its honesty. He tells us that we are not to uncover the nakedness of the person who is not our spouse. He is not telling us, as many people in our culture claim, that intercourse is harmful but outercourse (non-penetrating sex) is okay. He is telling us that it is wrong and harmful to even uncover the nakedness of another person—to look upon another person's nakedness and become aroused, and to engage in any other form of sexual activity with that person. This prohibition even applies to uncovering the nakedness of someone whose likeness appears in a pornographic magazine, a pornographic movie, or a pornographic Internet site.

We may fool ourselves with our clever parsing of sexual terms, but God is not fooled, and we can't fool nature. If we engage in the activities that God has forbidden, we will pay a heavy price for allowing our sexuality to overflow the banks God has designed for it.

## TWO REASONS FOR GOD'S PROHIBITION

Why does God prohibit sex with relatives? At first glance, this seems like a silly question. In our culture, the incest taboo is still strong, even while many other sexual taboos seemed to have fallen away. But in that ancient culture, the incest taboo was not an established fact. God had to issue a command so that the people would know His thoughts on the matter.

God clearly knew what medical science has come to understand only in recent centuries: Procreation with close relatives intensifies weaknesses in the genetic heritage of the family. For example, the royal families of Europe have shown a marked deterioration after generations of incestuous marriages. Charles II of Spain sat on the throne despite being so mentally and physically feeble that he could not walk until age ten, could barely chew his food or speak, and suffered from frequent seizures. The ruling Medici family of Italy produced generation after generation of offspring who lived, at most, into their twenties or thirties. This is a major reason why God's law and secular law forbid incest. Society has come to recognize that the children who result from such relationships are cruelly harmed as a result.

The Bible also reveals to us that there is a connection between illicit sexual practices and an openness to demonic influence. This is why God warns again and again throughout the Scriptures that nations and individuals who give themselves over to sexual permissiveness and perversion are inviting destructive attacks of demonic activity.

When a proper regard for the sexual limitations prescribed by God is broken down, the barrier that protects humankind from the unseen forces of darkness can quickly be erased. Individual lives, families, and societies can fall apart at that point. Paul described the decline that results from the misuse of human sexuality when he wrote:

> Therefore God gave them over in the sinful desires of their hearts to sexual impurity for the degrading of their bodies with one another. They exchanged the truth of God for a lie, and worshiped and served created things rather than the Creator—who is forever praised. Amen (Romans 1:24–25).

We see a similar principle as we continue on in Leviticus 18. Here, God addresses various sexual practices that produce harm in human lives and human society, and He suggests a connection between sexual sin and demonic activity.

> "'Do not approach a woman to have sexual relations during the uncleanness of her monthly period.
> "'Do not have sexual relations with your neighbor's wife and defile yourself with her.
> "'Do not give any of your children to be sacrificed to Molech, for you must not profane the name of your God. I am the LORD.
> "'Do not lie with a man as one lies with a woman; that is detestable.
> "'Do not have sexual relations with an animal and defile yourself with it. A woman must not present herself to an animal to have sexual relations with it; that is a perversion'" (Leviticus 18:19–23).

These verses gather up a number of prohibited activities in a single passage. God warns that even in marriage, a man should not make inordinate sexual demands on his wife, demanding sex from her during her menstrual period. He warns against adultery. Then God prohibits homosexual behavior. Then He forbids bestiality—that is, sex with animals.

In the middle of this passage, He warns against offering infants to Molech, the fiery brass god of the Canaanites. After stoking the fires within the idol so that it glowed red-hot, the idol worshipers laid living children in the searing arms of the idol, so that these innocents would writhe in torment as they were cremated alive.

The fact that God includes horrible practices of demon worship amid these prohibitions against certain sexual acts would seem to indicate several insights. First, idolatrous worship and human sacrifice to the demon Molech may well have had a sadistic sexual component; people engaged in such horrible behavior may well have derived some monstrous sexual pleasure from these horrible acts of ritual torture and infanticide. Second, God seems to view these forbidden sexual practices in much the same way that He views demon worship. Third, God seems to suggest a connection between sinful sexual practices and demonic activity.

All of these practices, the Bible suggests, provide open doors to the destruction of our humanity and human society by opening our lives to demonic influence. The spirits of darkness are looking for opportunities to take up residence in our humanity, and one way they gain a foothold is through sexual practices that God has forbidden. As Satan's influence grows in a human life, people become susceptible to demonic oppression and even possession.

## DEFILING THE LAND

The end of the process of the destruction of one's humanity through sexual sin is shown in the next few verses.

> "'Do not defile yourselves in any of these ways, because this is how the nations that I am going to drive out before you became defiled. Even the land was defiled; so I punished it for its sin, and the land vomited out its inhabitants. But you must keep my decrees and my laws. The native-born and the aliens living among you must not do any of these detestable things, for all these things were done by the people who lived in the land before you, and the land became defiled. And if you defile the land, it will vomit you out as it vomited out the nations that were before you.
>
> "'Everyone who does any of these detestable things—such persons must be cut off from their people. Keep my requirements and do not follow any of the detestable customs that were practiced before you came and do not defile yourselves with them. I am the LORD your God'" (Leviticus 18:24–30).

How tenderly God deals with His people! He graciously and faithfully warns us that by violating His statutes, we will only destroy ourselves. In fact, He warns that the ultimate effect of sexual depravity is ecological disaster: "And if you defile the land, it will vomit you out as it vomited out the nations that were before you."

This is an amazing revelation! It shows how little we understand life. We are so ignorant of our own humanity and of the way we are tied to each other and to our environment by the actions we take. We easily forget that all of human life comes from the earth. Milk doesn't come from a carton in the refrigerator—it comes from cows who feed on the grass of the land. Bread doesn't come out of plastic wrappers—it comes from grain that grows in the soil of the land. If we defile the land, we destroy our own lives.

Here, God tells us that there is a connection between wrongful sexual practices and ecological disaster. When human beings become distorted in their sexual practices, when their thinking becomes infected by demonic influences, people do things that harm the land and turn it against them. The land becomes defiled, and it vomits the people out—the land can't stand the people anymore, so it rejects them and destroys them.

If you think that the ecological problems in our world today are something new, you are wrong. Ecological disasters have occurred in many previous periods of human history. The inhabitants of the land of Canaan were cast out by the land itself because of the sexual depravity of the people. And there are many records of similar ecological disasters in human history.

If God hadn't pointed out to us the connection between sexual depravity and ecological calamity, we might never have observed it ourselves. But in His love and care for us, He wants us to know how humanity and nature interact. So He tells us, in effect, "If you go on in the way you are going, abusing yourselves and each other with degrading sexual practices, then you will ultimately abuse the land, and it will be repulsed by your presence. You will violate the land, so that it will expel you. Your sexual depravity will be your undoing."

Nature reflects the ravaged and ruined condition of the spirit of humanity. As society disintegrates due to rampant disobedience and the rejection of Jesus, the Savior, people become more and more deluded by satanic lies—and the very ground beneath their feet becomes defiled and sick. This principle is mirrored in the words spoken by God in 2 Chronicles 7:14—"If my people, who are called by my name, will humble themselves and pray and seek my face and turn from their wicked ways, then will I hear from heaven and will forgive their sin and will heal their land."

God's message to us is the same as the message He spoke to ancient Israel: Repent, trust God, and obey His commands, which He gave you to protect you, not to harm you. Only God has the wisdom and power to handle the problems and questions of this life. Only through God's power can we master our sexual desires and keep them channeled between the safe riverbanks that He has established.

CHAPTER 18

※——————————————※

# THE POWER TO DO
## LEVITICUS 19 AND 20

I'M SURE THAT Mark Twain spoke for all of us when he said, "It isn't the portions of the Bible which I don't understand that bother me; it's the ones I do!" The reason we are troubled by the Scripture passages we understand is that we don't want to do what they tell us to do! We don't like being accountable to God for what we know He wants us to do. So the challenge that faces us as Christians is not only to know what God's Word says but to obey it.

As we come to Leviticus 19 and Leviticus 20, we find a series of miscellaneous instructions covering various situations and problems that you and I face on a daily basis. Each of these instructions is worthy of a book in its own right, but we will take just a quick survey of this section. I hope you will take this study in Leviticus as merely a starting point and that you will continue to search these verses, increase your understanding of them, and above all, commit yourself to obeying their wise counsel for your life.

The first thing we notice about this passage is the striking format of these instructions. A remarkable phenomenon occurs again and again throughout these chapters. It is the way God links His name with these instructions.

> The LORD said to Moses, "Speak to the entire assembly of Israel and say to them: 'Be holy because I, the LORD your God, am holy.

"'Each of you must respect his mother and father, and you must observe my Sabbaths. I am the LORD your God.

"'Do not turn to idols or make gods of cast metal for yourselves. I am the LORD your God'" (Leviticus 19:1–4).

This pattern repeats again and again throughout Leviticus 19, and it continues into Leviticus 20. God clearly and specifically identifies Himself with each one of these instructions. He signs His name, as it were, after each one. He gives us a practical admonition, then underscores it with the words "I am the LORD your God." In the original Hebrew, the name He uses for Himself is His covenant name, YHWH or Yahweh (in English, Jehovah), a name that means "The Living One" or "The Eternal One" or "The All-Sufficient One."

What is God trying to impart to us by this pattern of repetition? He is underscoring two things: First, He is the ultimate authority. Second, He is the ultimate resource for all our needs.

The Israelites would understand this repeated statement to mean, "I am the Lord your God, distinct from all of the other gods of all the other nations around you." In Leviticus 18, God told the people, "You must not do as they do in Egypt, where you used to live, and you must not do as they do in the land of Canaan, where I am bringing you. Do not follow their practices" (Leviticus 18:3). In other words, "The Egyptians and the Canaanites have their own practices which are destructive and sinful, because they do not recognize me as Lord. But you have a relationship with me; I am the Lord your God. You must obey my commandments, not live according to their pagan and godless ways."

God's repeated statement of His relationship to His people underscores something very important: His people must know how to distinguish between right and wrong, truth and error. The basis for knowing right from wrong is the basis God has given us—His Law, which He has given us because of His relationship with us. He is the Lord our God.

This is practical truth because God is our ultimate reality. When He speaks to us, He tells us how life truly is. Any view of life that is at variance with God's Word is unrealistic, it is out of step with reality, it is an illusion. Such fantasy versions of reality were widespread in Egypt and Canaan, where the people worshiped such demonic deities as sun gods and fertility goddesses. These people ordered their lives around false beliefs in false gods.

But God tells His people, "You will not live as the Egyptians and Canaanites. I am the Lord your God, and I am telling you the truth about life as it really is. I am telling you what will hurt you and what will make you whole. So believe me, trust me, obey me—because I am the Lord your God."

This is so important to understand these days! God's view of reality, as expressed in His Word, has never been under such assault as it is in these days. A thousand voices shout at us—a cacophony of conflicting ideas. From philosophers to educators to politicians to media personalities, scores and scores of opinion leaders are telling us today that there is no absolute right or wrong, there is no authority in the area of morality—everything is relative. How can we know what is right? How can we discern truth from error?

In Leviticus 19, God tells us, in effect, "I determine what is right and wrong. I am the Authority. I am the Lord your God."

## THE ULTIMATE AUTHORITY

I once had a long phone conversation with a young man who fell victim to a modern-day false prophet, a so-called psychic counselor. This young man was being told that he could discover hidden powers of his personality through occult knowledge and astrology. He experimented with occult practices and seemed to gain useful information for making important decisions in his life. This is not uncommon, of course. Satan's age-old strategy is to mingle truth and deception together in a way that seduces the mind and soul.

I could see that this young man was being taken in by a line of thinking that was in direct opposition to the Word of God. Yet this young man was convinced that he had found the truth. He believed he had tapped into mystical and mysterious powers that would give him a sense of freedom and confidence in life that he had never known before. I told him that these teachings were in direct contradiction to the teaching of the Old and New Testaments, and I cited a number of specific passages that prohibited occult practices.

The young man refused to be convinced. Finally, I rested my case with these words: "You have to decide whose authority you will accept—the authority of the cultists and astrologers, or the authority of the Scriptures and of Jesus Christ. If you accept the authority of one, you must reject the other. There is no middle ground."

All of life ultimately reduces to this stark, black-and-white question of authority. None of us knows enough about life to make all of our own decisions, apart from the counsel of Scripture and the authority of Jesus Christ. We simply do not have God's omniscient perspective on reality. Only God knows all there is to know about life. We sometimes think we know everything, but we are just kidding ourselves—and we are setting ourselves up for tragic mistakes and disappointments in life.

So here is the great issue of our day: Who is the ultimate authority in your life? Who will you follow? Who will you believe?

In this passage, God helps His people, whom He loves, to see that He is the ultimate authority, that He is their God, and that He loves them and will tell them the truth about life—even if they don't like to hear it. That is why it is so dangerous to challenge the authority of Scripture. When you face the ultimate issues of the Bible, it is not just good advice—it is God's revelation of life as it is. I am a Christian not because I find the ideas in Christianity more agreeable or palatable than those of, say, Buddhism or Islam. I am a Christian because I am convinced that God's Word contains the only valid explanation of life, human nature, and the universe. When I compare what God tells me with my experiences and to the universe I see around me, it makes sense.

This is what God is saying by linking His divine name with these commands: "Here is the truth, and you have that on my authority. I am the Lord your God."

## THE ULTIMATE RESOURCE

But God is not only our ultimate authority; He is also our ultimate resource. This is the second reason He adds His name to each command. He is telling us, "I am the Lord your God. My strength is fully available to you. I will provide the power so that you can do whatever I command. I never tell you to do something without making available the power for you to do it."

I'm sure you can identify with the truth expressed by Paul in Romans 7. There he writes about the eternal struggle we all go through—the struggle between the good we ought to do versus the sins we can't keep from doing. We know what's right, and we want to do what's right, yet we keep doing wrong. It's as if there are two people occupying the same body, and they are continually at war with each other. We try to change our behavior and break bad habits by the force of our own will power, but no matter how hard we try, we inevitably fail. "I do not understand what I do," Paul laments. "For what I want to do I do not do, but what I hate I do" (Romans 7:15).

If you feel that way, God understands. It's the most common problem of life—and the reason you and all other Christians often feel that way is easy to understand: We lack the power to respond as we should. It is not that the power is not available to us; it is. But we fail to lay hold of the power God has provided for us.

So, in an effort to remind us of the great resource of power He has supplied for us in our times of temptation, God signs His name to each of these commands, saying, in effect, "I am the Lord your God—and I am ready and available, waiting for you to call upon me and draw upon my strength. My infinite resources are there for your use. I am the God whose power is enough for your needs. I am Jehovah."

There is no excuse for saying to God, "I can't." We can always say with the apostle Paul, "I can do everything through him who gives me strength" (Philippians 4:13). When we say, "I can't" to God, we are really saying, "I won't." When we say, "I can't resist temptation," we are really saying, "I love this sinful habit, and I don't want to change. I refuse to draw upon your resources for my life. I choose to continue in this sin."

God will never overrule your will. Only you can decide not to sin—God won't decide for you. Once you make the decision to rely on God to strengthen you to resist temptation, His power is available. All you have to do is act on the basis of the resources He has supplied, and His power will flow through you and meet you at your point of need.

## PROHIBITIONS THAT ARE ETERNALLY BINDING

Two types of prohibitions are given in Leviticus 19 and Leviticus 20.

First, there are certain acts and attitudes that are inherently wrong. The prohibitions against them are eternally binding upon the people of God. As you read through this passage you'll see that some things are always wrong and always to be avoided, by means of the strength that God supplies. Continuing through the passage, we first encounter some rules having to do with the eating of sacrifices and compassion for the poor and for strangers in the land.

> "'When you sacrifice a fellowship [peace] offering to the LORD, sacrifice it in such a way that it will be accepted on your behalf. It shall

be eaten on the day you sacrifice it or on the next day; anything left over until the third day must be burned up. If any of it is eaten on the third day, it is impure and will not be accepted. Whoever eats it will be held responsible because he has desecrated what is holy to the LORD; that person must be cut off from his people.

"'When you reap the harvest of your land, do not reap to the very edges of your field or gather the gleanings of your harvest. Do not go over your vineyard a second time or pickup the grapes that have fallen. Leave them for the poor and the alien. I am the LORD your God'" (Leviticus 19:5–10).

Our compassionate God wants to teach us to be compassionate people. So He tells us to leave some fruit on the vine for the poor to glean. Be kind to the strangers and aliens who pass through the land. In other words, we should not greedily snatch up everything we can lay our hands on.

What if you are not a farmer with vineyards to tend? Perhaps you are a merchant or a banker or an executive. Does this principle still apply to you? Of course it does. After all, it was God who enabled you to earn a good salary, so in thanks to God, don't spend it all on yourself. Leave some of your earnings aside for those who are less fortunate—the poor, the strangers, the aliens in the land. Not everyone has had the opportunities that you have had. So open your heart and your hand, and share with those who are less fortunate than you.

Next, we come to a series of eternally binding commandments. These commandments are as much in force for us today as they were in those ancient days.

"'Do not steal.

"'Do not lie.

"'Do not deceive one another.

"'Do not swear falsely by my name and so profane the name of your God. I am the LORD.

"'Do not defraud your neighbor or rob him.

"'Do not hold back the wages of a hired man overnight.

"'Do not curse the deaf or put a stumbling block in front of the blind, but fear your God. I am the LORD.

"'Do not pervert justice; do not show partiality to the poor or favoritism to the great, but judge your neighbor fairly.

"'Do not go about spreading slander among your people.

"'Do not do anything that endangers your neighbor's life. I am the Lord.

"'Do not hate your brother in your heart. Rebuke your neighbor frankly so you will not share in his guilt.

"'Do not seek revenge or bear a grudge against one of your people, but love your neighbor as yourself. I am the LORD'" (Leviticus 19:11–18).

The penalty for the violation of these prohibitions may no longer be in effect, due to the grace of God revealed in Jesus Christ. But these prohibitions are binding on us today and for all time. Another example of eternally binding prohibitions is this passage from Leviticus 20.

"'If a man sleeps with his daughter-in-law, both of them must be put to death. What they have done is a perversion; their blood will be on their own heads.

"'If a man lies with a man as one lies with a woman, both of them have done what is detestable. They must be put to death; their blood will be on their own heads.

"'If a man marries both a woman and her mother, it is wicked. Both he and they must be burned in the fire, so that no wickedness will be among you.

"'If a man has sexual relations with an animal, he must be put to death, and you must kill the animal.

"'If a woman approaches an animal to have sexual relations with it, kill both the woman and the animal. They must be put to death; their blood will be on their own heads'" (Leviticus 20:12–16).

Why did God insist upon the death penalty for these violations of His Law? Because it was the only way God could impress upon the people the seriousness of these sins. The behavior that is described in this passage was commonly accepted among the Canaanites and the Egyptians. But God said, in effect,

"You mustn't do these things that the Canaanites and Egyptians do, because they are destructive acts. They will destroy you as individuals and as a society. Therefore, in order to show you how serious these actions are, you must put to death those who do them. The death penalty will shock the people and awaken them to the seriousness and the damaging effects of sin."

Christ has come, and through Him God has graciously mitigated the penalty for such sins and has provided the opportunity for repentance and change. God no longer requires death for these offenses. But God continues to regard these as serious offenses that are destructive to individuals and to society as a whole.

## PROHIBITIONS CONCERNING SYMBOLIC PRACTICES AND RITUALS

The second general class of prohibitions in Leviticus 19 and Leviticus 20 are concerned with certain symbolic rituals and ceremonies. These practices no longer need to be observed, but the attitude they illustrate never changes. Underlying each of these rituals and ceremonies is an unchanging truth. For example:

> "'Keep my decrees.
> "'Do not mate different kinds of animals.
> "'Do not plant your field with two kinds of seed.
> "'Do not wear clothing woven of two kinds of material'"
> (Leviticus 19:19).

I'll bet you never suspected, when you purchased that wool-cotton blend suit or that poly-cotton sweatshirt, that you were breaking God's Law! The fact is, we no longer need to adhere strictly to this prohibition. The symbolism remains valid, but the restriction no longer applies to our lives. These symbols are meant to illustrate attitudes of mind and heart which were (and still are) spiritually harmful. The Israelites had to obey these restrictions literally, because that is how they learned the symbolic lessons that were portrayed in these laws. But as we study them today, we see that God is teaching that there are certain unmixable principles which are unalterably opposed to one another, and we are not to try to put the two together.

This principle is explicitly stated in various ways in both the Old Testament and the New. Here are two examples:

Do two walk together unless they have agreed to do so? (Amos 3:3).

Do not be yoked together with unbelievers. For what do righteous-ness and wickedness have in common? Or what fellowship can light have with darkness? What harmony is there between Christ and Belial? What does a believer have in common with an unbeliever? (2 Corinthians 6:14–15).

The most common application of this principle in the church today is this: A Christian believer should not marry or even date an unbeliever. To do so is to mix two ways of life that are categorically separated and at war with one another. When a Christian and a nonbeliever marry, the result is confusion and conflict.

This same principle applies in other areas of life as well. For example, a Christian and a nonbeliever should not form a business partnership together, because they will not agree on moral principles, business ethics, using the business for ministry purposes, and more. Another example is that Christians should think seriously before joining nonbelieving friends in certain activities which might jeopardize their Christian testimony—activities such as attend-ing certain parties, watching certain movies, going to certain theatrical plays or rock concerts, and so forth.

Clearly, God is not saying that we should cut off all contact with our non-believing friends. We are called to be witnesses, so we must be in the world yet not of the world. We must learn how to live as the Lord's representatives in our fallen society while making sure that we never mix righteousness with wicked-ness or light with darkness.

The remainder of Leviticus 19 contains an assortment of prohibitions, some of which are eternal in nature, others of which are symbolic and ceremonial.

"'If a man sleeps with a woman who is a slave girl promised to another man but who has not been ransomed or given her freedom, there must be due punishment. Yet they are not to be put to death, because she had not been freed. The man, however, must bring a ram to the entrance to the Tent of Meeting for a guilt offering to the LORD. With the ram of the guilt offering the priest is to make atonement for him before the LORD for the sin he has committed, and his sin will be forgiven.

"'When you enter the land and plant any kind of fruit tree, regard its fruit as forbidden. For three years you are to consider it forbidden; it must not be eaten. In the fourth year all its fruit will be holy, an offering of praise to the LORD. But in the fifth year you may eat its fruit. In this way your harvest will be increased. I am the LORD your God.

"'Do not eat any meat with the blood still in it.

"'Do not practice divination or sorcery.

"'Do not cut the hair at the sides of your head or clip off the edges of your beard.

"'Do not cut your bodies for the dead or put tattoo marks on yourselves. I am the LORD.

"'Do not degrade your daughter by making her a prostitute, or the land will turn to prostitution and be filled with wickedness.

"'Observe my Sabbaths and have reverence for my sanctuary. I am the LORD.

"'Do not turn to mediums or seek out spiritists, for you will be defiled by them. I am the LORD your God.

"'Rise in the presence of the aged, show respect for the elderly and revere your God. I am the LORD.

"'When an alien lives with you in your land, do not mistreat him. The alien living with you must be treated as one of your native-born. Love him as yourself, for you were aliens in Egypt. I am the LORD your God.

"'Do not use dishonest standards when measuring length, weight or quantity. Use honest scales and honest weights, an honest ephah and an honest hin. I am the LORD your God, who brought you out of Egypt.

"'Keep all my decrees and all my laws and follow them. I am the Lord'" (Leviticus 19:20–37).

Some of these decrees, such as the prohibitions against engaging in sorcery or seeking out mediums and spiritists, are literal, eternal decrees. There is nothing symbolic about them. It is always wrong to dabble in the occult, because occult practices expose an individual to demonic powers that can seize control of a personality.

Other decrees in this passage are more symbolic in nature—yet the people of Israel observed them all, strictly and literally, because God was teaching a lesson through those prohibitions.

Examples of symbolic prohibitions: They were not to eat flesh with blood in it; this was a symbolic lesson that blood is the life of the flesh, and the life belongs to God. The New Testament tells us clearly that such restrictions on food are mere shadows and pictures that are no longer in force; as literal rules of living, these restrictions have passed away, but their symbolic meaning abides.

## WHY OUR LOVING GOD SEEMS HARSH

Another remarkable example of God's symbolic prohibition is found at the beginning of Leviticus 20:

> The LORD said to Moses, "Say to the Israelites: 'Any Israelite or any alien living in Israel who gives any of his children to Molech must be put to death. The people of the community are to stone him. I will set my face against that man and I will cut him off from his people; for by giving his children to Molech, he has defiled my sanctuary and profaned my holy name. If the people of the community close their eyes when that man gives one of his children to Molech and they fail to put him to death, I will set my face against that man and his family and will cut off from their people both him and all who follow him in prostituting themselves to Molech'" (Leviticus 20:1–5).

As we have previously seen, Molech was a fertility god, represented by a great iron or brass statue that was heated until red-hot by a fire built within it. People would take their infants and lay them in the outstretched arms of this idol and stand by as the children screamed in agony, burned alive as an offering to Molech.

Why would parents do a thing like that? Because they believed that by placating their demon god with the sacrifice of an innocent life, they could increase the yield of their crops and enlarge their prosperity. God not only was intent upon ending this cruel practice but also wanted to establish an important principle: It is an offense and an outrage in the eyes of God for parents to sacrifice their children in order to benefit themselves.

Today, we see many parents sacrificing their children to a modern version of Molech. Status-conscious parents sacrifice their children on the altar of their own ego and selfishness, sending their children off to be raised by daycare centers and boarding schools so that they can work longer hours, make more money, and enjoy a more prestigious lifestyle (a larger home, a Lexus and a Mercedes in the driveway, a membership in the country club). Some parents sacrifice their children on the altar of their own convenience or pride; a baby might upset their career plans or cause them some shame and embarrassment, so they abort that child instead of giving the child life.

If we sacrifice children through neglect, abandonment, or abortion, how are we any better than those who offered their children to the demon god Molech? Sacrificing children was wrong thousands of years ago, and it is wrong today—even though it is socially acceptable and legally approved. God's law takes precedence over the law of the land.

The rest of Leviticus 20 recapitulates and expands on some of the prohibitions and penalties we have already seen, particularly in the area of sexual relations.

"'I will set my face against the person who turns to mediums and spiritists to prostitute himself by following them, and I will cut him off from his people.

"'Consecrate yourselves and be holy, because I am the LORD your God. Keep my decrees and follow them. I am the LORD, who makes you holy.

"'If anyone curses his father or mother, he must be put to death. He has cursed his father or his mother, and his blood will be on his own head.

"'If a man commits adultery with another man's wife—with the wife of his neighbor—both the adulterer and the adulteress must be put to death.

"'If a man sleeps with his father's wife, he has dishonored his father. Both the man and the woman must be put to death; their blood will be on their own heads.

"'If a man sleeps with his daughter-in-law, both of them must be put to death. What they have done is a perversion; their blood will be on their own heads.

"'If a man lies with a man as one lies with a woman, both of them have done what is detestable. They must be put to death; their blood will be on their own heads.

"'If a man marries both a woman and her mother, it is wicked. Both he and they must be burned in the fire, so that no wickedness will be among you.

"'If a man has sexual relations with an animal, he must be put to death, and you must kill the animal.

"'If a woman approaches an animal to have sexual relations with it, kill both the woman and the animal. They must be put to death; their blood will be on their own heads.

"'If a man marries his sister, the daughter of either his father or his mother, and they have sexual relations, it is a disgrace. They must be cut off before the eyes of their people. He has dishonored his sister and will be held responsible.

"'If a man lies with a woman during her monthly period and has sexual relations with her, he has exposed the source of her flow, and she has also uncovered it. Both of them must be cut off from their people.

"'Do not have sexual relations with the sister of either your mother or your father, for that would dishonor a close relative; both of you would be held responsible.

"'If a man sleeps with his aunt, he has dishonored his uncle. They will be held responsible; they will die childless.

"'If a man marries his brother's wife, it is an act of impurity; he has dishonored his brother. They will be childless.

"'Keep all my decrees and laws and follow them, so that the land where I am bringing you to live may not vomit you out. You must not live according to the customs of the nations I am going to drive out before you. Because they did all these things, I abhorred them. But I said to you, "You will possess their land; I will give it to you as an inheritance, a land flowing with milk and honey." I am the LORD your God, who has set you apart from the nations.

"'You must therefore make a distinction between clean and unclean animals and between unclean and clean birds. Do not defile yourselves by any animal or bird or anything that moves along the ground—those which I have set apart as unclean for you. You are to be holy to me because I, the LORD, am holy, and I have set you apart from the nations to be my own.

"'A man or woman who is a medium or spiritist among you must be put to death. You are to stone them; their blood will be on their own heads'" (Leviticus 20:6–27).

These prohibitions and death penalties seem harsh to our twenty-first century ears—especially since some of these condemned practices are tolerated or even approved in our culture. It is important for us to understand that the seeming harshness of God in these commands and regulations is an aspect of the love of God. If a little child wanders into the street where she could get run over by a car, a loving parent will probably yank that child away from the street and administer a few swats to her bottom. To the child, this seems harsh; the parent, however, feels nothing but love for that child.

So it is with our loving Father. When He sees humanity straying toward self-destructive activity with false gods and demons, or when He sees humanity engaging in self-destructive sexual activity, He lovingly seeks to bring us up short and shock us into understanding the harm we are doing to ourselves. But we see only that God is being too harsh.

It is the love of God that compels Him to give us pictures and symbols that explain to us how reality works. In His love, He symbolically pointed us to the new life that we can draw upon as a result of the shed blood of Jesus. In His love, He warned us against sacrificing our children and worshiping demons. In His love, He warned us against degrading ourselves, degrading others, and destroying our families with destructive and shameful sexual practices.

In His love, He established the Sabbath so that we would learn to rest in Him and not trust in our own works and efforts. In His love, He decreed that we should respect and care for the elderly, and we should treat the aliens in our land with the same respect as the native-born. In His love, He taught us to treat one another honestly in all of our business dealings and not take unfair advantage of anyone.

God has set high standards of behavior for His people because He loves us. If these standards sound familiar, it is because Jesus echoed these same standards when He delivered His Sermon on the Mount:

> "If you love those who love you, what credit is that to you? Even 'sinners' love those who love them. And if you do good to those who are good to you, what credit is that to you? Even 'sinners' do that. And if you lend to those from whom you expect repayment, what credit is that to you? Even 'sinners' lend to 'sinners,' expecting to be repaid in full. But love your enemies, do good to them, and lend to them without expecting to get anything back. Then your reward will be great, and you will be sons of the Most High, because he is kind to the ungrateful and wicked. Be merciful, just as your Father is merciful.
>
> "Do not judge, and you will not be judged. Do not condemn, and you will not be condemned. Forgive, and you will be forgiven" (Luke 6:32–37).

The same standard of life is proclaimed in the Old Testament as in the New. God's character—as expressed in His justice and His merciful love—is to be revealed through us, His children, by the power of an available God. He is our authority and He is our resource. In our own strength, we cannot live as we should; we are doomed to fail again and again. But God has provided all the power we need to keep His commandments. He stands ready to live His life through us as we daily draw upon His grace and power.

※———————※

# FREE TO SERVE

## LEVITICUS 21 AND 22

How HAVE YOU been a priest today? How have you served God and met the needs of other people around you? You do know that you are a priest, don't you?

As we come to chapters 21 and 22 of this book that could well be called The Gospel According to Leviticus, we encounter a section of the Scriptures that is specifically addressed to priests, to Aaron the high priest and his sons. This family was set aside to carry out a specific work of ministry for God and for the people of Israel. They did not choose their vocation; they did not apply for the job. All the members of Aaron's family were priests by birth. There was no other way to become a priest, and no other family in Israel was ever recognized as having membership in the priesthood.

But as we are about to see, being a member of Aaron's family didn't automatically qualify an individual to serve as a priest. A member of the priestly family still had to meet certain qualifications in order to serve. There was (and still is) a difference between merely being a priest and serving as a priest. This is an important distinction for us to grasp because, as we have seen, the priesthood of the family of Aaron is a symbolic picture of our priestly ministry as followers of Jesus Christ.

Every one of us who is born again—that is, who is born into the family of our Great High Priest Jesus Christ—is a priest. But that doesn't mean that we automatically serve as priests. One reason so many people feel bored and unfulfilled in the Christian life is that they aren't practicing their priestly ministry. They are priests, but they are not exercising their priesthood.

How, then, can we begin to exercise our priestly ministry? Where do we start? Answer: We start by making sure we are qualified to serve. Whether we can or cannot serve as a priest depends upon whether or not we meet God's qualifications for the priesthood.

## No More Exciting Way to Live

There are many specific tasks and responsibilities that are part of the calling of an Old Testament priest. Yet the essential ministry of a priest can be summed up in a single sentence in Leviticus 21:6:

> "They must be holy to their God and must not profane the name of their God. Because they present the offerings made to the LORD by fire, the food of their God, they are to be holy."

The two primary duties of a priest were to offer the sacrifices to the Lord and to offer the special bread, called the showbread, before the Lord in the tabernacle. These two duties are directly applicable to our lives and our role as priests in the priesthood of all believers. As Christians, we have the same essential ministry in the church that the Old Testament priests carried out in the tabernacle. The difference between us and the Old Testament priests is that the old Levitical practices involved shadows and symbols, whereas our ministry today is the reality that those shadows and symbols pointed to.

When the Levitical priests offered the sacrifices, they were dealing with the effects of Jesus' death. The slain animals represented the Lord Jesus, slain upon the cross. Every lamb, calf, goat, and bird that was slain in the Old Testament was a picture of the work of Christ upon the cross in giving up His life on our behalf. When the priests offered these sacrifices, they were symbolically applying the Lord's sacrifice to the lives of the people who brought those animals to be slain.

What does that mean to us today? As believers in Jesus Christ, we are called to apply Christ's sacrifice to people who are in desperate need around us, to other Christians and to non-Christians as well. We are to do so by sharing the truth of the Word of God with them—the good news that will deliver them from the burden of guilt for their sins and set them free from the power of sin in their lives. The sacrifice of Jesus Christ is the only solution to the central problem of our humanity. Helping people to discover the meaning of His sacrifice for their lives is the task of a priest—and an exciting task it is!

Have you ever had the privilege of sharing the good news of Jesus Christ with someone who was discouraged, defeated, and depressed? Someone whose entire outlook on life was darkened by a sense of guilt, shame, and failure? Have you had the privilege of setting someone free from the power of sin by pointing that person to a relationship with the eternal God who created the universe? That is the privilege given to us as priests. That is why God placed us on this earth.

So we, like the priests of old, are called to apply the sacrifice of Jesus Christ to the lives of hurting, needy people around us. And we, like the priests of old, are also called to offer bread.

The loaves of the showbread were baked in the tabernacle and offered before God along with the animal offerings. Bread speaks of strength and life. This is a beautiful picture, as we have already seen, of feeding upon the available life of our risen Lord, of taking from Him the strength we need to live effective, joyful, abundant lives of service to God and others. The Old Testament priests ate the showbread that was offered to the Lord, and we are called to do the same. We are to feed upon Jesus, the Bread of life, every day. As Jesus Himself said, "I am the bread of life. He who comes to me will never go hungry, and he who believes in me will never be thirsty" (John 6:35).

As priests, we are ministers of both the death of Christ and the life of Christ. We are ministers of His shed blood and of the Bread of life upon which we feed day by day. These two aspects of Christ's work in our lives—His death and His life—are beautifully symbolized by the Lord's Table. The wine and the bread represent the shed blood and the life of Christ.

When we take the cup and eat the bread, there is no magical hocus-pocus that takes place. Rather, these symbols apply the death of Jesus to our minds and hearts in a powerful, meaningful way. As we drink the cup and eat the bread, we feed upon the death and life of Christ. We realize in a fresh and emotionally stirring way that His life feeds us and strengthens us; it restores us and renews our hope; it encourages our hearts and lifts our spirits so that we can continue living for Him.

Somewhere near you—in your church, your neighborhood, your office, maybe even in your family—is someone who is right at the limit of his or her endurance. There is someone facing so much pain or discouragement that he or she can't imagine living one more day. Are you listening and watching for the symptoms of defeat and depression in the people around you? It may well be that you are the only person in a position to speak a healing word of God's grace. You may be the only one who can be God's priest to that person.

Are you eager and watchful for the opportunities God places in your path? Are you ready for the privilege of being God's priest to another person? There is no more exciting way to live than to be the one God chooses and uses to bring hope and healing to hurting people.

## QUALIFIED TO SERVE

In order to serve as a priest, a priest must be holy. This is what God says: "They must be holy to their God and must not profane the name of their God. Because they present the offerings made to the LORD by fire, the food of their God, they are to be holy" (Leviticus 21:6). As we have already seen, this word *holy* means nothing more or less than whole. Holiness is wholeness. It means to be complete and healed.

How can you help to heal someone if you are sick yourself? How can you confront sin in another person's life if your life is riddled with unrepented sin? How can you lift someone else out of a hole if you are at the bottom of an even deeper hole? You must be set free before you can liberate someone else. You must experience the joy and freedom of the Spirit of God in order to point others to the joy and freedom.

So Leviticus 21 and Leviticus 22 deal with the issue of how God's priests can be made whole and holy so that they can take part in this exciting ministry in His name. It is not enough to be born into the priesthood; a priest must be qualified to serve. These two chapters in Leviticus tell us what we need to do in order to be holy priests of God. We find the first qualification for service in the first few verses of Leviticus 21:

> The LORD said to Moses, "Speak to the priests, the sons of Aaron, and say to them: 'A priest must not make himself ceremonially unclean for any of his people who die, except for a close relative,

such as his mother or father, his son or daughter, his brother, or an unmarried sister who is dependent on him since she has no husband—for her he may make himself unclean. He must not make himself unclean for people related to him by marriage, and so defile himself.

"'Priests must not shave their heads or shave off the edges of their beards or cut their bodies. They must be holy to their God and must not profane the name of their God. Because they present the offerings made to the Lord by fire, the food of their God, they are to be holy'" (Leviticus 21:1–6).

The first qualification of a priest is that he must not defile himself with the dead. If an Israelite had to touch a dead body (as in the case of those who buried the dead), he was unclean until evening. But priests, who exercised ministry, were not permitted to be unclean, except for the sake of close blood relatives. A priest could not defile himself for a relative by marriage—not even his wife.

The touching of a dead body is a picture of a person's involvement with the flesh, the fallen nature, the old life within us. As Paul wrote, "For the mind of the flesh is death; but the mind of the Spirit is life and peace: because the mind of the flesh is enmity against God; for it is not subject to the law of God, neither indeed can it be: and they that are in the flesh cannot please God" (Romans 8:6–8 asv). So the prohibition against touching the dead is an illustration of the necessity of a priest to avoid the flesh—that is, the spirit of human self-sufficiency, self-will, and self-centeredness.

Those who minister as priests must have nothing to do with the flesh—except, as Scripture carefully notes, our flesh and blood, our next of kin. There is in each of us a nature inherited from Adam which is fleshly, and we can't avoid that. The exception of the next of kin symbolizes the fact that there is within each of us a fleshly dimension that we will never be freed from in this life. We can't escape it. We are too close to it. So we must deal with it.

We can be cleansed from our fleshly self when it arises. We can recognize it and renounce it by the power of God's Spirit. But there is no way that we can avoid the flesh altogether. There is no way we can be so spiritual that we never fall into sin. Even the most dedicated Christian, with the best of intentions and the strongest faith, will be tripped up from time to time by his or her own wily, deceitful flesh. The flesh never dies until our body dies and falls away. As long as our flesh keeps tripping us up, we must continually repent of it and cleanse ourselves from it.

The greatest warning implied by the prohibition against touching the dead is a warning to avoid contact with the flesh in the world around us—the deadly, fleshly, sinful attitudes, principles, and ideas by which the world operates. The flesh includes all worldly wisdom which sets itself against God's wisdom, all worldly self-confidence that rejects confidence in God, and all worldly pride which sets itself against godly humility. The world operates on a basis of ambition, greed, self-will, lust, and the drive for power and dominance over others. This is the dead flesh of the world which, God tells us, we should not touch. This is the dead corpse of worldliness that defiles God's priests.

God's commandment to avoid the contamination of worldliness and the flesh is carried to a deeper level in the next few verses:

> "'They must not marry women defiled by prostitution or divorced from their husbands, because priests are holy to their God. Regard them as holy, because they offer up the food of your God. Consider them holy, because I the LORD am holy—I who make you holy.
>
> "'If a priest's daughter defiles herself by becoming a prostitute, she disgraces her father; she must be burned in the fire'" (Leviticus 21:7–9).

Here, God warns His priests to have nothing to do with prostitutes. A prostitute represents worldliness and the flesh. On the surface, this prohibition is designed to keep the Levitical priests from polluting themselves and sullying their reputations by allying themselves with prostitutes. On a symbolic level, this passage can be applied to our lives as a prohibition against forming close alliances (as symbolized by marriage) with the flesh. Not only are priests not to have a momentary contact with worldliness and the flesh, but also they are forbidden to form long-term associations with the destructive values of the world. A priest who becomes contaminated by worldliness has compromised his right and his qualifications to minister. He can no longer apply the death of Christ to people's lives and feed them with the bread and blood of Christ.

So the prohibition against making alliance with prostitutes serves as a warning to us today. We should avoid mixing the programs and procedures of the world with the program of God. This is a challenge to the way we conduct ourselves in the church today.

Everywhere I look, I see that Christians are all too eager to use the methods of the world to advance the cause of Christ. They are willing to figuratively marry a prostitute in order to (in their mind) promote Jesus and His church. They seem to set aside any sense of dependence upon the life of Jesus Christ in them and simply borrow the attitudes and resources of the world to run the church. They evidently assume that a church is nothing but a business with a cross for a corporate logo. They run the church as if it were any other business. The result is that the church has very little effectiveness, very little life, and very little to show for all of the money and energy it expends in Christ's name.

Through these verses, God sends us a warning signal: "If you go about your priestly ministry this way, allying yourself with worldly means and methods, then you will do so without my blessing and without my power. No matter how hard you try, your efforts will come to nothing, because you are operating in the flesh and not by my Spirit and power."

This is not to say that our fleshly ministry won't look successful—it may be very impressive before the world, attracting praise, media attention, and donations. But if we build our ministry by worldly means instead of depending solely on Christ and His power, then our great worldly success will be nothing but a fleshly failure in the eyes of God. It will be one hundred percent ineffective by the only measure that counts. Nothing of eternal value ever results from the flesh. Worldly means always produce results that are hollow and worthless.

God is not fooled by our outward successes. He knows our hearts. He knows if we have violated His qualifications for ministry. If our hearts are wrong, if we have allied ourselves with the flesh and the world, our efforts are in vain, and God will not bless them.

## THE QUALIFICATIONS OF THE HIGH PRIEST

The next passage deals with the qualifications of the high priest—and his qualifications are the highest of all. He is the example to all the priests, as well as to the people. This is fitting, of course, because the high priest is a symbolic type of Jesus Himself. As we read this passage, we find beautiful symbols that graphically represent the way Jesus, our Great High Priest, lived among us:

"'The high priest, the one among his brothers who has had the anointing oil poured on his head and who has been ordained to wear the priestly garments, must not let his hair become unkempt or tear his clothes. He must not enter a place where there is a dead body. He must not make himself unclean, even for his father or mother, nor leave the sanctuary of his God or desecrate it, because he has been dedicated by the anointing oil of his God. I am the LORD.

"'The woman he marries must be a virgin. He must not marry a widow, a divorced woman, or a woman defiled by prostitution, but only a virgin from his own people, so he will not defile his offspring among his people. I am the LORD, who makes him holy'" (Leviticus 21:10–15).

We readily see how God has raised the requirements for the high priest. He cannot defile himself in any way for the dead—not even for his own blood relatives. In other words, he must have no contact whatsoever with the flesh, the fallenness of the world. How true this was of the Lord Jesus. He was born without a sinful flesh, and He never contaminated Himself in any way. His sinlessness is richly symbolized in these verses.

Here are the characteristics of the high priest.

First, the high priest was to have no loose hair. We have seen in earlier studies that hair is always the picture of beauty. Jesus' beauty was never in disarray. As you look at the record of our Great High Priest in the gospel accounts, you see how He met this requirement. There was no lack of orderliness or discipline in the beauty of His life, no looseness.

Even when expressing His righteous anger by cleansing the temple of moneychangers and merchants, Jesus was never out of control, never impatient or enraged, never unbalanced or hot-tempered. His life, His character, and His personality were all beautifully in order. Jesus was gentle, patient, compassionate, thoughtful, considerate, strong, courageous, obedient, and utterly determined to do the will of the Father, even if it meant the horrors of the cross. Everything in His life reflected order and beauty; there was no disarray to be found in Him.

Second, the high priest was to reflect the wholeness of God. He was never to tear his garments—for, as you remember, garments are a picture of the character of an individual. The character of the high priest is never to be fragmented, inconsistent, or defective but always balanced and whole. As you read through the four gospels you can see how fully Jesus fulfilled these requirements.

The prohibition against defilement with the dead extended even to the high priest's father and mother. In other words, he was not to defile himself even with those closest to him. When we see how perfectly Jesus embodied these high-priestly requirements, we can better understand His often strange-sounding words to His mother, Mary. There were occasions when she came to Him and presumed upon their natural human relationship, yet He would invariably disassociate Himself from the normal requirements of their mother-son relationship.

For example, when Mary pressed Jesus to change the water into wine at the wedding in Cana, His answer was, "Dear woman, why do you involve me?" (John 2:4). Though He loved and respected His mother, He did not take orders from her. Though He did the miracle she asked, He made it clear that it wasn't because she was His mother or because she had authority over Him. Moreover, He performed the miracle quietly, so that only a few people were aware of it, not in the spectacular way that Mary wanted Him to.

And do you remember how He answered His human parents when He was twelve years old? "Didn't you know I had to be in my Father's house?" (Luke 2:49). The Father Jesus spoke of was, of course, His heavenly Father. Jesus did not allow Himself to be derailed by fleshly human concerns, including the human concerns that were pressed upon Him by His mother. That is how spotless His character was, and that is the spotless, unsullied character that is symbolically set forth in these high-priestly requirements in Leviticus.

Third, the high priest was to have an unblemished marriage. The high priest was to marry only a virgin daughter of his people, and she was to be without any blemish. The meaning of this symbol is obvious: The virgin bride is the church. The requirement that the high priest marry an unblemished virgin reminds us of Paul's words:

> Husbands, love your wives, just as Christ loved the church and gave himself up for her to make her holy, cleansing her by the washing with water through the word, and to present her to himself as a

radiant church, without stain or wrinkle or any other blemish, but holy and blameless (Ephesians 5:25–27).

You might ask, "How can this be? We are part of the church, and we have all these blemishes and spots and sins! Just look at us!" Well, this is why the Lord has set aside everything that comes from the flesh. That is why, in His relationship with us, He will never accept or tolerate any evidences of the flesh, nor allow it to be exalted in His presence.

That is why He will not acknowledge any ministry that is based upon self-sufficiency, the feeling that "God is sure lucky I'm on His side because I've got something that He needs." God has set all of that aside. He has written off all of our blemishes, spots, and sins. They are a part of our daily experience, but He has dealt with them on the cross. The Lord has cleansed the church and washed it with the Word, and now He is eliminating these defects from our lives so that we might be without spot or blemish before Him. He will allow no activity that arises from the flesh to ever have any standing in His sight.

As Paul once wrote, "No flesh shall glory in his presence" (1 Corinthians 1:29 KJV). So if we operate in the flesh, in a spirit of ambition, in a desire to exalt ourselves, we will never accomplish anything in God's program. That is why God will never rest until we learn to draw from the strength of His life in us so that we can be qualified to serve Him as His priests.

## Blemishes That Disqualify

The remainder of the chapter deals with the various blemishes that would disqualify a person for the priesthood. These are things that come to us through our family connections, which in that sense are unavoidable, but which nevertheless disqualify us until they are dealt with.

The LORD said to Moses, "Say to Aaron: 'For the generations to come none of your descendants who has a defect may come near to offer the food of his God. No man who has any defect may come near: no man who is blind or lame, disfigured or deformed; no man with a crippled foot or hand, or who is hunchbacked or dwarfed, or who has any eye defect, or who has festering or running sores or damaged testicles. No descendant of Aaron the priest who has any defect is to come near to present the offerings made to the LORD by fire. He has a defect; he must not come near to offer the food of his God. He may eat the most holy food of his God, as well as the holy food; yet because of his defect, he must not go near the curtain or approach the altar, and so desecrate my sanctuary. I am the LORD, who makes them holy.'"

So Moses told this to Aaron and his sons and to all the Israelites (Leviticus 21:16–24).

Notice that all the members of the priestly family were privileged to eat the bread of God: "He may eat the most holy food of his God, as well as the holy food." There is no limitation against that. They could feed upon it. They could grow by its strength.

As we interpret that passage to apply to our lives in God's priesthood of all believers today, we understand that we can partake of the life of Christ, who is the Bread of Life, and we can draw upon it for our spiritual nourishment, even if our lives are blemished and imperfect. We are not cast out of the family of God, even though we have defects in our lives. But we can't pass this bread on to others if we have blemished lives. We cannot minister unless these issues are dealt with.

The priests of the Israelites were set aside for life because of their blemishes—even though their blemishes might be birth defects, which are no fault of their own. Why did God prevent people with physical blemishes and abnormalities from serving in the priesthood of Israel? It is certainly not because He loved such people any less. No, it is because the priests provided a visible lesson about the lives of His people: No one with a blemished life is qualified to minister in God's presence.

The beautiful lesson we find here is that these blemishes can be healed. Lives can be cleansed. We don't have to be forever set aside from ministering. Each of these blemishes has a symbolic meaning to us now, and these symbols have much to teach us about how God wants to work in our lives.

Were some of the Israelite priests blind? Yes. And so are some of us today. We don't see spiritual and moral truth very clearly. Our spiritual eyes are blinded.

Were some of the Israelite priests lame? Yes. And some of us are, too. We don't walk very well. We limp and stagger and fall on our faces at times.

Did some have deformed hands or feet? Yes. And some of us do as well. Our work and our walk may be faulty at times. Did some have deformed or stunted bodies? Yes. And some of us have lives that are warped by distorted views of God—possibly because we were abused or neglected or somehow hurt in childhood.

Some of us have vision defects—we see some measure of the truth, but we don't see clearly, perhaps because of some distortion caused by a painful experience with a fellow Christian. Some of us have festering or running sores in our souls and spirits—our lives ooze emotional pain because of some loss or hurt in our lives.

And what about damaged testicles? Why would God make a point of including that particular form of injury in this list of physical blemishes? Because the testicles symbolize our ability to spiritually reproduce—our ability to generate new converts for Christ.

Damaged testicles also speak of an area of many Christians' lives that hinders the ability to spiritually reproduce: sexual sin. Those who have brokenness in their sex life will have no ministry for Christ. They may try. They may even become popular Christian preachers, evangelists, or authors—yet all of their popularity in the church or in the world does not impress God in the least. He knows when there is sexual sin in a Christian's life, and He does not honor the ministry of a person who has not dealt with this area of brokenness and sin.

All these blemishes hinder our ministry as God's priests. They don't stop us from feeding upon the life of Christ, but they do prevent us from ministering effectively to others. Though we may perform an outward form of ministry, God withholds the power. The New Testament teaches this too. Paul wrote:

> In a large house there are articles not only of gold and silver, but also of wood and clay; some are for noble purposes and some for ignoble. If a man cleanses himself from the latter, he will be an instrument for noble purposes, made holy, useful to the Master and prepared to do any good work (2 Timothy 2:20–21).

We tend to think that we, as Christians, can be involved in sinful habits and unclean ways of thinking, with obscured spiritual vision and impaired hearing of the Word—yet God will bless our work anyway. So we live our lives with one foot in the world and one foot in the church, trying to do ministry for Christ and wondering why our ministry is not as full and satisfying as it should be.

I have seen this pattern in the lives of many people in the church and in other Christian ministries. Such people often feel a great deal of resistance to making changes in their lives and letting go of the pet sins and wrongful habits.

But whenever I have seen people, whether young or old, begin to take their priesthood seriously and clean up the dirty corners of their lives, I have seen them experience a newfound sweetness and freshness in their spiritual lives, plus a more potent effectiveness in their ministry for Christ. Again and again, I've heard Christians say, "I didn't understand. I didn't realize that this habit was limiting my ministry."

## LIVES OF MEANING AND WORTH

Leviticus 22 repeats many of the commands that we have already seen in Leviticus, so we will not explore that chapter in great detail. Here is the text of that chapter, along with a brief summary of the main themes and points of Leviticus 22.

> The LORD said to Moses, "Tell Aaron and his sons to treat with respect the sacred offerings the Israelites consecrate to me, so they will not profane my holy name. I am the LORD.
>
> "Say to them: 'For the generations to come, if any of your descendants is ceremonially unclean and yet comes near the sacred offerings that the Israelites consecrate to the LORD, that person must be cut off from my presence. I am the LORD.
>
> "'If a descendant of Aaron has an infectious skin disease or a bodily discharge, he may not eat the sacred offerings until he is cleansed. He will also be unclean if he touches something defiled by a corpse or by anyone who has an emission of semen, or if he touches any crawling thing that makes him unclean, or any person who makes him unclean, whatever the uncleanness may be. The one who touches any such thing will be unclean till evening. He must not eat any of the sacred offerings unless he has bathed himself with water. When the sun goes down, he will be clean, and after that he may eat the sacred offerings, for they are his food. He

must not eat anything found dead or torn by wild animals, and so become unclean through it. I am the LORD.

"'The priests are to keep my requirements so that they do not become guilty and die for treating them with contempt. I am the LORD, who makes them holy'" (Leviticus 22:1–9).

In these verses, God underscores His requirement that His people and their sacrifices to Him (that is, their worship of Him) must be cleansed in order to be useful for His service.

"'No one outside a priest's family may eat the sacred offering, nor may the guest of a priest or his hired worker eat it. But if a priest buys a slave with money, or if a slave is born in his household, that slave may eat his food. If a priest's daughter marries anyone other than a priest, she may not eat any of the sacred contributions. But if a priest's daughter becomes a widow or is divorced, yet has no children, and she returns to live in her father's house as in her youth, she may eat of her father's food. No unauthorized person, however, may eat any of it.

"'If anyone eats a sacred offering by mistake, he must make restitution to the priest for the offering and add a fifth of the value to it. The priests must not desecrate the sacred offerings the Israelites present to the LORD by allowing them to eat the sacred offerings and so bring upon them guilt requiring payment. I am the LORD, who makes them holy'" (Leviticus 22:10–16).

The preceding verses place restrictions upon strangers and foreigners— non-Israelites. No one other than the children of Aaron could serve as priests— and no non-Israelite could ever be admitted to the priesthood. This is a symbolic picture of the fact that God does not want people who are outside of His spiritual family doing spiritual work in His name. A nonbeliever cannot do the work of God. Only those who have been born again into the family of God can ever accomplish anything for Him.

Nonbelievers can perform works that appear to be of God, but God Himself will judge all works (see Romans 14:10; 2 Corinthians 5:10). Works that are done by His people according to His will, in reliance upon His power, will be revealed as gold, silver, and precious jewels; works done by nonbelievers, or done in the wrong spirit and for the wrong motives, will be revealed as nothing but wood, hay, and stubble, fit only to be burned to ashes (see 1 Corinthians 3:11–15).

Next, God continues to give Moses commands and requirements regarding the offerings and worship to be offered to Him by the priests.

> The LORD said to Moses, "Speak to Aaron and his sons and to all the Israelites and say to them: 'If any of you—either an Israelite or an alien living in Israel—presents a gift for a burnt offering to the LORD, either to fulfill a vow or as a freewill offering, you must present a male without defect from the cattle, sheep or goats in order that it may be accepted on your behalf. Do not bring anything with a defect, because it will not be accepted on your behalf. When anyone brings from the herd or flock a fellowship offering to the LORD to fulfill a special vow or as a freewill offering, it must be without defect or blemish to be acceptable. Do not offer to the LORD the blind, the injured or the maimed, or anything with warts or festering or running sores. Do not place any of these on the altar as an offering made to the LORD by fire. You may, however, present as a freewill offering an ox or a sheep that is deformed or stunted, but it will not be accepted in fulfillment of a vow. You must not offer to the LORD an animal whose testicles are bruised, crushed, torn or cut. You must not do this in your own land, and you must not accept such animals from the hand of a foreigner and offer them as the food of your God. They will not be accepted on your behalf, because they are deformed and have defects.'"
>
> The LORD said to Moses, "When a calf, a lamb or a goat is born, it is to remain with its mother for seven days. From the eighth day on, it will be acceptable as an offering made to the LORD by fire. Do not slaughter a cow or a sheep and its young on the same day.
>
> "When you sacrifice a thank offering to the LORD, sacrifice it in such a way that it will be accepted on your behalf. It must be

eaten that same day; leave none of it till morning. I am the LORD"
(Leviticus 22:17–30).

Here, God speaks about what makes sacrificial offerings acceptable or unacceptable in His sight. He says that there is to be no blemish in the offerings that are given. The sacrifices are to be perfect. Why is God so demanding? Because the sacrifices are a picture of the work of Jesus Christ. God insists that these sacrifices represent Jesus accurately, clearly, and without distortion.

Leviticus 22 concludes with these words of warning and compassion. We read:

> "Keep my commands and follow them. I am the LORD. Do not profane my holy name. I must be acknowledged as holy by the Israelites. I am the LORD, who makes you holy and who brought you out of Egypt to be your God. I am the LORD" (Leviticus 22:31–33).

These are the words of a tender and loving Father who cares for His children. "I am the Lord," He says, in effect, "who brought you out of bondage. I set you free. And I want to heal your life and bring you into a land of abundance and promise, of excitement and blessing, of fruitfulness and joy. I am your God, and my power is available to you. So follow my commands, keep my name holy, and you will be whole and holy, too."

When we submit to God's lordship over our lives, we discover that it is rich and exciting to be priests in His priesthood. When we live for Him as He intended, then He begins to enlarge our borders. He begins to use us in ways we never imagined before, and life becomes an adventure. We live with a new and exciting sense of purpose. Our lives have meaning and worth. That is what it means to serve as a priest of God.

We discover that God is not so much interested in our accomplishments as He is interested in our attitudes. We find out that we are approved by God because of what we are—His children—not because of what we do.

So if we have an attitude of joy, praise, and love for God, we can please Him while washing the dishes or driving the kids to the soccer game. We can be used by God while washing the car or going to the hardware store. God's life begins to flow through us, so that we are effective as priests no matter where we are, no matter what we do. Soon we find that God is sending people our way, so that we can minister to them right where we are—over the back fence, at the front door, in the checkout line, at the gas pump. We can pause from our chores and take time to encourage those people and feed them the Bread of Life. We can serve as God's whole and holy priests.

But before we can serve as priests, we must deal with the blemishes in our lives. May God give us the desire to let go of our sins and worthless habits, so that we can be qualified to serve Him as priests.

CHAPTER 20

≫———————≪

# GOD'S CALENDAR
## LEVITICUS 23

I HAVE A calendar that I use to plan out my entire year in advance. I write in all the important events and engagements of my personal and ministry life—a conference here, a trip there, a vacation a little later in the year, and so on. I use my calendar so that I can organize my time, schedule events that are important to me, and work more effectively to meet my goals and objectives. I don't always fulfill all of my intentions for the year, but having a calendar gives me an outline of what I hope to accomplish. It enables me to move along my timeline in a planned and coordinated way.

God, too, has a calendar, a program of events, and He is moving along its timeline with unerring precision. It is encouraging to me that God has given us His timeline in the Scriptures, so that we can clearly understand that His program is right on schedule. His plan has not deviated by one hour or even one second. Events are never out of His control. Even though we do not always understand His schedule, God is in total, sovereign control of history. That is a great reassurance to us in perilous times.

The twenty-third chapter of Leviticus is a remarkable portion of Scripture, because it gives us God's calendar for the appointed feasts of Israel. These feasts were observed by the nation on a regular basis, year after year. There were seven feasts throughout the year, in addition to the weekly Sabbath. The feasts were precisely spaced and dated because they represented God's timetable of events by which He is moving through history.

It would be a mistake to think of the feasts of Israel as mere holidays that were observed as we observe holidays today. The primary idea of a holiday observance in America is to give people a day off from work to have a backyard barbecue. Our holidays are usually observed on the Monday nearest the holiday in order to give people a three-day weekend. The feasts of Israel, by contrast, were instituted for a solemn and important purpose. Each was a symbolic occasion or season designed to teach a profound spiritual truth.

Because the feasts of Israel were created to teach truth to God's people, He spaced them and regulated them so that their observance would be a significant and specially appointed time in the lives of the people. As we examine God's calendar of feasts and observances, we will trace a symbolic picture of the history of the nation of Israel—where the nation has been, where it is now, and where it is going.

And, as we have seen throughout Leviticus, we will also see that things that were literally and historically true of the nation of Israel are also pictures of God's spiritual program for our lives today. Every believer in Jesus Christ proceeds through this same order of spiritual development. That is what makes Leviticus 23 such a fascinating and relevant chapter for our lives.

## THE TRUE MEANING OF THE SABBATH REST

Leviticus 23 begins with a reference to the institution of the Sabbath, the day of holy rest on the seventh day of every week.

> The LORD said to Moses, "Speak to the Israelites and say to them: 'These are my appointed feasts, the appointed feasts of the LORD, which you are to proclaim as sacred assemblies.
>
> "'There are six days when you may work, but the seventh day is a Sabbath of rest, a day of sacred assembly. You are not to do any work; wherever you live, it is a Sabbath to the LORD'" (Leviticus 23:1–3).

The weekly Sabbath was instituted at creation. We find the account of the first Sabbath in Genesis 2:2–3.

By the seventh day God had finished the work he had been doing; so on the seventh day he rested from all his work. And God blessed the seventh day and made it holy, because on it he rested from all the work of creating that he had done.

So God worked six days and then rested on the seventh day, the Sabbath. The Sabbath was reinstated and renewed when God gave the Law to Moses on Mount Sinai. At that time, God reminded His people that the Sabbath was at the heart of all His work.

"Remember the Sabbath day by keeping it holy. Six days you shall labor and do all your work, but the seventh day is a Sabbath to the LORD your God. On it you shall not do any work, neither you, nor your son or daughter, nor your manservant or maidservant, nor your animals, nor the alien within your gates. For in six days the LORD made the heavens and the earth, the sea, and all that is in them, but he rested on the seventh day. Therefore the LORD blessed the Sabbath day and made it holy" (Exodus 20:8–11).

We often hear Sunday referred to as the Sabbath. Many people seem to think that "Sabbath" is an old-fashioned word for Sunday, but that is wrong. Sunday is not the Sabbath and never was! The seventh day was Saturday, the Sabbath; the first day was Sunday. Biblically, the only day that is to be observed as the Sabbath is Saturday—and among observant Jews around the world, this is still true.

Our friends, the Seventh-day Adventists, feel that Christians still ought to observe the seventh day as God's day of rest. They tell us that Christians should worship on Saturday, not on Sunday. When they contend that God has never diminished the importance of the Sabbath, they are right. But, as we have already seen throughout Leviticus, the Levitical laws are shadows and symbols of a spiritual reality. It is the reality that is all-important, not the symbol. The observance of a day of rest is a picture of something else that God wants in our lives—something that is of great significance to Him. When the reality came, the shadow was done away with.

The apostle Paul specifically tells us that the observance of a day is one of those shadows which ended for the believer at the coming of Christ.

> Therefore do not let anyone judge you by what you eat or drink, or with regard to a religious festival, a New Moon celebration or a Sabbath day. These are a shadow of the things that were to come; the reality, however, is found in Christ (Colossians 2:16–17).

What, then, is the reality that the Sabbath points to? We find the answer to that question in a number of places in Scripture. We find it especially in Hebrews 4, where the writer to the Hebrews reminds us that Sabbath means "rest" and that this is a reference to the secret of life. Humans were made to operate out of rest, not out of haste, anxiety, and pressure. God never intended for us to be driven and harassed in a rat-race-like life. God intended for us to know rest and peace, and He provided for that need in our lives by means of the Sabbath. What is the rest God intended for us? Here is our answer.

> There remains, then, a Sabbath-rest for the people of God; for anyone who enters God's rest also rests from his own work, just as God did from his. Let us, therefore, make every effort to enter that rest, so that no one will fall by following their example of disobedience (Hebrews 4:9–11).

Those who enter into rest have stopped their own work and are resting on the work of others. So if you learn the principle of operating out of dependence upon God at work in you, then you no longer try to do the work of salvation by yourself. When you rest in God, you no longer feel that everything depends on you. The one who rests in God is observing the Sabbath as God intended it to be observed.

Rest is at the heart of everything God does. All of the feasts in Leviticus 23 are a form of the Sabbath and consist of one Sabbath or of several. All of these symbolic observances are intended to instruct us in the greatest secret of human existence: God created us to live and function for Him—not in a state of stress and worry but in a state of rest.

Notice how clearly and forcefully Jesus addressed the idea of resting when He preached the Sermon on the Mount.

> "Therefore I tell you, do not worry about your life, what you will eat or drink; or about your body, what you will wear. Is not life more

important than food, and the body more important than clothes? Look at the birds of the air; they do not sow or reap or store away in barns, and yet your heavenly Father feeds them. Are you not much more valuable than they? Who of you by worrying can add a single hour to his life?

"And why do you worry about clothes? See how the lilies of the field grow. They do not labor or spin. Yet I tell you that not even Solomon in all his splendor was dressed like one of these. If that is how God clothes the grass of the field, which is here today and tomorrow is thrown into the fire, will he not much more clothe you, O you of little faith? So do not worry, saying, 'What shall we eat?' or 'What shall we drink?' or 'What shall we wear?' For the pagans run after all these things, and your heavenly Father knows that you need them. But seek first his kingdom and his righteousness, and all these things will be given to you as well" (Matthew 6:25–33).

Our natural human tendency is to worry about our careers, our things-to-do list, our paycheck, our investments, our taxes, our mortgage, and on and on. But God does not want us to worry about these things. He wants us to rest. He wants us to enjoy His Sabbath. He wants us to trust Him and rely on Him for every need, task, and challenge in our lives.

A man once said to me, "I'm always finding that I've got a twelve-foot ditch to cross and only a ten-foot plank. No matter how hard I try, I can't figure out how to stretch that ten-foot plank so that it will cross that twelve-foot ditch." The secret of the Sabbath is that we don't need to try to stretch our ten-foot planks. God has already given us a bridge that is long enough and strong enough to span any ditch, chasm, or canyon we need to cross. That bridge is Jesus. When we rely on Him and depend on Him, we can relax and enjoy our Sabbath rest.

## THE GOSPEL ACCORDING TO THE PASSOVER

After setting forth the seventh day as a Sabbath of rest, God goes on to institute the first of several feasts, the Passover. This feast came in the spring, which was the beginning of the year in God's calendar for His people.

"'These are the LORD's appointed feasts, the sacred assemblies you are to proclaim at their appointed times: The LORD's Passover begins at twilight on the fourteenth day of the first month'" (Leviticus 23:4–5).

The details of this feast are given elsewhere in Scripture. The Passover was a reminder of that dramatic moment in Egypt when, because of Pharaoh's stubbornness, God sent the angel of death to pass throughout the land of Egypt and kill the firstborn son in every household. First, however, God made a provision for His people. If the people would kill a lamb and put its blood over the doorposts, the angel would see the blood and pass over that house (hence the name *Passover*).

The Passover was God's vivid and visual way of teaching humanity that the basis of His saving work on behalf of human beings always rests upon the death of Another. We can do nothing to save ourselves. The basis of our salvation is simply resting in the labor of Christ upon the cross. That is what the New Testament calls *justification*. When you place your trust in the work of Jesus Christ, who is our slain Passover Lamb, then you are saved by the infinite merit of His sacrifice. You cannot save yourself by your own effort; you can be saved only by resting in what Jesus has already done for you.

Both the original Passover event in Egypt and the annual Passover Feast were visual, symbolic representations of the Passover reality that would later be fulfilled in history. When the people of Israel ate the Passover, they thought that they were merely commemorating the night the angel of death passed through Egypt and passed over Israel. They didn't realize that they were also commemorating an event that was yet to take place.

The true Passover event began on the night that Jesus ate the last Passover Feast with His disciples in Jerusalem. Jesus and His friends ate together of the slain lamb that symbolized His death on the cross, just hours away. In the Exodus account of the first Passover night in Egypt, we read:

> Then Moses summoned all the elders of Israel and said to them, "Go at once and select the animals for your families and slaughter the Passover lamb. Take a bunch of hyssop, dip it into the blood in the basin and put some of the blood on the top and on both sides

of the doorframe. Not one of you shall go out the door of his house until morning. When the LORD goes through the land to strike down the Egyptians, he will see the blood on the top and sides of the doorframe and will pass over that doorway, and he will not permit the destroyer to enter your houses and strike you down" (Exodus 12:21–23).

God obviously did not need to see the blood on the doorposts of Israel to know who was His own and who was not. He knew every human heart in the land of Israel. The purpose of splashing blood on the top and both sides of the doorframe—on the upright posts and horizontal lintel—was to teach an important symbolic lesson to the people of Israel. The lamb's blood on the doorframe represented the human blood that would one day drench the upright post and horizontal crossbeam of a Roman cross.

Through the imagery of the Passover, God was saying to the entire human race, "If I see the blood of my Son Jesus splashed over the doorway of your life, if you hide behind His rugged and blood-drenched cross, then you will be safe from my wrath. You will be saved from the destruction that will be unleashed against the world in the day of judgment." That is the essence of the Passover and the Christian gospel: We are safe from the wrath of God under the blood of Christ.

## REMOVING THE CONTAMINATION OF YEAST

The next feast on God's calendar was closely linked to the Passover. It was called the Feast of Unleavened Bread.

"'On the fifteenth day of that month the LORD's Feast of Unleavened Bread begins; for seven days you must eat bread made without yeast. On the first day hold a sacred assembly and do no regular work. For seven days present an offering made to the LORD by fire. And on the seventh day hold a sacred assembly and do no regular work'" (Leviticus 23:6–8).

The Feast of Unleavened Bread always began on the fifteenth day of the month and lasted seven days. Like the Passover, this feast looked back to the time of captivity in Egypt, to the command that God gave the Israelites to remove all leaven (yeast) from their houses. To this day, orthodox Jews meticulously remove all yeast from their homes in preparation for the Passover season. (This is, in fact, the origin of the custom we now know as spring cleaning.)

Yeast causes bread to rise and swell. It is an apt symbol of that aspect of our humanity that tends to puff us up. There is something at work in human beings, God says, that causes us to inflate with pride, arrogance, and self-importance. There is a principle at work in our humanity that drives us to be self-centered and self-applauding. We have a compulsive need to have other people think we are important. We find subtle and not-so-subtle ways to let other people know what an important job we have, how exclusive a neighborhood we live in, how expensive a car we drive, who our influential friends and acquaintances are, and on and on.

Pride also induces us to hide our inadequacy. We don't want to appear insufficient or lacking in anything. We don't want to admit we have problems or need help. We protect our image of perfection, our image of power and status, our image of spiritual maturity. That is the yeast that swells us up, the leaven of human pride and ego.

Jesus often spoke of leaven. He said, "Be on your guard against the yeast of the Pharisees, which is hypocrisy" (Luke 12:1). Hypocrisy means pretending to be what we are not. As Christians, we easily engage in hypocrisy, don't we? We pretend to be super-spiritual when we're not. We pretend not to have any problems when we do. We pretend to be joyful when we're miserable inside. We pretend to tell the truth, but it's a lie. That is hypocrisy, the yeast of the Pharisees, which comes from an arrogant desire to have people think we are something better than we really are.

Jesus also warned against the yeast of another group. He said, "Be on your guard against the yeast of the . . . Sadducees" (Matthew 16:6). Like so many people around us today, the Sadducees were a rationalist group. They denied the existence of the supernatural. They believed that everything could be logically explained in terms of what you can see, taste, touch, smell, and feel; anything that cannot be so explained (such as the human spirit or the resurrection from the dead) cannot possibly exist. So Jesus warned against becoming contaminated by the yeast of the false teaching of the Sadducees.

Jesus also spoke of the yeast of the Herodians, the materialistic pleasure seekers who followed after King Herod (see Mark 8:15). Like so many people in our culture today, the Herodians lived for luxury, status, prestige, and the praise and favor of other people. They were immoral, manipulative, scheming people who constantly sought ways to advance themselves, even at the expense of others.

Paul also spoke about spiritual and moral yeast in our lives. He used the symbol of yeast to represent sin in various forms, including sexual immorality, pride, anger, and hypocrisy.

> Your boasting is not good. Don't you know that a little yeast works through the whole batch of dough? Get rid of the old yeast that you may be a new batch without yeast—as you really are. For Christ, our Passover lamb, has been sacrificed. Therefore let us keep the Festival, not with the old yeast, the yeast of malice and wickedness, but with bread without yeast, the bread of sincerity and truth (1 Corinthians 5:6–8).

Yeast, Paul warned, has a way of spreading and infecting everything. Put a little yeast in one little place in a large lump of dough, and soon it works its way through the entire batch. Sin spreads. Hypocrisy and pride are contagious. Sexually immoral practices, if tolerated by a few in the church, soon contaminate a congregation.

That is why God gave Israel the Feast of Unleavened Bread. He wanted to teach the people the importance of removing all the yeast of sin, pride, hypocrisy, and self-centeredness from their lives.

## THE FIRST FRUITS—A PICTURE OF THE RESURRECTION OF CHRIST

The third feast on God's calendar of observances was called the Feast of the First Fruits.

> The LORD said to Moses, "Speak to the Israelites and say to them: 'When you enter the land I am going to give you and you reap its harvest, bring to the priest a sheaf of the first grain you harvest. He is to wave the sheaf before the LORD so it will be accepted on

your behalf; the priest is to wave it on the day after the Sabbath. On the day you wave the sheaf, you must sacrifice as a burnt offering to the LORD a lamb a year old without defect, together with its grain offering of two-tenths of an ephah of fine flour mixed with oil—an offering made to the LORD by fire, a pleasing aroma—and its drink offering of a quarter of a hin of wine. You must not eat any bread, or roasted or new grain, until the very day you bring this offering to your God. This is to be a lasting ordinance for the generations to come, wherever you live'" (Leviticus 23:9–14).

In the land of Israel, barley was planted in the fall and was harvested in the springtime. (We read about Israel's barley harvest in the book of Ruth.) The harvest was preceded by the Feast of First Fruits in which the people took a sheaf of grain, cut it, and waved it before the Lord, offering Him the first and choicest reapings of the harvest. Along with the Feast of the First Fruits came certain sacrifices, which speak (as we previously saw) of the rest that is ours through the shed blood and sacrificial work of Another, Jesus. The people were specifically warned not to eat of this grain in any form until they had made this offering.

What was this feast a picture of? We don't have to guess. The apostle Paul tells us what this feast symbolizes in his letter to the church at Corinth.

But Christ has indeed been raised from the dead, the first fruits of those who have fallen asleep. For since death came through a man, the resurrection of the dead comes also through a man. For as in Adam all die, so in Christ all will be made alive. But each in his own turn: Christ, the first fruits; then, when he comes, those who belong to him (1 Corinthians 15:20–23).

When our Lord rose from the dead, He was the first fruits of God's harvest. When God initiates His saving work with humanity, He begins with the death of Another on our behalf. This saving work produces a harvest of risen lives. The Lord Himself, who was the first to rise from the grave on that beautiful Easter morning, was the first fruits of what will ultimately be a great harvest of resurrected lives. You and I, as believers in Christ, will be caught up in that great harvest, but we are preceded by Christ, the first to rise.

Notice that the first fruits were to be offered on the day after the Sabbath. The Sabbath is Saturday; the day after the Sabbath is Sunday. So the first fruits were to be offered on Sunday, the Lord's Day—the very day of the resurrection! In the gospel account of the resurrection, we find that the empty tomb was discovered "after the Sabbath, at dawn on the first day of the week" (Matthew 28:1).

On the day of the resurrection of Christ, a new life with a new kind of food was given to us. This is a reminder of the new life of the new creation which is ours through the resurrection. So the meaning of the Feast of First Fruits becomes clear in light of the resurrection: It symbolizes resurrection and new life, and that is why the Lord's Day, Sunday, is a day for all believers to celebrate.

## THE FEAST OF WEEKS

The next feast was called the Feast of Weeks, and it holds a special place in the Christian calendar and the calendar of Judaism.

> "'From the day after the Sabbath, the day you brought the sheaf of the wave offering, count off seven full weeks. Count off fifty days up to the day after the seventh Sabbath, and then present an offering of new grain to the LORD. From wherever you live, bring two loaves made of two-tenths of an ephah of fine flour, baked with yeast, as a wave offering of first fruits to the LORD. Present with this bread seven male lambs, each a year old and without defect, one young bull and two rams. They will be a burnt offering to the LORD, together with their grain offerings and drink offerings—an offering made by fire, an aroma pleasing to the LORD. Then sacrifice one male goat for a sin offering and two lambs, each a year old, for a fellowship offering. The priest is to wave the two lambs before the LORD as a wave offering, together with the bread of the firstfruits. They are a sacred offering to the LORD for the priest. On that same day you are to proclaim a sacred assembly and do no regular work. This is to be a lasting ordinance for the generations to come, wherever you live'" (Leviticus 23:15–21).

The people of Israel called this feast *Shavuot* or *Shabuoth*, which comes from the Hebrew words for "seven weeks." Seven weeks is literally forty-nine days; because God told Israel to count fifty days, to the day after the seventh Sabbath, this feast is known in English as Pentecost, from the Greek word *pentkost*, which means "fiftieth day." Notice that the Feast of Weeks or Pentecost fell on a Sunday, the day after a Sabbath, which is further evidence that God truly intended, following the resurrection of Jesus on a Sunday, to shift the day of celebration for believers to the first day of the week.

Remember also what took place on the first Pentecost following our Lord's resurrection. On that day, as the disciples were gathered in the upper room in Jerusalem, the Holy Spirit suddenly came upon them in a new way. A new body was formed, called the church, and it was to be made up not only of Jewish believers but also of Gentiles, non-Jewish people.

Notice that God commands, "From wherever you live, bring two loaves made of two-tenths of an ephah of fine flour, baked with yeast, as a wave offering of firstfruits to the LORD." What do the two loaves symbolize? That God's new community, His church, will be made up of Jews and Gentiles— two loaves baked with yeast.

Yeast, as we have seen, is a picture of the working of evil in our lives. And when the Holy Spirit came, He came upon people just like you and me, people still struggling with the yeast of sin in their lives, this deadly principle of human self-will, self-centeredness, and self-sufficiency. The people were filled with the Holy Spirit on Pentecost, just as you and I can be filled with God's Holy Spirit today.

The church today is beautifully symbolized by the two loaves of leavened bread—Jews and Gentiles together, filled with the Spirit, still tainted with yeast, still flawed and often failing, yet willing to approach God and allow Him to work through them.

The heart of this feast was these two loaves, baked with yeast. Baking is accomplished by heat from a fire. In the Scriptures, fire always symbolizes judgment. As the Holy Spirit takes up residence in men and women still capable of sin, the yeast is still there. This is God's testimony that He will work in His people and judge the yeast in their lives, bringing it under His control. The people in the church will never, in this life, be a flawless example of idealized Christianity. The only perfect example of Christianity is Christ Himself. But His followers still express God's fellowship with humanity.

Now, perhaps, you begin to see how these feasts in God's calendar anticipated the outline of history. The Feast of Pentecost occurred around the middle of May; from mid-May until the first day of the seventh month (about mid-September on our modern calendar), there were no more feasts in Israel. A long period of time would go by before another feast occurred—a long, hot summer without feasts. During that time, God made only one provision or stipulation for the people to observe.

"'When you reap the harvest of your land, do not reap to the very edges of your field or gather the gleanings of your harvest. Leave them for the poor and the alien. I am the LORD your God'" (Leviticus 23:22).

Here God says that when the Israelite people harvested the land, they should leave a portion for the poor and for aliens—that is, non-Jewish people who passed through the land. God showed, here in the Old Testament, that He cared about the Gentile people, those who were born outside of the house of Israel. It is significant that this commandment comes right after the Feast of Weeks, the Feast of Pentecost. On the New Testament day of Pentecost, many non-Jewish believers came into the church. Ever since that day, there has been a long, indeterminate, but definitely finite period of time during which the door is open to the Gentiles, and they may come in and feed upon the riches of Christ, just as the poor and the aliens could come in and feed on the richness of the fields of Israel.

The post-Pentecost age continues to this day. It has been many years since the day of the resurrection and since the day of Pentecost. We are in the summertime of human history, between the Feast of Pentecost and the next great feast, the next great moment in human history. For now, the door of the church is wide open to Jewish and non-Jewish people. In time, that door will be shut, but for now, all are welcome. This is where human history stands now.

The next feast gives us a glimpse into the future of the world.

## THE SOUND OF TRUMPETS AND WHAT THEY FORETELL

The next feast is the Feast of Trumpets, which, as we will see, symbolically represents a time in history that is yet to be fulfilled.

> The LORD said to Moses, "Say to the Israelites: 'On the first day of the seventh month you are to have a day of rest, a sacred assembly commemorated with trumpet blasts. Do no regular work, but present an offering made to the LORD by fire'" (Leviticus 23:23–25).

The central manifestation of this feast was a series of trumpet blasts. What does God mean by giving us this symbol? Once again we are not left to guess. If you turn to Matthew 24, Jesus describes how the age in which we are living shall end. The world will experience the rise of a great satanically inspired dictator, the antichrist; humanity will be divided between warring camps and tribes; and a great tribulation will spread across the earth unlike any time of trouble the earth has ever seen. Then, Jesus says, an even more dire event will take place.

> "Immediately after the distress of those days
> "'the sun will be darkened,
>     and the moon will not give its light;
> the stars will fall from the sky,
>     and the heavenly bodies will be shaken.'
> "At that time the sign of the Son of Man will appear in the sky, and all the nations of the earth will mourn. They will see the Son of Man coming on the clouds of the sky, with power and great glory. And he will send his angels with a loud trumpet call, and they will gather his elect from the four winds, from one end of the heavens to the other" (Matthew 24:29–31).

Here, Jesus describes the next event in God's program for His people Israel. The Son of Man will come, and the trumpet of God will herald the final gathering of Israel to the land. We saw a small foretaste of this event after World War II, when the Jewish state of Israel was established in Palestine. However, this small influx of Jews into their ancestral lands is not the final gathering that Jesus describes here. Strangely enough, there will be another dispersion, though it will not last long.

The prophet Zechariah describes in detail how the city of Jerusalem will again be taken captive and the people will be driven from it. It is only after they see returning the One whom they once rejected that they will be called back by the angels of God. In that day of trumpets, which the Feast of Trumpets only symbolizes, the Jews will return to Jerusalem, never to leave again. At that time, God will take up His work with Israel once again.

## THE DAY OF ATONEMENT—A DAY OF JUDGMENT

After the Feast of Trumpets comes the great Day of Atonement.

> The LORD said to Moses, "The tenth day of this seventh month is
> the Day of Atonement. Hold a sacred assembly and deny yourselves,
> and present an offering made to the LORD by fire. Do no work on
> that day, because it is the Day of Atonement, when atonement is
> made for you before the LORD your God. Anyone who does not
> deny himself on that day must be cut off from his people. I will
> destroy from among his people anyone who does any work on that
> day. You shall do no work at all. This is to be a lasting ordinance for
> the generations to come, wherever you live. It is a sabbath of rest for
> you, and you must deny yourselves. From the evening of the ninth
> day of the month until the following evening you are to observe
> your sabbath" (Leviticus 23:26–32).

In Leviticus 16, we saw certain offerings that were to be presented to God
in connection with the Day of Atonement. The distinctive feature of this day
is that it was to be a time of self-judgment, of looking inward and recognizing
the wasted years of our lives, and of mourning and regretting those lost opportunities. The true meaning of the Day of Atonement was described for us by
the prophet Zechariah:

> "And I will pour out on the house of David and the inhabitants
> of Jerusalem a spirit of grace and supplication. They will look on
> me, the one they have pierced, and they will mourn for him as one
> mourns for an only child, and grieve bitterly for him as one grieves
> for a firstborn son. On that day the weeping in Jerusalem will be
> great, like the weeping of Hadad Rimmon in the plain of Megiddo"
> (Zechariah 12:10–11).

Here we see a time when the people of Israel will regret their long centuries of unbelief. Christians, too, will experience a time of mourning, but
it will come in the form of a review of the wasted opportunities of life—a
review that will occur at the judgment seat of Christ, when every Christian

will "receive what is due him for the things done while in the body, whether good or bad" (2 Corinthians 5:10). At that time, we will learn how much of our life was spent in the flesh, following the inclinations of our fallen humanity, and how much of it was spent in the Spirit, rejoicing in the work of Jesus on our behalf. At that time we will discover how much of our lives can be considered to be made of gold, silver, and precious stones—and how much is just so much wood, hay, and stubble, fit only to be burned up by fire.

## THE FEAST OF TABERNACLES

Finally, we come to the last of the feasts on God's calendar, the Feast of Tabernacles.

> The LORD said to Moses, "Say to the Israelites: 'On the fifteenth day of the seventh month the LORD's Feast of Tabernacles begins, and it lasts for seven days. The first day is a sacred assembly; do no regular work. For seven days present offerings made to the LORD by fire, and on the eighth day hold a sacred assembly and present an offering made to the LORD by fire. It is the closing assembly; do no regular work.
>
> ("'These are the LORD's appointed feasts, which you are to proclaim as sacred assemblies for bringing offerings made to the LORD by fire—the burnt offerings and grain offerings, sacrifices and drink offerings required for each day. These offerings are in addition to those for the LORD's Sabbaths and in addition to your gifts and whatever you have vowed and all the freewill offerings you give to the LORD.)
>
> "'So beginning with the fifteenth day of the seventh month, after you have gathered the crops of the land, celebrate the festival to the LORD for seven days; the first day is a day of rest, and the eighth day also is a day of rest. On the first day you are to take choice fruit from the trees, and palm fronds, leafy branches and poplars, and rejoice before the LORD your God for seven days. Celebrate this as a festival to the LORD for seven days each year. This is to be a lasting ordinance for the generations to come; celebrate it in

the seventh month. Live in booths for seven days: All native-born Israelites are to live in booths so your descendants will know that I had the Israelites live in booths when I brought them out of Egypt. I am the LORD your God.'"

So Moses announced to the Israelites the appointed feasts of the LORD (Leviticus 23:33–44).

These verses contain a beautiful picture of what is often called the millennium, the time which follows Israel's restoration to faith in God. At that time, the people of Israel will return to a relationship with nature in which the curse of sin shall be removed and God will bless the earth. Then, the desert will blossom like the rose. The secret of peace will be found and nations will not make war any more, and humanity will rejoice throughout the earth. The centerpiece of God's program for the future is the nation of Israel.

As C. S. Lewis has said, "The ultimate purpose of God in all His work is to increase joy." The Feast of Tabernacles is a beautiful picture of the radiant joy which is always the final product of God at work in a human life. God leads from wrath and judgment to the place of rest in the sacrifice of Jesus, our Passover lamb. He leads us through a gradual separation from evil, from the yeast of sin, pride, selfishness, and hypocrisy, and toward a new life imparted by the Holy Spirit. He leads us through the gathering of believers into one body, through the breaking down of the walls between Jew and Gentile, through the restoration of the wasted years of our life, and finally into the experience of radiant joy with God Himself. That is God's program in human history, and in your life and mine.

I once met with a pastor who had been serving God for years but had recently seen his ministry collapse in ruins. It was an embarrassing, humbling experience for this dedicated pastor. We sat down and talked about his painful experience, and he told me, "I prided myself on my own faithfulness and dedication to God. I looked down on people who were not as dedicated as I was. I thought I was being very spiritual and committed, a true servant of God. Now I look back and realize that I was only feeding my own pride and ego, telling myself what a wonderful servant of God I was, and how lucky God was to have me on His team!

"After my ministry collapsed, I was baffled and disillusioned. How could

God allow that to happen to me, after all I had done for Him? Then, as I was praying, God opened my eyes to the kind of servant I had truly been. I had been a proud Pharisee, looking down my nose at those sinners who were not as holy and righteous as I was. And then I understood why God allowed my ministry to fail. He took away the thing that I took pride in, the thing that fed my ego. He allowed me to fall so that I could learn that my efforts, my dedication, my commitment are worth nothing. God wants me to simply rest in Him, and give Him the glory. I've learned that I don't have any standing before God except His forgiving grace."

As this pastor said these words, his face was tear-stained yet radiant with joy. "What a relief!" he said. "What a relief! God reduced me to a place where He can finally begin to use me!"

That is what God seeks to do in your life and mine. He wants none of our feeble effort, our pitiful self-made righteousness, our yeast-infected, prideful good works. He simply wants us to take our Sabbath rest in Him. As long as we are operating in our own prideful strength, He will find a way to pull the rug out from under us and humble us. Only when we are clinging in total dependence upon Him can He truly use us as His servants and priests.

So this is how we are to live—resting in the work of Another. That is God's program for His people, that is what we see again and again in God's calendar, in one observance after another. As we look at this calendar of feasts, we can clearly see where we are in history. We can see how these feasts recapitulate the Passover sacrifice of Christ upon the cross, the first fruits of His resurrection, the founding of the church at Pentecost, and the coming sound of trumpets that will announce the final days of human history.

Now the question that confronts us is this: Where are we in God's calendar? Have we aligned our lives with God's eternal plan in human history? Have we made Jesus the Lord of our lives? Will we serve Him throughout our lives and reign with Him throughout eternity?

Or will we wake up one day to discover that we have wasted our lives and the opportunity God so patiently gave us to know Him and serve Him? As God brings human history to a close, will we stand with our Lord, our faces radiant with joy?

Or will we mourn?

I have made my decision. I am assured of my place on God's calendar. I know where I will spend the end of time and all of eternity.

What will you decide?

※────────────≪

# CHAPTER 21

# THE PATTERN OF
# HUMANITY

## LEVITICUS 24

I WAS ONCE asked to teach on Leviticus in a home Bible study in Dallas. The group consisted primarily of young believers, mostly college-age. At the end of the meeting, one of the young women in the group came to me and said, "I used to think that Leviticus was dull and didn't have very much to say to Christians in our century—but that's because I never really understood it. I'm studying psychology in school, and we've been studying the fundamental emotional needs of human beings. The amazing thing is that everything I've learned about human needs in psychology is what you've shown the book of Leviticus to be saying. The difference is that psychology explains the problem but Leviticus explains the solution."

What this young woman said is true. Leviticus—and, indeed, the entire Bible—tells us how to understand human beings—our drives, needs, and problems. The Bible tells us who we are, how we think, and what God has done to enable us to solve our problems and live as we were created to live. Leviticus reveals to us our basic human pattern and discloses to us the hidden potential that is available to us through the Spirit of God.

The key to understanding God's pattern of humanity is a building called the tabernacle. The New International Version of the Bible uses the term "the

Tent of Meeting." The tabernacle or Tent of Meeting was designed by God to symbolically represent humanity. All of the functions of the tabernacle are intended to reveal what takes place within our humanity, within our body, soul, and spirit. This same three-part structure was later reproduced when the permanent temple was built in Jerusalem.

Why is there so much emphasis on the tabernacle and the temple throughout the Bible? Because the tabernacle and the temple were designed by God to teach us His truth about ourselves. The pattern for the tabernacle was part of the great revelation God gave Moses upon the mountain when Moses was with Him for forty days and forty nights, while all of Israel waited below. God meticulously laid out for Moses the exact plan for constructing this building and for carrying on the functions within it. It is, therefore, an extremely important revelation, on par with the Ten Commandments.

## THE THREE DIVISIONS OF HUMANITY AND OF THE TABERNACLE

The reason the tabernacle and the temple were constructed to symbolize our humanity is that these structures were to be the dwelling place of God among the people of Israel in the Old Testament. After the coming of the Holy Spirit at Pentecost, humanity itself—ordinary believers like you and me—would become God's dwelling place. The apostle Paul told the Christians at Corinth:

> Don't you know that you yourselves are God's temple and that God's Spirit lives in you? If anyone destroys God's temple, God will destroy him; for God's temple is sacred, and you are that temple (1 Corinthians 3:16–17).

Since the tabernacle symbolized God's ultimate dwelling place—humanity itself—God made the design of the tabernacle clear to Moses in precise terms. As God instructed Moses, the tabernacle was to consist of three parts or divisions, just as human beings consist of three divisions:

First, there was the outer court. This corresponds to the human body. Even the Gentiles could enter the outer court. The body is the membrane of contact between our inner being and the outer world. Through the body, we experience the material universe in which we live. The outer court surrounded the structure of the tabernacle, which contained the next two divisions.

The second division was the Holy Place, one of the two divisions of the tabernacle structure. This corresponds to the soul. The soul is the conscious life, the realm of ideas, knowledge, rationality, emotion, decision-making, conscience, and memory.

Third, there is a mysterious area within the Holy Place that is kept hidden behind a veil. This is the secret place called the Holy of Holies. It corresponds to the spirit of humanity, a realm of mystery where all the deepest longings of our humanity are buried. This is where our longing for God and for heaven arises. This is where that sense of emptiness is found in all of those who don't know God and who have no relationship with Him. This human spirit is the place God intended to serve as His dwelling place. In the same way, we see that in the tabernacle, the Shekinah glory—the light that represents the presence of God—dwelt in the Holy of Holies.

## THE FURNISHINGS OF THE
## HOLY PLACE: THE CANDELABRUM

Leviticus 24 opens with a revealing description of the functions that took place in the Holy Place of the tabernacle. While this chapter is actually a summary of truths that are taught elsewhere in the Pentateuch (the first five books of the Bible), these are important truths. This chapter deals with the furniture that was in the Holy Place—furniture that corresponds to the soul, or the conscious life, of a human being.

There were three pieces of furniture. First, the golden candelabrum or *menorah* with its seven branches; the menorah is still one of the most recognizable symbols among the Jewish people. Second, the golden table of the show bread, upon which were displayed the twelve loaves that was the food of the priests. Third, the golden altar of incense, which stood directly before the veil that separated the Holy Place from the Holy of Holies; there, the fragrant frankincense was burned before God as an offering.

Those three pieces of furniture symbolize the three major functions of our soul—the mind, the emotions, and the will. They show how God intended a human soul to operate when filled and led by the Holy Spirit of God. The passage begins with a series of specific commands regarding the seven-branched candelabrum.

> The LORD said to Moses, "Command the Israelites to bring you clear oil of pressed olives for the light so that the lamps may be kept burning continually. Outside the curtain of the Testimony in the Tent of Meeting, Aaron is to tend the lamps before the LORD from evening till morning, continually. This is to be a lasting ordinance for the generations to come. The lamps on the pure gold lampstand before the LORD must be tended continually" (Leviticus 24:1–4).

Notice the elements of this passage. The candelabrum was to stand on a lampstand of pure gold. Pure olive oil was to be brought by the people as fuel to light the candelabrum. The flames were to burn continuously and never go out. The candelabrum was to burn at night; from evening to morning, Aaron was primarily responsible to keep the light going, because the candelabrum was the sole source of illumination in the tabernacle at night. What do these requirements mean?

The symbols of this passage are consistent with other Old Testament symbols, making this passage easy to interpret. The function of the human soul, of our conscious life, is to give us light—the light of truth. To this day, we speak of truth as being illuminating, and when we gain insight into a problem, we say, "Oh, now I see the light!" Light is a universally understood symbol for truth and knowledge. It is the mind that receives truth; when the mind grasps an illuminating idea, it is as if a light comes on. The function of the mind is to perceive, think, reason, explore, study, investigate, correlate, and understand. The mind is designed to sift through information, ideas, and opinions in order to arrive at truth.

Next, notice how specific this passage is in describing how the candelabrum is to be fueled: "clear oil of pressed olives." Here, God specifies that only a very pure oil—clear, without any adulterating solids—may be used to light the candelabrum. Throughout Scripture, oil is always a symbol of the Holy Spirit. So the light of truth is produced and made known to the human mind by means of the Holy Spirit, who anoints the mind with revealed truth. Our basic understanding of who we are, why we are here, what life is all about, and how the universe works all comes from the Holy Spirit.

The candelabrum is supported by a golden candlestick. Gold is always the symbol of deity in Scripture. So it is the life of God within us that sustains the light which illuminates our minds. This is a beautiful picture of how believers are to perceive and think.

We start with a mind that is taught by God to see life as God sees it. Most of the problems that come into our lives originate because we fail to begin with God's perspective on life. We tend to approach our problems, plans, and challenges from a natural point of view. We think about life as the world thinks. We accept as true all the illusions that the world teaches about life. We act and react just as the world does—then we wonder why our lives are in such disarray! Our minds must be governed not by natural thinking but by God's illuminating truth. Only then can we see life as it really is.

There is no more urgent need among Christians than that we continually expose our minds to the revelation of God's truth, then habitually put that truth into practice. We need to practice looking at life as God sees it—*not* as it is filtered and distorted by worldly writers, pundits, professors, philosophers, dramatists, songwriters, and others. If we feel confused and troubled by the events we see on the news and by the false spiritual and moral ideas on our television and movie screens, it is because we are looking at life through worldly eyes instead of God's eyes.

I am sad to say that many people go to church every Sunday and hear sermons that reflect the world's view of life, not God's view. I remember one pastor, a man who became a very dear friend of mine. When I first became acquainted with him, his preaching came primarily out of books and journals of politics and social issues. He might squeeze in a Bible verse here, a saying of Jesus there, if it applied to the social comment he wanted to make. But he didn't preach from the Scriptures, he didn't believe in God's Word, and he didn't have a personal relationship with Jesus Christ.

One day, this pastor and I had lunch together, and he told me, "I recently came to understand how bankrupt my beliefs have been. I have spent years in the pulpit, yet I haven't brought anyone in my congregation any nearer to God. My own life was falling apart, and I finally had to cast myself completely on the grace of Jesus Christ. I was prepared to do anything, if only God would meet me!"

"What kind of price did you expect to pay?" I asked.

"For one thing," he replied, "I thought that in order to believe in Jesus, I would have to lock up my reasoning ability in cold storage. I didn't like the idea, but I was ready to do it if God would come into my life and straighten out the mess I had made of it. But I made an amazing discovery after I invited Jesus to become my Lord and Savior—I became a better thinker than ever before! The Scriptures challenge and sharpen my mind and clarify my thinking in ways I could never have imagined! Being a believer doesn't mean I have to crucify my intellect. It means that I can search out the truth about life more honestly, deeply, and clearly than ever before!"

Though he faced opposition from some of his parishioners, my pastor friend succeeded in turning his church into a Christ-centered, Bible-teaching church. He and his church were still involved in social concerns and meeting human needs, but now their compassion for people grew out of the teaching of Jesus about justice for the poor and oppressed—not out of mere worldly political activism.

I have enjoyed a number of conversations with Dr. John McIntyre, who was an instructor in nuclear physics at Stanford and Texas A & M. He told me that when he became a Christian, he was impressed to discover that biblical truth was so much like the truth of science and nature. He investigated the world of nature all the time, and he said that nature, on the surface, looks rather simple. But the more deeply you probe, the more complex and difficult it becomes, until it ultimately staggers the intellect.

"I have found the same thing to be true of the Bible," he said. "On the surface, the Bible seems so simple that even a child can understand and believe it. But as you begin to investigate it and search out its relationships and go deeper and deeper into it, the fuses of your mind begin to blow, until you stand absolutely amazed and astonished before God."

God created the world of nature, the world of spiritual reality, and the mind of human beings. Nature and spiritual reality are both astonishingly complex, yet comprehensible to the human mind. The gold candelabrum on the gold lampstand symbolizes our God-given ability to comprehend the world around us, as God reveals it in His Word.

## THE TABLE OF THE SHOW BREAD— AND THE NEED FOR BODY LIFE

The next piece of furniture in the Holy Place was the table of the show bread. This passage explains not only the table but also how the show bread should be baked.

> "Take fine flour and bake twelve loaves of bread, using two-tenths of an ephah for each loaf. Set them in two rows, six in each row, on the table of pure gold before the LORD. Along each row put some pure incense as a memorial portion to represent the bread and to be an offering made to the LORD by fire. This bread is to be set out before the LORD regularly, Sabbath after Sabbath, on behalf of the Israelites, as a lasting covenant. It belongs to Aaron and his sons, who are to eat it in a holy place, because it is a most holy part of their regular share of the offerings made to the LORD by fire" (Leviticus 24:5–9).

As we learn in Exodus 25:23–30, the table was made of acacia wood and overlaid and ornamented with pure gold. It was set with plates, dishes, pitchers, and bowls of pure gold. Every Sabbath day, the golden table was spread with freshly baked, unleavened show bread—twelve loaves made of fine flour. These were to be displayed for a week with frankincense spread on top of them. At the end of the week the frankincense was offered on the golden altar of incense and the bread was consumed by the priests as part of their diet.

What is the meaning of these symbols? The twelve loaves are a picture of the twelve tribes of Israel. In other words, they symbolize all of the people of God. Fine flour, as we saw in Leviticus 2, is a picture of redeemed or idealized humanity. It is an apt symbol because fine flour contains no lumps or coarseness. Our natural humanity, apart from Jesus Christ, would be pictured as something like coarse, rough-cut oatmeal, with chips of husk and straw and other chaff. But humanity as God made us to be, and as He intends us to be, is smooth, refined, and consistent.

This fine flour is without yeast, without leaven, and therefore (symbolically) without sin. This represents the uncontaminated new nature that the Spirit of God has imparted to us because of our new life in Christ. The unleavened fine flour is all mixed together, representing believers joined together in communion with God, sharing their lives together. This is a beautiful picture of the realm of relationships in the community of believers—a realm that involves the whole range of emotions: joy, sorrow, love, peace, grief, elation, and more.

This realm of communion and community can be summed up in a single phrase: Body Life. At our church, Peninsula Bible Church in Palo Alto, California, we use the phrase "Body Life" to sum up the way God intends Christians to live together in a caring, accepting, forgiving community. The essence of Body Life involves living out the "one another" admonitions in Scripture. That is, we believe it is our joyful duty as believers to: bear one another's burdens; confess our faults one to another; admonish and exhort one another; forgive and restore one another; minister to each other with our spiritual gifts; be sensitive to one another's needs; grieve with those who are grieving and rejoice with those who are rejoicing; pray for one another; and encourage one another.

The communion and community of the fellowship of God's people is symbolized by the show bread. These twelve loaves, baked from fine unleavened flour, depict for us the need of God's people to have fellowship with one another while experiencing communion with God—the need for Body Life. [Editor's Note: The revised and updated edition of Ray Stedman's classic book on the nature of Christian community, *Body Life*, is available from Discovery House.]

## THE ALTAR OF INCENSE AND THE FRAGRANCE OF SUFFERING

The third piece of furniture in the Holy Place was the altar of incense, where the frankincense was burned. God always insisted that the incense be frankincense and no other kind. You will recall that, in Leviticus 10, two of Aaron's sons were killed because they burned the wrong kind of incense—"strange fire"—before the Lord. Why is the particular kind of incense so important to God? Because frankincense has a special symbolic significance: it yields its fragrance only when it is burned.

Frankincense symbolizes the fragrance that comes out of suffering. It is a picture of the obedient heart. The human mind, illuminated by the Spirit of God (represented by the candelabrum), sharing the communion and community of life in the body of Christ (represented by the show bread), makes a choice, a decision, an act of the will to walk in obedience before God. Our obedience yields a sweet fragrance, like clouds of fragrant incense-laden smoke, that is pleasing to God.

Jesus is our example of obedience. He did what the Father told Him to do. He was obedient even to suffering and death upon the cross. His life was like frankincense that was burned and gave off a sweet fragrance—the fragrance of obedience, the fragrance of suffering, the fragrance of a mind and will that was submitted wholly and completely to the will of God the Father.

## A THREAT TO THE COMMUNITY OF GOD'S PEOPLE

The closing section of Leviticus 24 is a picture of the kind of sin that threatens the entire community of God's people.

> Now the son of an Israelite mother and an Egyptian father went out among the Israelites, and a fight broke out in the camp between him and an Israelite. The son of the Israelite woman blasphemed the Name with a curse; so they brought him to Moses. (His mother's name was Shelomith, the daughter of Dibri the Danite.) They put him in custody until the will of the LORD should be made clear to them.
>
> Then the LORD said to Moses: "Take the blasphemer outside the camp. All those who heard him are to lay their hands on his head, and the entire assembly is to stone him. Say to the Israelites: 'If anyone curses his God, he will be held responsible; anyone who blasphemes the name of the LORD must be put to death. The entire assembly must stone him. Whether an alien or native-born, when he blasphemes the Name, he must be put to death'" (Leviticus 24:10–16).

The first half of Leviticus 24 dealt with symbols of the tabernacle that depict the inner life of humanity. Now we come to the second half of Leviticus 24, and we encounter an incident that threatens the very relationship that has just been described to us.

The story involves a man who is half-Egyptian, half-Israelite. Why is the man's mixed ethnic heritage important? After the captivity in Egypt, there were undoubtedly many people who were the offspring of mixed Israelite-Egyptian ancestry. Yet this man's mixed heritage is considered worthy of mention in this account, so it must be symbolically significant. I believe that this man's life depicts for us a spiritual conflict.

In the Scriptures, Israel is a picture of the Holy Spirit of God at work within us—a picture of new life, redeemed life. Egypt, by contrast, is always a picture of the world, of the old life. Here is a man who is a mixture of the two—he is Israelite and Egyptian, he is of God and of the world. He depicts those who try to live as a friend of God and a friend of the world. He symbolizes those who try to mix a worldly outlook with a godly outlook.

This man had gotten into a quarrel with someone in the camp. In the heat of anger, he blurted out something that was deep down within his thoughts but which he had always kept hidden. This man had undoubtedly harbored ill feelings about God. Perhaps he had heard his Egyptian father speak out against the Hebrew God, and he had adopted his father's resentment against the Lord. When he became angry, his long-suppressed resentment came spilling out of his mouth. He cursed the Name.

Today, we often hear people use the name of God as a curse. We often hear people invoke the name of God while calling down damnation on someone. Though our culture has become tolerant and complacent about such blasphemy, the Bible is clear that using God's name in this way is a vile and horrible sin.

Even so, that is not what this Egyptian-Israelite man did. He didn't merely use God's name in connection with a curse. He literally cursed God. He called down damnation upon God Himself. He blasphemed the Name with a curse.

So the people brought the man to Moses for judgment. Moses said, in effect, "I don't know how to handle this. Take him to God. Let's let God decide what to do." So God told Moses to take the man out of the camp, let all who heard the curse lay hands upon his head, and then let him be stoned to death by the congregation. That was the judgment of God in this case.

Why did God render such a harsh sentence against this man? Was it because He was offended by what the man said? Was it because God is vindictive and malicious? No. God is patient and loving. He could have borne this affront for centuries, as He has borne our cursing and bitterness. But He prescribed immediate death for this blasphemer because the people of Israel needed to learn an important truth: The person who curses God and rejects God has denied the basis of life.

Jesus said, "It is written: 'Man does not live on bread alone, but on every word that comes from the mouth of God'" (Matthew 4:4). If a professed believer denies God, then he has denied the very basis of his life, the only way he can live. To reject God is death. So to make this truth graphically clear to all the people, He ordered this man put to death. What physically happened to this man is a picture of what spiritually happens to us if we reject God.

We don't need to point the finger of blame at this man, because we are often guilty of the same offense! We become angry with God when life doesn't go as we expect or when He doesn't answer our prayers as quickly as we think He should. We even get angry with God when we receive the rightful consequences for our sins. So we shake our fists at Him, we complain to Him, we blame Him. We accuse God of not caring. We may even blaspheme the Name.

When we take that attitude, God says, our spiritual life stops dead. No, we are not lost, we haven't lost our salvation—but we have lost the supply of life, power, strength, and joy that we need to live day by day.

The good news, of course, is that we can regain our life in Him. God's grace restores us. His love and forgiveness enables us to begin anew.

## A BASIC LAW OF LIFE

Leviticus 24 ends with a series of laws by which conduct within the Israelite community was to be governed.

> "'If anyone takes the life of a human being, he must be put to death. Anyone who takes the life of someone's animal must make restitution—life for life. If anyone injures his neighbor, whatever he has done must be done to him: fracture for fracture, eye for eye, tooth for tooth. As he has injured the other, so he is to be injured. Whoever kills an animal must make restitution, but whoever kills a man must be put to death. You are to have the same law for the alien and the native-born. I am the LORD your God'" (Leviticus 24:17–22).

This passage reminds us of the law that Jesus stated: "For in the same way you judge others, you will be judged, and with the measure you use, it will be measured to you" (Matthew 7:2). In other words, the way you treat others is the way you will be treated. If you don't like the way you are being treated, take a look at the way you treat other people. Or, in today's vernacular, "What goes around, comes around."

It is strange but true: We all want to live by a double standard. We all want the privilege of judging others harshly, yet we feel that we deserve leniency and mercy. But God says that we can't live that way. The treatment we dish out to others will eventually come back to us—so we'd better not dish it out if we can't take it.

If we want others to change their ways, then we must change ours. It is amazing how often, when we change, others change as well. True, it doesn't always work that way. But one of the most wonderful discoveries we ever make is the discovery that our decision to let go of anger, bitterness, and sin often causes other people to notice and to want to change their ways as well.

We often think, *If I could just get other people to change!* If we only knew— they're often thinking the same thing about us! Once we realize that we are the problem, and once we deal with that problem, we often find that others readily respond by becoming more of what we want them to be.

The last verse of Leviticus 24 shows, in a powerfully symbolic and graphic way, the end of all people who reject God.

> Then Moses spoke to the Israelites, and they took the blasphemer outside the camp and stoned him. The Israelites did as the LORD commanded Moses (Leviticus 24:23).

For the Egyptian-Israelite man who died beneath a hail of stones, there was nothing symbolic about that event. This was the moment of his physical death, and it was a horrible way to die. This is a sobering moment in Scripture, and we should all remember that spiritual death is no less real—and no less horrible. Are we listening to the message God wants us to hear? Are we serious about life, about death, and about our eternal destiny?

The apostle Peter wrote that God "is patient with you, not wanting anyone to perish, but everyone to come to repentance" (2 Peter 3:9). Let's not reject His patience but obediently submit ourselves to Jesus as our Lord and Savior. Let us place our minds under the control of the Spirit, so that we can see every problem of our lives from God's perspective. Let's join ourselves to His community of believers and live in a state of Body Life, living out all of God's "one another" commands as He intended. And let's offer to God the frankincense fragrance of an obedient heart—a heart that gladly lifts prayer, praise, and even suffering to God, knowing that it is a sweet fragrance to Him.

Through the visual symbols of the tabernacle, God has shown us what our life is all about and how it should be lived. Let us be living tabernacles of our God, human houses of worship and dwelling places for Him. This is the pattern for living that He intended. This is life as God created us to live.

≫———————≪

# CHAPTER 22

# LIBERTY AND REST
## LEVITICUS 25

ONE OF THE great symbols of American freedom is the Liberty Bell, a massive bronze bell located in Philadelphia, Pennsylvania. The bell was cast in 1752 by the Whitechapel Bell Foundry and was hung in the Pennsylvania State House, now better known as Independence Hall. A hairline crack appeared in the bell the first time it was rung in March 1753, and the crack lengthened and widened with successive ringings until the bell became unusable.

Most people think that it is called the Liberty Bell because of its connection to the founding of United States of America. While it is true that the Liberty Bell was rung on July 8, 1776, to call citizens from their homes to hear the first public reading of the Declaration of Independence, it was not known as the Liberty Bell until seventy years after America became a nation. Why, then, was it called the Liberty Bell?

In 1837, the growing abolitionist (anti-slavery) movement in America was looking for a symbol of human freedom. The abolitionist leaders seized upon the famous cracked bell when someone pointed out the inscription that was cast into the metal surface of the bell: "Proclaim liberty throughout all the land unto all the inhabitants thereof." The source of that inscription? Leviticus 25:10.

The abolitionists proclaimed that bell to be the Liberty Bell, and they used it as a symbol in their fight to end the practice of human slavery in America. So the word *liberty* in the name of the Liberty Bell does not refer to America's liberty from British colonialism, as most people believe. It refers to liberty for the millions of Africans who were in bondage prior to their emancipation during the Civil War. Those words from Leviticus 25:10 are God's Emancipation Proclamation, issued centuries before Abraham Lincoln freed the slaves.

Here, in Leviticus 25, we will study that beautiful inscription, and we will see that it speaks of God's intense concern for human liberty and social justice for all people. This chapter of Leviticus reveals God's heart of concern for the poor, the oppressed, and the downtrodden. This is a chapter that has great significance for our individual lives and for the life of our nation today.

## THE SABBATICAL YEAR

One question that occurs to many people as they read through the Old Testament is, "Why did God choose Israel to be His nation among all the nations?" The answer that becomes clear as we read through Leviticus is that God intended for Israel to be an example to the world of how God deals with all people and nations.

The people of Israel were no better and no worse than any other nation on earth. They had their moments of great faith and great courage, and they had their moments of apostasy and weakness, when they fell away from God and worshiped false gods. It may well be that God chose the Hebrew people precisely because they were so typical of the human race—because they exemplified human greatness and human failings. They were people with whom we all can identify.

God chose the people of Israel as a model nation to teach the rest of the nations of the earth how God operates in the world—how He wants all nations to be run. That is why God's instructions to Israel are so significant. From God's instructions to Israel, we learn how God wants us to deal with social issues and social problems in our nation today. God hasn't changed, and neither has His desire to see people everywhere treated with respect, compassion, dignity, and justice.

In the first seven verses of Leviticus 25, we find God's instructions to Israel concerning the use of the land.

> The LORD said to Moses on Mount Sinai, "Speak to the Israelites and say to them: 'When you enter the land I am going to give you,

the land itself must observe a sabbath to the LORD. For six years sow your fields, and for six years prune your vineyards and gather their crops. But in the seventh year the land is to have a sabbath of rest, a sabbath to the LORD. Do not sow your fields or prune your vineyards. Do not reap what grows of itself or harvest the grapes of your untended vines. The land is to have a year of rest. Whatever the land yields during the sabbath year will be food for you—for yourself, your manservant and maidservant, and the hired worker and temporary resident who live among you, as well as for your livestock and the wild animals in your land. Whatever the land produces may be eaten'" (Leviticus 25:1–7).

We are already familiar with the weekly Sabbath, the day of rest that was observed every Saturday in Israel. The Sabbath lies at the heart of everything God does, from creation on, because He is trying to drive home to human hearts a truth that is fundamental to our humanity: We must operate from a state of rest. Our salvation does not depend on our labor. Our forgiveness, our self-worth, our acceptance by God does not depend on our good works. God has done all the work for us through His Son, Jesus, and our response is to rest in what He has accomplished.

Now, in Leviticus 25, God introduces a new application of the concept of the Sabbath: the sabbatical year. Not only were the people to rest one day out of seven, but they were also to rest one year out of seven. Every seventh year, Israel was to let the land rest for a year. They were not to plant any crops or reap anything. They were not even to prune the vineyards but were to let the trees and the vines grow without hindrance. They were not even permitted to eat anything that grew of itself but were to let the land lie fallow.

If you have any experience with farming, you will immediately recognize an important principle of agriculture: Let the land rest every few years. This is advice that the U.S. Department of Agriculture gives to farmers in their official pamphlets. It is sound practical wisdom.

This advice was ignored in the American Midwest during the 1920s and 1930s—with tragic results. Year after year, farmers planted crops and worked the land without giving it time to replenish itself. Soon the land was depleted and crops wouldn't grow. Prairie winds carried off the weakened topsoil, and an estimated 100 million acres of land became useless due to soil erosion. The result was the infamous Dust Bowl of the 1930s, which drove the bankrupt farmers and their families out of the land in a great migration. The loss of agricultural production in the Dust Bowl region contributed to the collapse of the American economy and to the global Great Depression.

Today, soil conservation scientists teach the importance of crop rotation and resting the land to keep it rich and fertile for years to come. Though it is rare to hear either government officials or agriculture scientists openly acknowledge the wisdom of God and His laws, they tacitly honor His wisdom by urging farmers to rest the land as God commanded. Even an atheist farmer will be materially blessed if he follows God's advice for living in harmony with nature and the land. As God promises in Leviticus 25:18–19, "Follow my decrees and be careful to obey my laws, and you will live safely in the land. Then the land will yield its fruit, and you will eat your fill and live there in safety."

It would be a mistake, however, if we interpreted God's commandments in Leviticus 25 on a merely superficial level, the level of nature and physical life. There is a deeper meaning to God's instruction about the sabbatical year, and this meaning affects society at large. We tend to think of humanity's relationship to God as being essentially a matter of each individual believer relating to God in the privacy of his or her prayers, worship, and obedience. But God's instructions in Leviticus apply beyond the life of the individual to society at large.

God wants entire societies, entire nations, to live in dependence on His wisdom, power, and mercy. Leviticus spells out God's plan not only for individual lives and relationships but also for governments and societies. If nations would follow God's instructions in Leviticus, then the people of those nations would enjoy blessings and fruitfulness that can be obtained in no other way. We will see God's plan for human society developed and explained further as we move through this passage, for that is the true significance of God's instructions regarding the sabbatical year.

## THE YEAR OF JUBILEE

Linked to the sabbatical year is the Year of Jubilee, which occurs every fiftieth year.

"'Count off seven sabbaths of years—seven times seven years—so that the seven sabbaths of years amount to a period of forty-nine years. Then have the trumpet sounded everywhere on the tenth day of the seventh month; on the Day of Atonement sound the trumpet throughout your land. Consecrate the fiftieth year and proclaim liberty throughout the land to all its inhabitants. It shall be a jubilee for you; each one of you is to return to his family property and each to his own clan. The fiftieth year shall be a jubilee for you; do not sow and do not reap what grows of itself or harvest the untended vines. For it is a jubilee and is to be holy for you; eat only what is taken directly from the fields'" (Leviticus 25:8–12).

Notice that the Year of Jubilee is nothing more or less than an intensified version of the sabbatical year. The sabbatical year was to be observed every seventh year. And when seven times seven had passed—forty-nine years—the next year was declared the Year of Jubilee. These numbers were chosen because they are symbolically significant. Seven is the number of perfection. So seven times seven is perfection fully manifested. In other words, God is saying that whatever the Sabbath year stands for, if you allow it to run its full course, will become clear and well-demonstrated after the seven times seven years are fulfilled.

What is the perfection that will be fully manifested after seven times seven years? The answer is stated in Leviticus 25:10—the same verse that is cast in raised letters of bronze around the top of the Liberty Bell: "Consecrate the fiftieth year and proclaim liberty throughout the land to all its inhabitants." Liberty! God is instructing His people in His plan to liberate people from social problems, injustice, and oppression. This work of liberation is accomplished every fifty years in the Year of Jubilee.

God is telling us that Sabbath rest must be at the heart not only of the life of an individual but of society as well. There must be a dependence upon the working of Another, upon the fact that God is the Architect and unseen Mover in human events. Only when a society acknowledges Him, follows His instructions, and lives in dependence upon Him can there be true liberty in that society.

Notice, by the way, that there were two consecutive years observed as

Sabbath years during the time of Jubilee. The forty-ninth year would be a sabbatical year, and then the next year, the fiftieth, would be a Sabbath Year of Jubilee. This meant that two years would pass without the planting of crops. How were people expected to eat during two years without crops? We will discover the answer to that question later in this chapter.

The Year of Jubilee was to be announced by a trumpet. In fact, the word *jubilee* derives from a Hebrew word having to do with trumpets. The word comes from the Latin *iubilaeus,* by way of the Greek *iobelaios,* via the Hebrew *yobel,* which meant a ram's horn. The ancient Jews used a ram's horn as a trumpet to announce the Year of Jubilee.

In Scripture, trumpets always herald a new beginning. The first day of the seventh month was the feast of trumpets every year, and trumpets were sent out to announce the new year, a new beginning. Now in the fiftieth year, on the tenth day of the seventh month, was the great Day of Atonement. At that time, when the blood of a bull and the blood of a goat were offered in the Holy of Holies, God made atonement for all the people. On that day the trumpet went abroad, announcing that the people were set at liberty. This is God's memorable way of teaching us that all liberty arises from redemption. When God redeems us, He cleanses, forgives, heals, restores, and liberates us.

What does liberty mean, according to God? We tend to think that liberty means doing whatever we want to do whenever we want to do it. But that is not true liberty. That is actually a greater form of slavery. You need to experience only a little of that wide-open, no-responsibility liberty to discover how empty, boring, and ultimately enslaving it is.

I have been privileged to travel extensively and have often been invited to speak before some very affluent audiences. I once spoke to a group in Hollywood, Florida, on the famed Gold Coast, the southeastern coast of Florida. For several mornings, I taught the Scriptures to a crowd of people who, I was told, represented well over a billion dollars' worth of accumulated wealth. I talked with many of them individually. Most of them, by their own admission, had all the money they needed to buy anything they could ever want—yet many of them were not happy.

A large number of these people suffered from what has been called destination sickness—the problem of having everything that you want but not wanting anything you have. Sufferers of this malady no longer have hopes and

dreams to aim for in life, because they have already arrived. They can go yacht-
ing or golfing or jetting off to the Riviera, yet they are empty, lonely, and miserable inside because they can do anything they want to do, and none of it
satisfies.

The license to do anything you want is not liberty, as God defines it. Liberty,
God says, is being freed from inner bondage, inner shackles of guilt, fear, anxiety, and hostility. True liberty begins with redemption, with the atoning work
of Jesus Christ.

In the second half of Leviticus 25:10, we see that the authentic liberty that
God gives to people in the Jubilee year is a two-sided liberty. That is, God's liberty consists of two beautiful elements, like two sides of a single coin. Do you
see what those two elements are? Leviticus 25:10 tells us, "It shall be a jubilee
for you; each one of you is to return to his family property and each to his own
clan."

The first element is this: The liberty God grants in the Jubilee year restores
to us our lost inheritance. We return to our family property, our family estate,
our family inheritance. We get back what God intended us to have—our lost
property, our lost birthright. And what is our lost inheritance? It is our ability to live as God created us to live. God made human beings in His perfect
image, but that image was shattered like a broken mirror when Adam sinned.
Now God has acted to restore to us what we once had in the Garden of Eden,
before sin entered the world. He is restoring His image in us, the image that
was marred by sin. In the Jubilee year, God has reversed the effects of the fall
and has restored us to the garden.

The second element is this: The liberty God grants us in the Jubilee year
restores our broken, fragmented relationships. All the walls and partitions that
separate people from each other and from God have been broken down. Our
relationship with Him was severed in the fall of Adam. Now God has acted
to draw us back into fellowship with Him. As our relationship with God is
restored, so is our relationship with other people. All distinctions of skin color,
economic class, and culture quickly evaporate in the warm sunshine of God's
love. We can return to our own clan—the human family—and experience
complete healing in all of our relationships.

That is the beauty of this picture of the Jubilee year, the Sabbath-year of rest
and restoration.

## THE LIFE OF THE LAND IS PRESERVED IN RIGHTEOUSNESS

The passage goes on to tell us some important aspects of the Year of Jubilee that God declared to His people.

> "'In this Year of Jubilee everyone is to return to his own property.
>
> "'If you sell land to one of your countrymen or buy any from him, do not take advantage of each other. You are to buy from your countryman on the basis of the number of years since the Jubilee. And he is to sell to you on the basis of the number of years left for harvesting crops. When the years are many, you are to increase the price, and when the years are few, you are to decrease the price, because what he is really selling you is the number of crops. Do not take advantage of each other, but fear your God. I am the LORD your God'" (Leviticus 25:13–17).

The Year of Jubilee was to be the center of all commercial enterprise. The entire economy of Israel looked toward this year of liberation, this freeing of individuals. The price of a tract of land was based on the number of years remaining before the Year of Jubilee. A buyer paid a reduced price if the Year of Jubilee was near, because in that year the land had to revert to its original owner, no matter who owned it at the time. But if the Jubilee year was decades in the future, the land was worth much more.

In Leviticus 25:16, God said, "When the years are many, you are to increase the price, and when the years are few, you are to decrease the price, because what he is really selling you is the number of crops." God was teaching His people an important truth: When they purchased real estate, they were not buying a chunk of the planet, a patch of dirt. They were buying all the crops that would be raised on that land for years to come.

This is a paramount principle that is developed further in the next few verses—verses which truly form the heart of this chapter. Here, God teaches us that He is as concerned about governments and societies as He is about the hearts of individual human beings. We must make room for God to act not just in our individual lives but in our culture as well. When we invite God into the life of our nation, everyone in the nation will be blessed.

"'Follow my decrees and be careful to obey my laws, and you will live safely in the land. Then the land will yield its fruit, and you will eat your fill and live there in safety. You may ask, "What will we eat in the seventh year if we do not plant or harvest our crops?" I will send you such a blessing in the sixth year that the land will yield enough for three years. While you plant during the eighth year, you will eat from the old crop and will continue to eat from it until the harvest of the ninth year comes in'" (Leviticus 25:18–22).

Here is the answer to the question we raised earlier: The forty-ninth and fiftieth years are both sabbatical years—years in which the land must lie fallow and unplanted. How were people expected to eat during two years without crops?

And God replies, in effect, "That's exactly what I wanted you to ask, because it is not the land that supports you and feeds you. It is I. And I will make the land produce enough food in one year to last three years. I want you to know that I will take care of you, regardless of outward circumstances. I want you to depend on me, not the land, not your own effort. Yes, the land is part of the picture, and so is your work in planting, tilling, and harvesting. But it is I who gives you food and life. Every sixth year, I will increase the crops to carry you through the seventh year, the eighth Year of Jubilee, and into the ninth year, as the next harvest is maturing. If you rely on me and trust in me, you will always have everything you need."

In this passage, God makes a beautiful threefold promise.

First, He promises safety and security. "Follow my decrees and be careful to obey my laws," He says, "and you will live safely in the land. Then the land will yield its fruit, and you will eat your fill and live there in safety." He promises the people of Israel that no enemy will attack and there will be food and safety in the land.

Second, He promises a bountiful harvest without excessive toil. "The land will yield its fruit," He says. Arduous toil, sweat, pain, and tears won't be necessary. The land will readily produce its crop.

Third, He promises a sufficient supply: "You will eat your fill." Imagine: God promised His people an all-you-can-eat buffet! Every seventh year and every fiftieth year, His people will have all they want, and God will pick up the check.

This is what God wants His people to learn—and not just the people of Israel in the days of Moses but also the people of His church today. How sad it is that we Christians have neglected God's truth about the Sabbath year and the Year of Jubilee! We have stamped on our coins, "In God We Trust." We have written God's Emancipation Proclamation on our Liberty Bell. But in recent years, we have forgotten that a nation must depend upon God. We no longer make any allowance for God to work in our society. We have erased God's name from our national monuments, blotted all mention of Him from our children's textbooks. We are forgetting our heritage as "one nation under God," and we are rapidly becoming a secular and godless society.

When God no longer reigns over a nation, that nation begins to disintegrate. Remember that God has set up the nation of Israel as an example. Through Israel, God demonstrates how He deals with nations that honor Him—and with nations that fall away from Him. That is why these words in Leviticus are so vitally important to us in the times in which we now live.

I have always been impressed by the motto of the state of Hawaii: *Ua Mau ke Ea o ka Aina i ka Pono.* Translated, this motto means, "The life of the land is preserved in righteousness." This saying is believed to have been coined by King Kamehameha III in 1843 and is thought to reflect the influence of the Christian missionaries who first came to Hawaii in 1820.

It isn't the Declaration of Independence or the Constitution that preserves a nation. It isn't Congress or the Supreme Court or the president. It isn't the army, the navy, the air force, or the marines. It is righteousness that preserves a nation—the righteousness of God as reflected in the lives of the people.

The truly tragic fact is that Israel never experienced the sabbatical year that God intended for them. In the entire history of the nation, Israel never trusted God enough to take Him at His word and see what He would do. So the people of Israel never saw God's abundant supply.

The people planted their crops year after year. Six years passed, and though the people knew that they were to let the ground rest while they observed a seventh, sabbatical year, they ignored God's instruction. They didn't trust God's promise, so they planted their crops in the seventh year. And God let them do as they pleased. If God's people insist on rejecting His instruction, He doesn't force them; instead, He lets them reap the consequences of their choices. But God kept a record of the people's deeds for 490 years. Out of those 490 years, 70 should have been sabbatical years.

At the end of that time, God said to Israel, in effect, "You have ignored my instruction. You have not allowed the land to rest. Now I will make sure the land has its rest. I will allow the Babylonians to sweep you off the land and take you into captivity." The nation of Israel committed other sins, including the sin of idolatry. But there is no mistaking the significance of the 490-year period of the neglect of God's law, followed by 70 years of captivity. The people of Israel remained captives in Babylon for 70 years because that was the number of sabbatical years they had failed to observe.

The Babylonian captivity underscores the fact that God is sovereign. You can never cheat God. He counted up all the years Israel had forgotten to observe the sabbatical year—then He presented the bill. For seventy years, no one farmed the land of Israel. The people of Israel were forced to serve in an alien land.

## THREE PRINCIPLES OF THE JUBILEE YEAR

Next, God explains the purpose of the Jubilee year by means of three important principles.

> "'The land must not be sold permanently, because the land is mine and you are but aliens and my tenants. Throughout the country that you hold as a possession, you must provide for the redemption of the land'" (Leviticus 25:23–24).

The first of the three principles we see in this passage is simply this: The land belongs to God. "The land is mine," God says. This is still true today, isn't it? We may hold the deed, we may even have the mortgage paid off, but we don't really own the land. We are tenants in the land. Other people occupied it before we came along. When we leave, more people will take our place. And they will not own the land either. God says, "The land is mine."

One of the great and troublesome questions of our age is the question of who has the right to occupy the land called Palestine. The Jewish people say that it is their land, the land of Israel. The Palestinian Arabs say it is their land, and the Palestine Liberation Organization (PLO) publishes special maps of the region which do not show the state of Israel. Arguments rage in the United Nations over whether the land should belong to the Israelis or to the Palestinians. The Israelis try to solidify their claim by building settlements in the territories that have been occupied since the Six Day War in 1967. The Palestinians stake their claim by sending suicide bombers into Israel to spread death and terror.

Who owns Palestine? There is only one answer: God owns the land. He will sovereignly choose who will be the tenants of that land at any given time, whether Arabs or Jews. It is not up to the Knesset, the Israeli Parliament. It is not up to the PLO. It is not up to the Russians, the British, the French, the Americans, or even the United Nations. The land belongs to God, and He alone will decide.

The second great principle we see in this passage is: We human beings are strangers and temporary tenants in the land God owns. "You are but aliens and my tenants," God says. If we are aliens and tenants in the land, then it logically follows that earth is not our home. We are only passing through this world on our way to our ultimate destination. What we do here on earth is important, but it is not the sum of our existence. This life on earth is like a school that prepares us for the real life which still lies ahead of us. So it is important that we do not focus on things like real estate and material possessions, because those are temporal and ephemeral. This physical world is just a fleeting stage in our existence, and we are aliens in the land.

The third great principle we see in this passage is this: God is very concerned about justice, including economic justice. He does not want people to be trapped in poverty and oppression, with no hope for the future. That is why He instructed the people to observe the Year of Jubilee, when displaced people could return to their land, when personal property would be restored, when slaves would be set free, when people who were bankrupt and impoverished could get a new start in life.

God wants governments to practice this kind of justice and compassion toward people, so that they will have the ability to recover from injury, damage, loss, and personal disaster. God says that governments must safeguard the right of people to recover from a low economic state. This is an indispensable principle for just and godly government.

## THE PROBLEM OF POVERTY

In the rest of Leviticus 25, God deals with the problem of poverty—a problem that remains with us today.

> "If one of your countrymen becomes poor and sells some of his property, his nearest relative is to come and redeem what his

countryman has sold. If, however, a man has no one to redeem it for him but he himself prospers and acquires sufficient means to redeem it, he is to determine the value for the years since he sold it and refund the balance to the man to whom he sold it; he can then go back to his own property. But if he does not acquire the means to repay him, what he sold will remain in the possession of the buyer until the Year of Jubilee. It will be returned in the Jubilee, and he can then go back to his property.

"'If a man sells a house in a walled city, he retains the right of redemption a full year after its sale. During that time he may redeem it. If it is not redeemed before a full year has passed, the house in the walled city shall belong permanently to the buyer and his descendants. It is not to be returned in the Jubilee. But houses in villages without walls around them are to be considered as open country. They can be redeemed, and they are to be returned in the Jubilee.

"'The Levites always have the right to redeem their houses in the Levitical towns, which they possess. So the property of the Levites is redeemable—that is, a house sold in any town they hold—and is to be returned in the Jubilee, because the houses in the towns of the Levites are their property among the Israelites. But the pastureland belonging to their towns must not be sold; it is their permanent possession.

"'If one of your countrymen becomes poor and is unable to support himself among you, help him as you would an alien or a temporary resident, so he can continue to live among you. Do not take interest of any kind from him, but fear your God, so that your countryman may continue to live among you. You must not lend him money at interest or sell him food at a profit. I am the LORD your God, who brought you out of Egypt to give you the land of Canaan and to be your God.

"'If one of your countrymen becomes poor among you and sells himself to you, do not make him work as a slave. He is to be treated as a hired worker or a temporary resident among you; he is to work for you until the Year of Jubilee. Then he and his children are to be released, and he will go back to his own clan and to the property of his forefathers. Because the Israelites are my servants, whom I brought out of Egypt, they must not be sold as slaves. Do not rule over them ruthlessly, but fear your God.

"'Your male and female slaves are to come from the nations around you; from them you may buy slaves. You may also buy some of the temporary residents living among you and members of their clans born in your country, and they will become your property. You can will them to your children as inherited property and can make them slaves for life, but you must not rule over your fellow Israelites ruthlessly.

"'If an alien or a temporary resident among you becomes rich and one of your countrymen becomes poor and sells himself to the alien living among you or to a member of the alien's clan, he retains the right of redemption after he has sold himself. One of his relatives may redeem him: An uncle or a cousin or any blood relative in his clan may redeem him. Or if he prospers, he may redeem himself. He and his buyer are to count the time from the year he sold himself up to the Year of Jubilee. The price for his release is to be based on the rate paid to a hired man for that number of years. If many years remain, he must pay for his redemption a larger share of the price paid for him. If only a few years remain until the Year of Jubilee, he is to compute that and pay for his redemption accordingly. He is to be treated as a man hired from year to year; you must see to it that his owner does not rule over him ruthlessly.

"'Even if he is not redeemed in any of these ways, he and his children are to be released in the Year of Jubilee, for the Israelites belong to me as servants. They are my servants, whom I brought out of Egypt. I am the LORD your God'" (Leviticus 25:25–55).

The central issue of this passage is the problem of poverty. Again and again we see the phrase "If one of your countrymen becomes poor."

These are God's instructions on how to deal with poverty. This entire section serves to amplify and explain the great statement in Leviticus 25:24: "Throughout the country that you hold as a possession, you must provide for the redemption of the land." This section could be restated this way: "You must give the poor an opportunity to recover from their poverty. You must not merely shrug your shoulders and say, 'Well, the poor are poor because they are too lazy to work.' You must give them a chance to recover. Do not lock them into poverty."

God tells us that one of the basic functions of government is to protect the right of people to recover from poverty. "You must do something about injustice and poverty," He says in effect. "You must help those who are trapped in a place of hopelessness and destitution. You must help them find opportunities to better themselves. You must help to place their feet on the rungs of the economic ladder so that they can begin to climb out of the pit of despair." Governments, organizations, corporations, churches, and individuals all need to listen and hear what God is saying to them.

This passage goes on to outline specific solutions to the common economic plights of those times. In Leviticus 25:25–34, God says that people must be given the right to redeem their own land. Then, in Leviticus 25:35–38, He goes on to say that if the poor are unable to redeem their own land, then the people of the land should assist the poor: lend to them without collecting interest; sell them food at cost, without profit; give them the same kind of help that would be given to strangers and aliens in the land. If you have been materially blessed, do not forget the poor, do not leave them to starve, do not ignore them. God cares about the poor; so should we.

Leviticus 25:39–46 deals with the issue of slavery. The people of Israel knew what it was like to be slaves, for their entire nation had been enslaved in Egypt. So God decreed that no Israelite was ever to be a slave again. Because the Israelites were servants of God, He would not allow them to be slaves to any other master. "If one of your countrymen becomes poor among you and sells himself to you," God said, "do not make him work as a slave. He is to be treated as a hired worker or a temporary resident among you." In other words, treat him with dignity, as an employee, not as a piece of property to be bought and sold.

Leviticus 25:47–55 sets forth the right to redeem people from slavery—to buy people back and restore to them their human dignity. This is God's way of teaching us that God is in the business of redeeming people—of liberating them, purchasing them out of the slave market of sin, and restoring their humanity to them. Because the practice of slavery is so removed from our daily experience, we easily forget what it truly means when we call Jesus our Redeemer. On the cross, He paid the debt we could not pay, and He redeemed us from slavery to sin, death, and Satan. We have been bought at the price of our Lord's own blood, and He is our master now. We are no longer slaves to sin.

Another truth we find in these verses is that God is able to change human hearts and human society. He seeks to create communities of people who live according to the principle of Sabbath rest, of dependence on the work of Another, of complete trust and reliance upon God. He seeks to create communities of justice, fairness, compassion, opportunity, hope, and liberty.

Down through the centuries, God has raised up individuals and great movements as His instruments of social and moral justice. In 1784, a British member of Parliament, William Wilberforce, committed his life to Jesus Christ. Convicted by the biblical message of liberation for the oppressed and justice for the poor, Wilberforce made a decision to devote the rest of his life to the cause of ending the practice of human slavery. He spent the next five decades of his life battling the pro-slavery forces in the Parliament. Ultimately, Wilberforce won that battle—though he did not live to see the victory. He died on July 29, 1833, and the Parliament passed the Slavery Abolition Act one month later.

In America, the fight against slavery went on. In 1858, the newly formed Republican Party named a forty-nine-year-old attorney, Abraham Lincoln, as its candidate for the U.S. Senate. In June of that year, at the close of the Republican State Convention in Illinois, Lincoln gave his famous "house divided" speech. The speech was widely reprinted and it electrified the nation. "'A house divided against itself cannot stand,'" he said, quoting the words of Jesus from Mark 3:25. Then he added, "I believe this government cannot endure, permanently, half slave and half free."

Lincoln was elected president of the United States in the fall of 1860; between the time he was elected and the day of his inauguration in March 1861, seven Southern states seceded from the Union. Soon after his inauguration, another wave of states seceded. The Civil War began practically as he was taking office. On January 1, 1863, Lincoln issued the Emancipation Proclamation, declaring that all slaves on American soil were henceforth and forever free. By the fall of 1864, as the Union was advancing across the battlefield, Lincoln won reelection. On March 4, 1865, he delivered his second inaugural address, which the

London *Spectator* has called "the noblest political document known to history." In that speech, Lincoln said:

> Fondly do we hope—fervently do we pray—that this mighty scourge of war may speedily pass away. Yet, if God wills that it continue, until all the wealth piled by the bond-man's two hundred and fifty years of unrequited toil shall be sunk, and until every drop of blood drawn with the lash, shall be paid by another drawn with the sword, as was said three thousand years ago, so still it must be said "the judgments of the Lord, are true and righteous altogether."
>
> With malice toward none; with charity for all; with firmness in the right, as God gives us to see the right, let us strive on to finish the work we are in; to bind up the nation's wounds; to care for him who shall have borne the battle, and for his widow, and his orphan—to do all which may achieve and cherish a just and lasting peace, among ourselves, and with all nations.

These words show that, like Wilberforce before him, Abraham Lincoln was motivated by faith in God and an understanding of God's Word. Lincoln's heart reflected God's own passion for justice and His compassion for suffering humanity. On Good Friday, 1865, just five and a half weeks after he delivered that speech, Abraham Lincoln, the Great Emancipator, was shot by an assassin at Ford's Theater in Washington, D.C. After redeeming America's slaves, he paid the price in his own blood.

The great lesson we learn from the lives of such servants as William Wilberforce and Abraham Lincoln is this: "The life of the land is preserved in righteousness." That is the lesson God wants us to draw from Leviticus 25.

God is at work in human history. He is at work in your life as an individual, and in the life of your nation and your world. He wants to give you a Sabbath rest. He wants you to learn to live and work and minister in a state of rest, of total reliance and dependence upon His wisdom and power.

God wants every person and every nation to find His rest. He wants to break down the walls that divide Jew and Gentile, black and white, Democrat and Republican, liberal and conservative, Northerner and Southerner, Easterner and Westerner. He wants to bring rest and peace to all nations, so that they will operate out of a dependence upon Him instead of operating out of racial tension and political hostility.

God has given us the gifts of the Sabbath rest, the sabbatical year, and the Year of Jubilee. Let us receive His gifts with joy and gratitude—and let's rest in them. "Come to me," Jesus said, "all you who are weary and burdened, and I will give you rest" (Matthew 11:28). That is the message of Leviticus 25. That is the message of the gospel.

≫———————≪

# EITHER/OR

## LEVITICUS 26

DURING A VISIT to Israel, I drove to the Shomron Valley and stood in the shadow of the twin peaks of Mount Ebal and Mount Gerizim. As Joshua 8 records, that is the place where Joshua read the Book of the Law to all the people and renewed the covenant between God and the nation of Israel. Half of the people of Israel stood in front of Mount Ebal and half stood in front of Mount Gerizim. The Scripture that Joshua read included the passage we are about to explore, Leviticus 26. It is a passage that contains blessings for those who keep God's Law—and penalties for those who violate the Law.

As Joshua read, those two mountains visually represented the blessings and the penalties. Mount Ebal was the taller of the two mountains, and its bleak, rocky slopes were strewn with gray rubble. That desolate mountain represented the penalties that awaited those who would rebel against God's Law. Mount Gerizim, by contrast, had green, forested slopes. The beautiful Mount Gerizim represented good life and bountiful blessings that awaited those who remained faithful to God's Law.

Joshua set before the people of Israel the same choice that is set before us today—a choice represented by those two mountains: Shall we obey God and receive His blessings? Or shall we turn our backs on God and receive the just penalties for our disobedience?

## THE CURSE OF IDOLATRY, THE BLESSING OF REST

Leviticus 26 is a particularly noteworthy passage of the Old Testament, because we have already seen its promises fulfilled in history. We can compare what God promised with what has taken place. As we go through this chapter, we will see a remarkable confirmation of the way God keeps His promises in His dealings with His people. As the chapter opens, we find that God repeats two of the Ten Commandments.

> "'Do not make idols or set up an image or a sacred stone for your-selves, and do not place a carved stone in your land to bow down before it. I am the LORD your God. Observe my Sabbaths and have reverence for my sanctuary. I am the LORD'" (Leviticus 26:1–2).

Here, God restates the second commandment, which forbids idol worship, and the fourth commandment, which tells the people to keep the Sabbath day holy. There is an important reason why these two commandments are restated here. Leviticus 26 is divided into two parts. Leviticus 26:1–13 deals with the blessings of obedience; Leviticus 26:14–46 deals with the penalties for disobedience. Disobeying the second commandment produces a penalty, a punishment, a curse in our lives. Obeying the fourth commandment produces blessings and rewards. These first two verses set the theme for the rest of the chapter.

Idolatry means worshiping any god besides God. Many people think that idolatry consists only of bowing down to images of false gods. This is a mistaken notion. America is one of the most idolatrous nations in the history of the world. The most common form of idolatry in America does not involve praying to statues—we are far too sophisticated for such obvious forms of idolatry! Our paganism is much more subtle than that of the ancient pagans, such as the Greeks or Romans.

The Greeks worshiped Aphrodite, the goddess of love and beauty; the Romans called her Venus. We Americans simply call her Sex, and we worship her at the altar of our television screens or in those dark suburban temples where R-rated movies are shown. We worship her with our thoughts, our fantasies, our talk, and our adulterous relationships.

The Greeks worshiped Hermes, the god of wealth, trade, and commerce; the Romans called him Mercury. We Americans call him Money or Success.

We worship him with our obsessive fascination with the stock market or our 401(k) plan or our relentless ambition to get that promotion or the key to the executive washroom.

The Greeks worshiped Dionysus, the god of wine and merriment; the Romans called him Bacchus. We Americans call him Pleasure or Materialism, and we drink in his honor, we throw parties to worship him, we accumulate cars and big houses and country club memberships, and we seek to gratify our senses in any way we can.

The Greeks worshiped Tyche, the goddess of fortune; the Romans called her Fortuna. We Americans call her Fame or Status, and we do anything to gain her favor. We can't imagine a worse fate than to spend our lives in anonymity, serving God and others in obscurity. No, we want the whole world to know our names—even if only for fifteen minutes. We want the whole world to envy our awards, our lifestyle, our achievements, our titles.

The Greeks worshiped Ares, the god of war and power; the Romans called him Mars. We Americans call him Power, and we pursue him by trying to be the boss, the alpha male, the top dog. The sacrament of the god called Power is to have everyone snap to attention and call you sir (or ma'am) whenever you enter the room.

We worship the same gods as the ancient pagans. We just happen to know them by different names. Oh, and we have also added some new gods that the ancients never even dreamed of. For example, on Sunday mornings as I drive to church, I often see people out in their driveways, polishing their gods. Others spend hours and hours mumbling incantations and imprecations to Microsoft or Apple while surfing the Internet on their glowing gods.

Whether we idolize a bronze statue or we worship Sex, Money, Success, Pleasure, Materialism, Fame, Status, or Power, it is all idolatry. We have replaced the one true God with a substitute god. Make no mistake: Idolatry always produces punishment. Idolatry always brings a curse upon our lives.

And just as idolatry produces punishment, so the Sabbath produces blessing. As we have seen throughout Leviticus, the Sabbath day is a symbol, a picture of the rest God wants us to experience as we learn to live in complete dependence upon Him. Sabbath rest is the result of our dependence upon the work of Another. It frees us from stress and anxiety. It releases us from that nagging sense that our best efforts are never good enough. As we rest in God's ability to work through us, we no longer have to do it all ourselves. Sabbath rest liberates us, body, soul, and spirit. That is why the observance of God's Sabbath rest produces blessings in our lives.

## THE PROMISE OF SIX BLESSINGS

Following these two introductory commandments, we have the list of six promised blessings for those who are obedient to God's Law. Read the text and see if you can identify those six blessings.

> "'If you follow my decrees and are careful to obey my commands, I will send you rain in its season, and the ground will yield its crops and the trees of the field their fruit. Your threshing will continue until grape harvest and the grape harvest will continue until planting, and you will eat all the food you want and live in safety in your land.
>
> "'I will grant peace in the land, and you will lie down and no one will make you afraid. I will remove savage beasts from the land, and the sword will not pass through your country. You will pursue your enemies, and they will fall by the sword before you. Five of you will chase a hundred, and a hundred of you will chase ten thousand, and your enemies will fall by the sword before you.
>
> "'I will look on you with favor and make you fruitful and increase your numbers, and I will keep my covenant with you. You will still be eating last year's harvest when you will have to move it out to make room for the new. I will put my dwelling place among you, and I will not abhor you. I will walk among you and be your God, and you will be my people. I am the LORD your God, who brought you out of Egypt so that you would no longer be slaves to the Egyptians; I broke the bars of your yoke and enabled you to walk with heads held high'" (Leviticus 26:3–13).

This is a beautiful array of promises—and God meant every word! When He told His people to observe His commandments, He wasn't merely referring to the Ten Commandments. He was referring to the entire program of observances, offerings, sacrifices, cleansings, sabbaths, and feasts. Clearly, God knew that these people, in their fallen human nature, would never be able to keep all of His commandments. He didn't expect them to. In fact, that is precisely why He provided the sacrifices and other observances—because they pointed to Jesus Christ. It was not the rituals that saved the people from their sins; it was their faith that granted them access to God's forgiving grace—a faith expressed by keeping God's program of offerings and sacrifices.

So God was saying to the people, in effect, "If you walk before me, living by the provision I have made available to you, dealing with your sins on a regular basis, experiencing forgiveness and wholeness from day to day, these blessings will be yours."

The blessings God promised are sixfold. As we go through this list of blessings, you will see that there is a counterpart for each of these blessings in our spiritual life today. In this passage, God spoke of material, physical blessings for His people in Israel, but these blessings are also a picture of the spiritual benefits that are ours today if we will obey God. So this passage has a direct application to our lives.

*The first promise: Fruitfulness.* God said to Israel, "I will send you rain in its season, and the ground will yield its crops and the trees of the field their fruit." God promised that if the nation of Israel obeyed His commands, they would receive the blessings of fruitfulness, an abundance of food to enjoy and to sustain their life.

This same promise is ours today in the spiritual realm. If we will obey God's commands, then our lives will be fruitful. We will experience a spiritual abundance, a rich harvest of joy. Our lives will bring blessing and life to the lives of other people. We will have a beneficial impact upon our family and friends, our churches and neighborhoods, our nation and our world.

*The second promise: A full supply.* God said, "Your threshing will continue until grape harvest and the grape harvest will continue until planting, and you will eat all the food you want." God promised the people of Israel that they would always have a plentiful harvest if they obeyed His commands. They would never know want or hunger. They would never lack for any resource. They would eat their fill all year round.

Again, this promise is ours today in the spiritual realm. If we will obey God's commands, then He will make His infinite resources available to us. He will supply all our needs, and we will never lack for any resource that we need for life, for joy, or for ministering in His name.

*The third promise: Safety and security.* God said that, if the people obeyed, they would "live in safety" in their land. He went on to say that the people would have peace in the land, freedom from the fear of the sword or from savage beasts, and victory over their enemies. "Five of you will chase a hundred," he said, "and a hundred of you will chase ten thousand."

We have this same promise in the spiritual realm today. If we obey God's commands, we will have peace and confidence in our lives. No enemy can overwhelm us, no threat can intimidate us, no attack can overthrow us. In Christ, we are safe and secure. As Paul tells us, "Such confidence as this is ours through Christ before God" (2 Corinthians 3:4).

*The fourth promise: Increase.* God told His people, "I will look on you with favor and make you fruitful and increase your numbers, and I will keep my covenant with you." Here, God speaks of a different kind of fruitfulness: Israel would be blessed with children, with growth in numbers, growth in the numerical strength of its people.

Once again, we have this same promise in the spiritual realm today. If we obey God's commandments, we will experience numerical growth. Our lives will shine for Christ, influencing others, drawing more and more people into His kingdom. As we serve others and witness to them about our faith, more and more people will give their lives to Christ. The family of faith will be blessed with an increase in spiritual children.

*The fifth promise: God's presence.* God told Israel, "I will walk among you and be your God, and you will be my people." This is the promise of communion and fellowship with the living God, the Creator of heaven and earth. Of course, there is no need to translate this promise into spiritual terms, because this is, in itself, a powerful spiritual promise. Just as the people of Israel experienced the presence of God in powerful ways, so can we. If we keep His commandments, then He will walk among us. He will be our God, and we will be His people.

*The sixth promise: Deliverance and dignity.* God concluded His list of blessings with these words: "I am the LORD your God, who brought you out of Egypt so that you would no longer be slaves to the Egyptians; I broke the bars of your yoke and enabled you to walk with heads held high." God delivers His people from the shame and humiliation of bondage. He enables us to walk tall and free, as men and women ought to. He restores dignity and self-respect to people who have been held in chains.

What is the thing that keeps you in bondage today? What is the sin of the past that fills you with shame? What is the circumstance that has robbed you of your dignity and self-respect? What keeps you from standing tall and holding your head high? God has promised that if you keep His commandments, He will shatter your yoke, break your chains, and deliver you from your shame and humiliation. He will release you, so that you can walk tall and free—free to enjoy your God-given dignity and self-respect.

This is the God we serve. This is what He says He will do. These are the promises of blessing that we can count on if we will lay hold of the provision that He has made for us in Jesus Christ and if we will deal honestly and openly with Him about our faults and failings. This is all He asks.

God doesn't expect us to be sinless and perfect. He asks us to be honest with Him. He asks us to stop kidding ourselves and pretending to be what we are not. He asks us to drop our hypocritical façade, the mask we hide behind. If we confess our sins to Him and repent of them, we can be forgiven and restored. These are the blessings that God promised to His people in ancient Israel, and they are the same blessings He promises us today.

## THE PENALTY FOR DISOBEDIENCE

The tragic fact of history is that Israel did not keep God's commandments and did not receive these blessings. So the next section of the book deals with the penalties for disobedience. As history records, these are the penalties that Israel incurred for failing to keep God's Law. These penalties fall into six definite stages, each one worse than the one before. God tells us that these are the stages that individuals, churches, or entire nations go through if they turn against Him and refuse to heed His words.

> "'But if you will not listen to me and carryout all these commands, and if you reject my decrees and abhor my laws and fail to carry out all my commands and so violate my covenant, then I will do this to you: I will bring upon you sudden terror, wasting diseases and fever that will destroy your sight and drain away your life. You will plant seed in vain, because your enemies will eat it. I will set my face against you so that you will be defeated by your enemies; those who hate you will rule over you, and you will flee even when no one is pursuing you.

"'If after all this you will not listen to me, I will punish you for your sins seven times over. I will break down your stubborn pride and make the sky above you like iron and the ground beneath you like bronze. Your strength will be spent in vain, because your soil will not yield its crops, nor will the trees of the land yield their fruit.

"'If you remain hostile toward me and refuse to listen to me, I will multiply your afflictions seven times over, as your sins deserve. I will send wild animals against you, and they will rob you of your children, destroy your cattle and make you so few in number that your roads will be deserted.

"'If in spite of these things you do not accept my correction but continue to be hostile toward me, I myself will be hostile toward you and will afflict you for your sins seven times over. And I will bring the sword upon you to avenge the breaking of the covenant. When you withdraw into your cities, I will send a plague among you, and you will be given into enemy hands. When I cut off your supply of bread, ten women will be able to bake your bread in one oven, and they will dole out the bread by weight. You will eat, but you will not be satisfied.

"'If in spite of this you still do not listen to me but continue to be hostile toward me, then in my anger I will be hostile toward you, and I myself will punish you for your sins seven times over. You will eat the flesh of your sons and the flesh of your daughters. I will destroy your high places, cut down your incense altars and pile your dead bodies on the lifeless forms of your idols, and I will abhor you. I will turn your cities into ruins and lay waste your sanctuaries, and I will take no delight in the pleasing aroma of your offerings. I will lay waste the land, so that your enemies who live there will be appalled. I will scatter you among the nations and will draw out my sword and pursue you. Your land will be laid waste, and your cities will lie in ruins. Then the land will enjoy its sabbath years all the time that it lies desolate and you are in the country of your enemies; then the land will rest and enjoy its sabbaths. All the time that it lies desolate, the land will have the rest it did not have during the sabbaths you lived in it.

"'As for those of you who are left, I will make their hearts so fearful in the lands of their enemies that the sound of a wind-blown leaf will put them to flight. They will run as though fleeing from the sword, and they will fall, even though no one is pursuing them. They will stumble over one another as though fleeing from the sword, even though no one is pursuing them. So you will not be able to stand before your enemies. You will perish among the nations; the land of your enemies will devour you. Those of you who are left will waste away in the lands of their enemies because of their sins; also because of their fathers' sins they will waste away'" (Leviticus 26:14–39).

These punishments follow disobedience as surely as blessings follow faithfulness and obedience. These are the tragic consequences of disobedience, and these warnings are as valid today as they were in centuries past. Notice the six stages of punishment as we examine this passage.

*The first stage: Fear, sickness, and conflict.* God says, "I will bring upon you sudden terror, wasting diseases and fever that will destroy your sight and drain away your life. You will plant seed in vain, because your enemies will eat it. I will set my face against you so that you will be defeated by your enemies; those who hate you will rule over you, and you will flee even when no one is pursuing you."

Notice that there are three parts to this first stage of God's discipline. The first part is fear and terror. Those who trust God and obey Him live in confidence and security. Those who disobey God know that they live as enemies of God. This knowledge makes them afraid, so that they jump at their own shadows and flee even when no one is chasing them. Disobedience produces fear. This is as true for us today as it was in Old Testament times. If you live in unreasoning fear right now, a fear that seems to have no cause, then you are probably not living in a trusting, obedient relationship with God. Get right with God, and He will take away your fear.

The next part of this first stage is sickness. God promised that disobedience would cause disease to break out among the people. As you read the record of Israel's forty-year sojourn in the wilderness, from Egypt to the borders of the Promised Land, you find that the people were not afflicted with disease except during special punishments for specific events of temporary disobedience. God preserved them from the illnesses that were common among the Egyptians, the Canaanites, and other nations around them. When disease erupted in Israel, it was a sign that they had turned away from God and His Law.

In the Bible, disease symbolizes the moral and spiritual leprosy, cancer, and contagion of our lives. When we disobey God's commandments, we develop soul-destroying lesions of pride, lust, resentment, malice, selfishness, and indifference. These are some of the spiritual diseases that can afflict the believer. When these sicknesses begin to appear in your life, they are an indication of disobedience, that you have fallen away from Christ. These are warnings that you need to turn back to God and find healing.

The third part of this first stage of discipline is conflict. You find yourself at odds with the people around you. You find yourself living in a state of constant strife, schism, and division. You are hindered in your life and your ministry by the attacks of enemies. As God says, "You will plant seed in vain, because your enemies will eat it. I will set my face against you so that you will be defeated by your enemies; those who hate you will rule over you."

Now, a certain amount of conflict is to be expected in anyone's life. In fact, if we live in obedience to God, we can expect that worldly people will sometimes be offended by our witness and our righteous way of life. That is why righteous Christians are often persecuted for their faith. But that is not the kind of conflict God speaks of here. He is saying that because of our disobedient state, we will attract conflict and discord into our own lives. We will make enemies. We will cause people to resent us, to lose respect for us, and they will attack us and obstruct whatever we try to do. We will even stir up discord, factions, and conflict in our own churches.

So these three elements—fear, sickness, and conflict—mark the first stage of God's punishment of our disobedience. The purpose of this first stage of punishment is not to hurt us but to discipline us and turn us back to God and His love. God does not want to hurt us. He wants to heal us. But if we choose to continue in disobedience, He will not overrule our decision. He has promised us blessings if we obey, He has warned us of discipline if we disobey, and He allows us to decide between the two. If we choose disobedience, we move to the second stage of punishment.

*The second stage: Drought.* God says, "If after all this you will not listen to me, I will punish you for your sins seven times over. I will break down your stubborn pride and make the sky above you like iron and the ground beneath you like bronze. Your strength will be spent in vain, because your soil will not yield its crops, nor will the trees of the land yield their fruit." So the second stage consisted, first, of an immediate sevenfold increase of all the woes of the first stage—plus drought!

If the heavens are like iron, there is no rain. If the ground is like bronze, it is too hard to plow and plant crops. If the soil yields no crops and the trees no fruit, it is because the earth has dried up. This is a vivid description of drought and famine—which is exactly what took place in the history of Israel, time and again.

In the spiritual realm, drought speaks of barrenness, hopelessness, depression, and despair. Someone going through a time of spiritual drought experience lifelessness, listlessness, and futility. Food has no taste. Days pass in dreary, meaningless succession. If we still choose disobedience, then we move to the third stage of punishment.

*The third stage: Attack and desolation.* God says, "If you remain hostile toward me and refuse to listen to me, I will multiply your afflictions seven times over, as your sins deserve. I will send wild animals against you, and they will rob you of your children, destroy your cattle and make you so few in number that your roads will be deserted." Once again, those who disobey God's Law experience a compounding of misery, seven times over. Then, added to those sufferings, come attacks of wild animals that kill herds and flocks, people in the streets, and children in their yards.

Here again, this is a vivid picture of something that we can experience in our spiritual lives if we choose to disobey God. The attack of wild beasts is a picture of the kind of unprovoked attacks that come suddenly and unexpectedly, even when we think we are safe. Though loss and attack can also come to the righteous (as we see in the life of Job, for example), a sudden and unprovoked attack of this kind can often be a mark of spiritual decline. To the person who trusts in God, a time of attack and persecution serves to test and grow one's faith; but to the person who is living in willful disobedience, a time of attack produces desolation.

Amazingly, even after all of these multiplied woes, some people will still choose disobedience. If so, then they move to the fourth stage of punishment.

*The fourth stage: Invasion.* God says, "If in spite of these things you do not accept my correction but continue to be hostile toward me, I myself will be hostile toward you and will afflict you for your sins seven times over. And I will bring the sword upon you to avenge the breaking of the covenant. When you withdraw into your cities, I will send a plague among you, and you will be given into enemy hands."

Again, the afflictions multiply seven times over—and this time, there will be an invasion of the land. Enemies will be permitted to come in and take over. This invasion will be accompanied by pestilence and famine among the people. Bread will be so scarce that it will be eaten up, yet the people will remain unsatisfied.

You can read of the historical fulfillment of this dire warning in the records of the Old Testament books of 1 and 2 Kings and 1 and 2 Chronicles. These terrible events befell the people of Israel as they persisted in their disobedience. This should serve as a warning to us today. These warnings have a spiritual counterpart in our lives now, and if we are disobedient, then we will surely experience a profound sense of moral famine and spiritual despair. And if, after all of this, we still choose disobedience, then we move to the fifth stage of punishment.

*The fifth stage: Destruction.* Again, God warns that the troubles that have already been described in the first four stages will be multiplied seven times— and worse, the people will see their civilization destroyed and be reduced to feeding on the bodies of their children. "You will eat the flesh of your sons and the flesh of your daughters," He says. "I will destroy your high places, cut down your incense altars and pile your dead bodies on the lifeless forms of your idols, and I will abhor you. I will turn your cities into ruins and lay waste your sanctuaries, and I will take no delight in the pleasing aroma of your offerings. I will lay waste the land, so that your enemies who live there will be appalled." Imagine being so utterly destroyed and disgraced that even your enemies are horrified at your fate!

This remarkable prediction was fulfilled in history. The Jewish historian Josephus records that just as God predicted in Leviticus, the people in Jerusalem ate the bodies of their children in the terrible famine that occurred when the Roman armies under Titus laid siege to Jerusalem in A.D. 70.

The spiritual counterpart of this disastrous spiritual decline is the destruction of families, the loss of sons and daughters, and the unspeakable moral perversions that are becoming increasingly common in our society today. The result is utter devastation and a miserable exile from the presence and power of God. This leads, ultimately, to the sixth and final stage of punishment.

*The sixth stage: Scattering.* God says, "I will scatter you among the nations and will draw out my sword and pursue you. Your land will be laid waste, and your cities will lie in ruins . . . . As for those of you who are left, I will make their hearts so fearful in the lands of their enemies that the sound of a wind-blown leaf will put them to flight. They will run as though fleeing from the sword, and they will fall, even though no one is pursuing them. They will stumble over one another as though fleeing from the sword, even though no one is pursuing them. So you will not be able to stand before your enemies. You will perish among the nations; the land of your enemies will devour you. Those of you who are left will waste away in the lands of their enemies because of their sins; also because of their fathers' sins they will waste away."

This warning speaks prophetically of the diaspora, the great dispersion of the Jewish people among the nations outside of Palestine. The diaspora began in the sixth century B.C., when the Jewish people were taken in bondage to Babylon. Another great shockwave of dispersion occurred in A.D. 70, when the city of Jerusalem was destroyed by Rome. To this day, Jews living outside of modern Israel (more than 8.3 million in 2000) greatly out number Jews living within Israel's borders (5.4 million). Over the centuries, the Jewish people have been spread around the world, hunted, persecuted, and exterminated.

Here again, we see that this warning has a parallel in our spiritual lives today. If we disobey God's Law, if we reject His love, if we ignore His repeated warnings, then we face spiritual alienation. We will be spiritually homeless, without a foundation for our souls. Our spirits will be laid waste, our hearts will be full of fear, we will not be able to stand before the enemies of our souls, and we will perish. We will utterly waste away and our enemy, Satan, will devour us.

God has fulfilled these ominous words down through history in the life of Israel. He will fulfill them as well in an individual life—in your life or mine. May we remain true to God and to His commandments, so that this tragic fate may never befall us.

## Relentless Love

So much tragedy! So much punishment! But notice where all of this is driving—toward redemption and restoration. God always has a loving and redemptive goal toward which He is aiming.

> "'But if they will confess their sins and the sins of their fathers—their treachery against me and their hostility toward me, which made me hostile toward them so that I sent them into the land of their enemies—then when their uncircumcised hearts are humbled and they pay for their sin, I will remember my covenant with Jacob and my covenant with Isaac and my covenant with Abraham, and I will remember the land. For the land will be deserted by them and will enjoy its sabbaths while it lies desolate without them. They will pay for their sins because they rejected my laws and abhorred my decrees. Yet in spite of this, when they are in the land of their enemies, I will not reject them or abhor them so as to destroy them completely, breaking my covenant with them. I am the Lord their God. But for their sake I will remember the covenant with their ancestors whom I brought out of Egypt in the sight of the nations to be their God. I am the Lord.'"
>
> These are the decrees, the laws and the regulations that the Lord established on Mount Sinai between himself and the Israelites through Moses (Leviticus 26:40–46).

The disobedience of the people of Israel brought down God's punishment—but not His hatred. God has always loved the Jewish people, and He always will. No matter how much they disobeyed Him in the past, He will not destroy them utterly. He will not allow them to be wiped off the face of the earth. Instead, He will accomplish His purpose and bring them back to the land. The history of Israel is proof that God means what He says in Leviticus 26; He means what He says about the punishments for disobedience—and about the blessings of remaining faithful to God and His Law.

Frederick the Great was king of Prussia from 1740 to 1786. He once debated the existence of God with a representative of the Lutheran church. "If your

Bible is truly the Word of God, then you should be able to demonstrate its truth by some simple proof."

"Your Majesty," the churchman replied, "I can demonstrate the truth of the Bible with a single word."

"Oh?" King Frederick said, surprised. "And what is this single word that can prove that the entire Bible is true?"

"Israel," said the churchman.

The existence of Israel as a distinct people, with a distinct culture, religion, and national identity—even after centuries of dispersion, centuries of persecution, centuries of genocidal exterminations, centuries without any homeland!—is proof positive that God's Word is truth. God has dealt severely with His people, yet He loves them and has a plan for them that is unfolding before our eyes.

If you have read this passage and have concluded that the schedule of punishments in Leviticus 26 mean that God is cruel, heartless, and harshly demanding, then you have misread the Scriptures. This is not a story of God's rage and malice toward Israel. It is the story of His relentless love, His ruthless grace, His unyielding compassion, His inflexible caring. There is as much of God's love behind this schedule of punishments as there is behind the list of blessings. Every verse, every line, every word of Leviticus 26 is about the loving heart of God.

Notice what God is doing through these stages of punishment. At each stage, God says, in effect, "I will discipline Israel, the people I love, in the hope that they will turn back to me. If they repent and return, then the punishments will end and the blessings will resume. If they continue in sin, then I will go to the next stage. I will never give up on my people, Israel. I will discipline them and plead with them, and I will ultimately see that they return to me."

So the process moves from stage to stage, and God gradually pushes them to a place of despair. When they finally hit bottom, when there is no way to go but up, they will turn to God. That is how God works. This is, apparently, an invariable law of human nature and spiritual reality. Human beings seem to have a perverse inclination to choose punishment over blessing. When God presents us with a moral choice, we have a genius for choosing the wrong thing. God will never violate our free will, but at the same time, He does not shield us from the consequences of our decisions. If we choose to reject Him, then we accept the responsibility for that choice. Usually, those heart breaking consequences are persuasive in turning us back to God.

C. S. Lewis wrote in *The Problem of Pain,* "God whispers to us in our pleasures, speaks in our conscience, but shouts in our pains; it is His megaphone to rouse a deaf world." Out of His great love for us, God must sometimes break our hearts in order to get through to us, so that we will take Him seriously.

I have a friend, an eminent psychiatrist, who was for many years an agnostic, an enemy of the Christian faith. He spoke out against Christianity in public lectures and ridiculed the Bible.

Without warning, this man's world fell apart when his little son accidentally drowned in a swimming pool. Devastated by grief, this man longed to be with his son again. He wondered if what the Bible said about life after death might be true. He began reading the Bible and books on Christianity. While reading a book by C. S. Lewis, he was suddenly overcome by a sense that God is real. He regretted the way he had publicly ridiculed the Christian faith. Angry with himself, he dropped the book on the floor and shouted aloud, "I've been such a fool!"

Then he got down on his knees and begged God to forgive him, cleanse him, and take control of his life. At that instant, he sensed the Spirit of God come into him—and he knew that his life was forever changed. He has been growing in grace ever since.

This man's story is a metaphor of what God has done in the life of the nation of Israel. The people turned away from God and ignored His Law. Only pain and loss could get Israel's attention and turn the nation back to God.

God has promised us a life of blessing if we will remain faithful to Him. He has promised us punishment if we turn away from Him. If we reject the light, we must endure the darkness. If we refuse His warmth, we must suffer the cold. If we will not go in, then we must stay out. Either/or—that is the choice we must make. There is no third alternative.

Our Lord still deals with us today as He dealt with Israel of old. What seems cruel and harsh on the surface is actually God's relentless love. He says to us, "I will never let you go. I will never give up on you. I love you too much to let you turn your back on me. I love you, and you mean that much to me." That is the message of Leviticus 26. That is the way God works with us. We sing it in the wonderful old hymn by George Matheson:

O Love that will not let me go,
I rest my weary soul in Thee;
I give Thee back the life I owe,
That in Thine ocean depths its flow
May richer, fuller be.

Thank God for His wonderful, inflexible, relentless love!

※────────────≪

# PROMISES, PROMISES
## LEVITICUS 27

I AM TOLD that a pastor once went to visit a wealthy businessman who was in the hospital and not expected to live. During their visit together, the businessman said, "Pastor, I'm making a promise to God, with you as my witness, that if He will heal me and raise me out of this sickbed, I'll give a million dollars to the church!"

The pastor saw how pale and weak the businessman looked, and he was sure that the man would not last the night. The preacher prayed for the man's healing, but he left the sickroom shaking his head.

To the pastor's amazement, however, the man was miraculously healed the following day. He was released from the hospital and soon returned to a full schedule of work at his office. The pastor remembered the man's promise and waited for the businessman's million-dollar check to arrive. Weeks passed—but no check. So the pastor went to the businessman's office.

When the businessman saw the minister at his office door, he tugged nervously at his collar. "Oh, hello, Pastor," he said. "What a surprise to see you here."

"You're surprised?" the pastor said. "I thought you'd be expecting me. When you were in the hospital, you made a promise to God. You said that if He let you live, you would give the church a million dollars."

"Did I say that?" the businessman asked. "I guess that shows how sick I was!"

The last chapter of Leviticus deals with the promises we make to God in response for what He has done for us. People often make promises in times of danger, when they want God to save them, or when there is something they want very badly ("God, if you'll just give me this one thing, I will do anything you ask!"). If you have ever made such a promise to God, then you will be very interested to learn what God says in Leviticus 27.

## VOWS ARE VOLUNTARY

In beginning this study, I must point out that God never commands people to make a vow or promise to Him. You can search the Old and New Testaments, and you will never find a single instance where God commands a person to make a promise. A vow to God is always voluntary, never mandatory. You don't have to promise God anything in order to receive blessings from Him. God is a Giver, and it delights Him to shower us with blessings. That is His nature. Because God is love, He delights in giving. The apostle James tells us, "Every good and perfect gift is from above, coming down from the Father of the heavenly lights, who does not change like shifting shadows" (James 1:17).

Yet there is something innate in human beings that makes us want to make a vow, a promise, a resolution before God. So God, in recognizing this tendency within us, makes room for it and gives us instructions about making promises to Him. Scripture records many instances where people made vows and bargains with God. This is a feature of human nature that we can all identify with.

Even though God never demands that we make a vow, the Scriptures teach that once we voluntarily make a vow, God expects us to keep it. In the book of Numbers, we see this principle clearly stated:

> Moses said to the heads of the tribes of Israel: "This is what the LORD commands: When a man makes a vow to the LORD or takes an oath to obligate himself by a pledge, he must not break his word but must do everything he said" (Numbers 30:1–2).

And in the wisdom book of Ecclesiastes we read:

> When you make a vow to God, do not delay in fulfilling it. He has no pleasure in fools; fulfill your vow. It is better not to vow than to make a vow and not fulfill it (Ecclesiastes 5:4–5).

You never have to make a vow to God. But if you make a vow, keep it. God expects us to keep our promises.

## LAW VERSUS GRACE

Several categories of vows are listed in Leviticus 27. The details of these vows apply largely to the social conditions in Israel during those days, so we will not dwell here on those details. The underlying principles of these vows, however, apply to our lives today, so our emphasis will largely be on those principles.

The first category involves vows made regarding people.

> The LORD said to Moses, "Speak to the Israelites and say to them: 'If anyone makes a special vow to dedicate persons to the LORD by giving equivalent values, set the value of a male between the ages of twenty and sixty at fifty shekels of silver, according to the sanctuary shekel; and if it is a female, set her value at thirty shekels. If it is a person between the ages of five and twenty, set the value of a male at twenty shekels and of a female at ten shekels. If it is a person between one month and five years, set the value of a male at five shekels of silver and that of a female at three shekels of silver. If it is a person sixty years old or more, set the value of a male at fifteen shekels and of a female at ten shekels. If anyone making the vow is too poor to pay the specified amount, he is to present the person to the priest, who will set the value for him according to what the man making the vow can afford'" (Leviticus 27:1–8).

Several items in this passage require comment. First, notice that this vow involves dedicating people to the Lord. What does that mean? In the ancient Hebrew culture, people would sometimes make a vow to God, asking God to benefit or bless themselves or a parent, child, spouse, friend, or servant. They would pray, "Lord, if you do such-and-such for me or for this person, then I promise to invest in your work." This was called dedicating a person to the Lord.

When a promise of this nature was made, there was a scale of monetary values which God had determined and communicated through Moses. These values were set according to the age and sex of the person who was being dedicated to God. This amount had to be paid if the blessing or benefit was received. It was to be paid to Moses as the representative of the government of Israel.

Some people may find it troubling or offensive that a lower rate was established for females than for males. But we must remember that this does not mean that women were worth less than men in God's eyes. The Old and the New Testaments clearly state that men and women are of equal value as persons before God. As Paul writes in Galatians, "There is neither Jew nor Greek, slave nor free, male nor female, for you are all one in Christ Jesus" (Galatians 3:28). All distinctions of race, class, gender, and so forth are erased when we stand in the presence of God.

The difference in monetary values that are expressed here relate to the differences in the opportunities for service to the community. That is why there are distinctions of age as well as sex. Both the very old and the very young have a much lower monetary value assessed than those who are in the prime of their working years, ages twenty to sixty. This passage recognizes that those who have greater opportunities for service to the community have a greater obligation to contribute.

A provision was also made for those who were unable to pay. It is important to note that the poor did not make their payment to Moses, as others did. Instead, God said, "If anyone making the vow is too poor to pay the specified amount, he is to present the person to the priest, who will set the value for him according to what the man making the vow can afford." The poor were to make their payment to the priest instead of to Moses. Moses represented the throne of Israel, the government of the nation, the power of and justice of God; the priest represented the grace and mercy of God, the tender character of God's love.

This indicates that if a person were bargaining with God on a legalistic basis ("I'll do this for you, if you'll do that for me"), then he had to pay the full price. Moses could not reduce the demand of the Law. But if a person approached God on the basis of his or her poverty in the presence of God's grace (as represented by the priest), then that person did not have to pay what the Law demanded.

It is clear to see how this principle applies to us on a spiritual level. If we make a promise to God in a time of need, offering Him something from ourselves in exchange for His work on our behalf, then God expects us to pay in full exactly what we promise. A bargain is a legal transaction.

But if a person approaches God and says, "I am too poor to pay the price, but I promise you, God, to give what I can out of a heart full of thanksgiving and gratitude for your grace," then the priest enters the picture as the representative of God's mercy and grace. The priest intercedes on the poor person's behalf and establishes a valuation that the poor person is able to meet.

This is a beautiful picture of how God works in our lives. What we cannot gain by the Law, God gives to us by His grace. Our merciful and gracious God "is able to do immeasurably more than all we ask or imagine, according to his power that is at work within us" (Ephesians 3:20).

## THE PAYMENT OF VOWS

The rest of this chapter deals with detailed instructions as to how these vows should be paid.

> "'If what he vowed is an animal that is acceptable as an offering to the LORD, such an animal given to the LORD becomes holy. He must not exchange it or substitute a good one for a bad one, or a bad one for a good one; if he should substitute one animal for another, both it and the substitute become holy. If what he vowed is a ceremonially unclean animal—one that is not acceptable as an offering to the LORD—the animal must be presented to the priest, who will judge its quality as good or bad. Whatever value the priest then sets, that is what it will be. If the owner wishes to redeem the animal, he must add a fifth to its value.
>
> "'If a man dedicates his house as something holy to the LORD, the priest will judge its quality as good or bad. Whatever value the priest then sets, so it will remain. If the man who dedicates his house redeems it, he must add a fifth to its value, and the house will again become his.
>
> "'If a man dedicates to the LORD part of his family land, its value is to be set according to the amount of seed required for it—fifty shekels of silver to a homer of barley seed. If he dedicates his field during the Year of Jubilee, the value that has been set remains. But if he dedicates his field after the Jubilee, the priest will determine the value according to the number of years that remain until the

next Year of Jubilee, and its set value will be reduced. If the man who dedicates the field wishes to redeem it, he must add a fifth to its value, and the field will again become his. If, however, he does not redeem the field, or if he has sold it to someone else, it can never be redeemed. When the field is released in the Jubilee, it will become holy, like a field devoted to the Lord; it will become the property of the priests.

"'If a man dedicates to the LORD a field he has bought, which is not part of his family land, the priest will determine its value up to the Year of Jubilee, and the man must pay its value on that day as something holy to the LORD. In the Year of Jubilee the field will revert to the person from whom he bought it, the one whose land it was. Every value is to be set according to the sanctuary shekel, twenty gerahs to the shekel.

"'No one, however, may dedicate the firstborn of an animal, since the firstborn already belongs to the LORD; whether an ox or a sheep, it is the LORD's. If it is one of the unclean animals, he may buy it back at its set value, adding a fifth of the value to it. If he does not redeem it, it is to be sold at its set value.

"'But nothing that a man owns and devotes to the LORD—whether man or animal or family land—may be sold or redeemed; everything so devoted is most holy to the LORD.

"'No person devoted to destruction may be ransomed; he must be put to death.

"'A tithe of everything from the land, whether grain from the soil or fruit from the trees, belongs to the LORD; it is holy to the LORD. If a man redeems any of his tithe, he must add a fifth of the value to it. The entire tithe of the herd and flock—every tenth animal that passes under the shepherd's rod—will be holy to the LORD. He must not pick out the good from the bad or make any substitution. If he does make a substitution, both the animal and its substitute become holy and cannot be redeemed.'"

These are the commands the LORD gave Moses on Mount Sinai for the Israelites (Leviticus 27:9–34).

Leviticus 27:9–13 deals with the vowing of animals to the Lord. Leviticus 27:14–15 specifies that houses could be dedicated to God in payment of a vow.

In Leviticus 27:16–25, God makes provision for the dedication of land, in connection with the Year of Jubilee, when all land had to return to its original owner. Implicit throughout these verses is the principle that human beings are tenants of the land; only God holds absolute title to the land.

Leviticus 27:26–34 deals with the exclusion of certain items as payment of vows. For example, the firstlings of animals could not be used to pay a vow because God had already told the people, "Consecrate to me every firstborn male. The first offspring of every womb among the Israelites belongs to me, whether man or animal" (Exodus 13:2). The firstborn animals could not be used because they already belonged to God.

An important exclusion is listed in Leviticus 27:28, which deals with people, animals, or land that may not be vowed to God because it is already devoted to God:

> "'But nothing that a man owns and devotes to the LORD—whether man or animal or family land—may be sold or redeemed; everything so devoted is most holy to the LORD'" (Leviticus 27:28).

In Israel it was possible to devote a child, servant, or animal for an entire span of life to the service of God. Hannah did this with her son Samuel (see 1 Samuel 1:1–28). Even before Samuel was born, she promised him to God. And when her boy grew old enough, she took him to the temple and gave him to God to be used in the service there. Samuel the prophet grew up in the temple as a man devoted to God.

This verse may also help explain an incident in the book of Judges that has puzzled and troubled believers over the years. In Judges 11, we find the story of Jephthah, a mighty warrior of Israel who delivered Israel from the oppression of the Ammonites and was a judge in Israel for six years. Jephthah made a rash and tragic vow before God. Before going out to battle against the enemies of Israel, he told God, "If you give the Ammonites into my hands, whatever comes out of the door of my house to meet me when I return in triumph from the Ammonites will be the LORD's, and I will sacrifice it as a burnt offering" (Judges 11:30–31).

Then Jephthah went out and defeated the Ammonite armies. When he returned to his home, he was greeted by what should have been a wonderful, joyful sight—but because of his vow, he was horrified. There, emerging from the door of his house, was his only child, his beloved daughter, who was probably in her early teens. "Oh! My daughter!" he cried. "You have made me miserable and wretched, because I have made a vow to the LORD that I cannot break."

"My father," the girl bravely replied, "you have given your word to the LORD. Do to me just as you promised, now that the LORD has avenged you of your enemies, the Ammonites. But grant me this one request. Give me two months to roam the hills and weep with my friends, because I will never marry."

So she spent two months mourning her own life, accompanied by her friends. At the end of that time, the Scriptures record, "she returned to her father and he did to her as he had vowed. And she was a virgin. From this comes the Israelite custom that each year the young women of Israel go out for four days to commemorate the daughter of Jephthah the Gileadite" (Judges 11:39–40).

Many people have recoiled at this story, and understandably so. They ask, "How could a man of God offer Him a human sacrifice—especially the sacrifice of his own daughter?" Some Bible scholars have tried to avoid the obvious meaning of this passage by suggesting that Jephthah must have paid redemption money for his daughter. They translate Jephthah's vow this way: "Whatever comes out of the door of my house will be dedicated to the Lord, or I will sacrifice it as a burnt offering." Perhaps the statement that "she was a virgin" suggests that instead of sacrificing his daughter, Jephthah dedicated his daughter to God, so that she had to remain a virgin for the rest of her life. After all, the passage doesn't specifically say that Jephthah sacrificed his daughter— only that "he did to her as he had vowed."

But if Jephthah had vowed to either dedicate or sacrifice whatever came out of the house, then why was he so upset when he saw his daughter? Why did he tear his clothes? Why did he cry out, "Oh! My daughter! You have made me miserable and wretched, because I have made a vow to the LORD that I cannot break"? These are the words and actions of a man who is experiencing overwhelming grief because he knows his daughter must die. Jephthah knew the Law, as stated in Leviticus 27:28: "But nothing that a man owns and devotes to the LORD—whether man or animal or family land— may be sold or redeemed; everything so devoted is most holy to the LORD."

This incident in Judges 11 cannot be explained away. The reality of it must be accepted and understood. My opinion is that Jephthah did offer his daughter as a burnt offering. This was not the kind of offering God wanted. The reason Jephthah's daughter died is not that God demanded a human sacrifice but because Jephthah made a foolish vow—a promise to God that he had no business making in the first place. This story occurs during a time of moral decline in the nation of Israel. The whole period of the Judges was a moral low point in the life of the Hebrew nation. It serves as a warning to us that we should not make any rash or thoughtless pledge to God.

Leviticus 27:29–33 tells us that no condemned person could be dedicated to God in payment of a vow, because such people belonged to God already. Nor could tithes be used to pay a vow, because they also belonged to the Lord already.

We must ask ourselves: "What do these regulations about vows mean to us today? What is the function of vows in our lives?" It is impossible not to make vows. Every time we deal with God, we tend to make a vow or a promise in some sense. On the one hand, the flesh within us wants to bargain with God. We have all felt this way. We have all wanted to say to God, whether we've actually said it or not, "Lord, I want this so badly. If you'll just do this for me, I'll do something for you." We tend to approach God on that legalistic, bargaining basis. And when we come on that basis, God says, "All right, whatever you say. But remember, you will have to fulfill your end of the bargain."

During the era of the Vietnam War, a young man came to speak to me after a Sunday morning worship service. He said, "Two years ago, I was in Vietnam. Our company was pinned down under an enemy barrage. I was in an exposed position, bullets were whistling over my head, shrapnel was exploding all around me, and I was scared to death. I was sure I would not get out of that situation alive. Being a Christian, I prayed and said, 'Lord, if you'll get me out of this, I'll go to seminary and become a minister.' Well, God answered my prayer and He got me out of that situation.

"I came back to the States, got out of the army, started my own business, and began making money. Every time I remembered the promise I'd made to God, I tucked it into the back of my mind. Time passed, and my business became very successful. I almost forgot the promise I had made in Vietnam— and I thought God had forgotten it, too. But soon some strange things started happening. Though conditions were favorable for my business, though I was doing everything right, my business started to fall apart. Yesterday, I lost the whole business. I know what God is saying to me through those circumstances. I know what He wants me to do. He was taking me at my word. I had made a promise, and He was making sure I kept it. I just wanted you to hear my story."

He enrolled in seminary the next day and, true to his promise, he became a pastor. God holds us to our legalistic bargains—even foxhole bargains.

Christians sometimes make another kind of vow: "Lord, you have done so much for me! My heart is so moved that I want to promise to devote this or that to you. I don't know how I will be able to pay this vow, but I ask you, Lord, to help me fulfill it." God loves this kind of promise. If we make this kind of vow to Him, He will make the fulfillment of that vow more rich and full and meaningful than we could ever imagine, "according to his power that is at work within us" (Ephesians 3:20). God uses such vows to stretch us, to grow our character, to increase our faith.

Our hymns, too, reflect promises we make to God. I once heard Dr. Charles Allen, then pastor of the First Methodist Church of Houston, tell of an experience he had during a morning worship service. In the middle of a hymn, he broke into loud laughter. After the service, his wife rebuked him. "I was so embarrassed," she said, "that you would start laughing right in the middle of a hymn for no reason at all!"

"I couldn't help it," he told her. "We were singing 'Take my life and let it be consecrated, Lord, to Thee.' And while we were singing the third verse, the words of the song leaped out at me: 'Take my silver and my gold, Not a mite would I withhold.' It suddenly struck me: There are so many millionaires sitting in this congregation. What if God held them to the promise of that hymn? What if every one of those rich men had to carry out the words that they were singing, and had to give God every mite of their silver and gold? Some of them would be very upset with God!"

When we sing hymns in church, I often think of Jesus' admonition that we will have to give an account for every idle word that we utter. We should not sing any hymn unless we truly mean what we say. I must candidly tell you that sometimes when I'm singing a hymn and I see what the words are, I shut up! Why? Because I'm not ready to say that yet, and I know that God is listening.

We don't sing hymns in a worship service just to fill up the time. We sing those songs in order to lift our souls to God and express the feelings that are in our hearts. If the hymn does not express our heart's own song, we should not sing it!

So what are vows? They are a way God has of drawing us along toward maturity. They are His way of claiming His rightful ownership of us. If you read Leviticus 27 carefully, you will see that, in every case—whether it is persons, animals, houses, lands, or any other object being pledged—everything ultimately belongs to God. It is all His.

That is the meaning of the words of the apostle Paul: "You are not your own; you were bought at a price" (1 Corinthians 6:19–20). Since we are already His, then it only makes sense that we should offer ourselves to Him, utterly and completely.

A woman I knew was diagnosed with terminal cancer. She'd had an operation that gave her a reprieve for a while, but she knew that she was approaching the end of her life. "I don't how long I have to live," she told me, "whether it's measured in months or years. But I have promised the Lord that whatever time remains to me, I will give to Him in a way I never have before. I'll be available for whatever He wants me to do." Through her trial of cancer, God had led her to a place of deep faith and maturity, so that she was able to acknowledge God's rightful claim on her entire life.

I think it is instructive that the book of Leviticus closes on precisely the same note that is sounded by the apostle Paul in Romans 12:1:

> Therefore, I urge you, brothers, in view of God's mercy, to offer your bodies as living sacrifices, holy and pleasing to God—this is your spiritual act of worship.

Notice that closing phrase—"your spiritual act of worship." The original Greek word translated "spiritual" can also be translated "reasonable" or "logical." You see, it is only reasonable and logical that we present our bodies to God as living sacrifices. Why? Because we are already His. He already owns us. It would be irrational for us to try to withhold from Him that which He already owns.

Notice, too, that when Paul writes, "I urge you . . . to offer your bodies as living sacrifices," that word "offer" means to continuously, repeatedly, uninterruptedly present yourself to God. How do we do that? By giving God every moment of our lives.

That means that when you are annoyed with your spouse, and you are tempted to say something caustic or sarcastic, you hold your tongue, you give that moment to God, and you ask Him to help you respond in love. That means that in the privacy of your thoughts, when you are tempted by images of lust, you give that moment to God and ask Him to cleanse your mind. That means that when you see a person in need, you give that moment to God, you set aside your busy schedule and your crowded agenda, and you present yourself as a priest and an agent of God's healing grace to that person.

The closing verses of Leviticus 27 call us to say to God, "Lord, here I am; I give myself to you. Here are my possessions; I lay them at your feet. Here are my children; live your life through them. Here are my relationships, my friendships, my career, my abilities, everything I am and everything I have and everything I do—Lord, it's all yours. Help me to fulfill my promises to you in the moment-by-moment living of my life." It makes no sense to hold any of these things back, because they all belong to Him.

If we hold back anything from God, we are only robbing God of what He rightfully owns. My prayer as we come to these closing verses of Leviticus is this: "Our Father, may we not bargain with you. May we not offer you rash promises that we cannot fulfill or which would only hurt ourselves and others. Instead, may we offer you all that we are and all that we have, our very lives, because that is our reasonable, logical, spiritual act of worship."

If we will live every day of our lives with such a prayer on our lips, then we will have solved the mystery of the book of Leviticus. Remember, at the beginning of this study, I said that all of the secrets of Leviticus are unlocked by one verse, Leviticus 20:26:

> You are to be holy to me because I, the LORD, am holy, and I have
> set you apart from the nations to be my own.

To be holy is to be whole. In order to be whole and holy, we must offer our total selves to God as a living sacrifice, holy and pleasing to God, nothing held back. God has set us apart from the nations to be His own. He owns us. He loves us. He cherishes us more than we can imagine. If you long to be whole and holy, if you desire to rid yourself of your brokenness, then don't wait another day, another minute, another moment. Offer yourself as a living sacrifice, and discover the beauty and splendor of God's wholeness and holiness.

That is what God is after in your life and mine. That is what the book of Leviticus is all about. And that is God's wonderful plan and purpose for our lives.

# NOTE TO THE READER